About the author

Rhondda Valley born and educated, long time writer and journalist Jonathan Isaacs cannot remember a time during his younger days when travelling almost anywhere didn't mean hopping aboard a maroon coloured bus.

That vehicle was more than likely operated by Rhondda Transport and as well as a ride to his destination they were without doubt the spark for a lifelong interest in the bus industry.

He recalls that the highlight of most days was the bus ride to and from school — always a double decker in the morning and a saloon on the afternoon home run.

Lunchtimes often meant sneaking out of school, and heading for the depot which was just down the hill and then having to trespass on a railway line to catch sight of the long rows of buses parked there.

He laments the demise in 1970 of the original, long-serving, legendary Rhondda Transport Company and hopes this book will be seen as a fitting salute to the company's 65 year long existence.

Jonathan Isaacs

Jonathan left the valley soon after the demise of Rhondda Transport, but his passion for the company endured and has now resulted in this book which records the life and times of a unique company that had a profound influence on the life of almost everyone who lived in the valley.

Jonathan worked for Wales' biggest selling regional daily newspaper, the South Wales Evening Post, for more than 30 years, first as a reporter and finally as the publication's News Editor. He lives in Swansea.

Remembering Rhondda is Jonathan's second book on South Wales bus fleets. His first which received much acclaim, detailed the life and times of the Swansea-based South Wales Transport Company.

This book is a fascinating, long-awaited first-ever record of the life and times of a company that played its part in helping Britain win the Second World War and certainly left its mark on the Rhondda Valley.

Itinerary

Foreword

There are many meticulously researched histories of public transport operators in various parts of the world which British transport authors are particularly good at producing.

There must be a well documented history of almost every one of the more significant British company and municipal public transport operators, tracing their evolution from the days of horse drawn forms of public transport through the electric tram and trolleybus era to the present day modern bus fleets.

Until now, there was one significant exception. There had never been such a detailed history of Rhondda Transport. Although a relatively small bus company with never more than 230 buses, it nevertheless, played a vital role in day to day life, tucked away in the twin Rhondda Valley mining communities.

Rhondda Transport's proudest moment was during the Second World War when the company was called upon to transport thousands of passengers daily to and from the coal mines, factories and munition arsenals so vital to the war effort.

When word reached me in Hong Kong that Bryngold Books had engaged Jonathan Isaacs to produce a long overdue history of the company, I was overjoyed since my first recollected contact with a Rhondda bus was way back in 1942. I grew up surrounded by Rhondda's impressive fleet of AEC buses which gripped my enthusiasm and thirst for knowledge of the fascinatingly intricate bus industry. I have felt a close affinity for the company ever since and had assembled a mass of material over the years which I thought one day to publish myself.

I wasn't interested in just the bus fleet, but curious to know what went on behind the scenes such as, how they were maintained and what was involved in the organisation of the timetables and crew duties.

With this in mind, I was most fortunate to be offered a position in the Traffic Department at Porth in the late 1950s and spent the two happiest years of my life totally absorbed in the management methods of this fascinating and intensively operated bus fleet. Indeed, I often made myself a nuisance pestering everyone who had the patience to respond to my never ending thirst for knowledge.

The Rhondda Transport staff were a particularly friendly team of colleagues and, in true Welsh valley tradition, everyone knew each other or, had a family member somewhere or other in the company. When, after two years, I was told by the General Manager, Ivor Gray, that he wanted to move me on to our larger sister company, Western Welsh, for career development, I felt a mixture of emotions.

Unlike the relaxed and friendly atmosphere at Porth, I initially found the environment at Cardiff HQ to be stuffy, formal and exceedingly conservative but soon learned to cope and challenge it.

The foundations of my bus experience at Porth have served me well in my subsequent long transport career overseas where, particularly on the hilly and difficult operating terrain of Hong Kong Island, there are strong bus operating similarities to the Rhondda valley routes. I am everlastingly grateful for the time I spent at Porth.

Jonathan has produced an excellent definitive history of the company. I congratulate him for his tireless efforts in researching this excellent publication which is not only a great credit to him, but an everlasting tribute to the thousands of loyal staff who worked for the company over the years from the earlier days of the trams.

**Lyndon Rees, MBE,
Hong Kong.**

A transport tale of two valleys

Rough roads, dogs, children and the sacred sheep of the valleys all conspired to make life difficult for the Rhondda Transport Company which at its height employed 1,000 staff, operated 214 vehicles and boasted the largest bus depot in Wales.

That's without even taking into account the steep hills that presented problems from the time it ran its first trams in 1908, when it operated as the Rhondda Tramways Company, to 1971 when it was taken over by its larger, sister company, Western Welsh.

Rhondda is actually two valleys, the Fawr (large) and the Fach (small) and its narrow streets, with their long rows of terraced homes built at seemingly impossible angles along the valley sides, were the children's playground. Sheep wandered at will around the area's unfenced hillsides, inevitably finding their way down to the streets to seek scraps of food among the houses where they took their chances with dogs which were also allowed to roam freely. Collisions were always a possibility and there were few tram or bus drivers who didn't hit the brakes at one time or another to avoid a child, sheep or dog suddenly running into the road.

The biggest problem however, was the valley roads. In the company's early days these were in appalling condition, something made worse by subsidence caused by extensive underground mine workings. Poor roads forced the trams to run excessively slowly and there were frequent derailments. They were also the reason that Rhondda's trolleybuses lasted less than three months, the shortest lifespan of such a system in the UK. Motorbuses were introduced in 1920 and they had to tackle severe gradients on most routes. This resulted in significant wear and tear on the vehicles and made them expensive to operate.

Rhondda Transport, as it was renamed in 1934 when the trams were withdrawn, also suffered from the effects of the Great Depression between the two world wars. Pits closed and the area lost a staggering 36 per cent of its population as 50,000 people left the valley in the hunt for employment. Poverty, deprivation, soup kitchens and despair led to Rhondda being referred to at the time as Heartbreak Valley. Yet in defiance of these challenges, Rhondda Transport grew from an antiquated tramway system to a modern bus company. At the beginning it connected valley communities which, clustered round the local pits, had previously been isolated from one another. Later, as pits closed, factories sprang up outside the valley to provide new work for the unemployed and it was to the company's buses that the role of transporting people there — and back again — fell.

After the Second World War the desire for a return to normality brought with it a huge growth in the demand for travel and at its peak in the early 1950s Rhondda Transport carried more than 43 million passengers a year. For work, school, shopping or leisure, everyone travelled on a Rhondda bus.

A highlight for many was the annual chapel, pit or social club outing to the seaside in long convoys. Sometimes as many as 40 of the company's familiar red, double deck buses headed off on the route to happiness. Most of these were AEC vehicles, a company with which Rhondda Transport developed a bond that spanned more than 50 years. It also had a large fleet of Leyland Tiger Cub single deckers.

By the end of the 1950s however, the company's boom days were coming to an end. Passenger figures began to fall as TV and the family car began to play an increasingly important role in daily life. The company suffered losses and cut the number of vehicles in the fleet. By the end of the 1960s just 20 million passengers a year were using its buses. Even so it continued to operate a sizeable fleet of 164 buses and employed a staff of almost 800.

Rhondda Transport was taken over by Western Welsh on January 1, 1971, and its identity soon vanished in the major upheavals that afflicted the bus industry during the remainder of that decade. The company may be long gone, but even today it is still fondly remembered by those who worked for it and those for whom its buses provided a lifeline.

Few other bus operators in the UK were more closely identified with the communities they served than Rhondda Transport. The company's legacy continues in the shape of routes operated from the Porth depot by Stagecoach in South Wales which are largely those developed in the 1920s.

There is little doubt that without the advent of Rhondda Transport, the valley's history would have been far different.

Jonathan Isaacs
September 2015.

Trams changed a valley's lifestyle

Thousands of people lined Rhondda's streets on July 11,1908, for one of the most important events in the valley's history. After many delays, the trams were running at last! There was huge excitement among the crowds as the first tramcar pulled out of Porth depot to inaugurate the eagerly awaited, life-changing new transport system.

Adorned with Union flags and to loud cheers from the throng of onlookers, tramcar number 41, driven by Mr CW Furness, who represented the consulting engineers, rolled out of the depot and into the history books. Also on board were leading representatives from the tramway builders and the company that would run the service — the Rhondda Tramways Company.

Another nine tramcars followed soon after and the service got underway, initially covering six and a half miles of track from Rhondda Urban District Council's southern boundary at Trehafod, known originally as Hafod, to Partridge Road, Llwynypia, in the Rhondda Fawr and to Pontygwaith in the Rhondda Fach.

Delays had plagued the start of the service. Work on the track had started in 1906 but subsidence from mineworkings caused huge problems and only short sections of no more than 100 yards could be constructed at a time. The new trams were also vociferously opposed by the Taff Vale Railway Company which feared they would dent its profits. It raised continual objections during the construction phase and this further delayed matters. Even when the service finally started, for the first two months only 10 tramcars could run because of delivery problems with generating plant.

Despite this by September 1, 1908, the trams had carried no fewer than 597,638 passengers bringing in sizeable takings of £3,115.6s.6d. In reality many more people than this were carried for everyone wanted a ride and they packed every available space on the cars

The driver and conductor of tramcar 23 spare a moment for the photographer as they prepare to leave the depot and head off to Maerdy, early 1920s.

during those first weeks making it impossible for the conductors to collect every fare.

On September 2 the sections from Partridge Road to Pentre and Pontygwaith to Ferndale opened and between that time and September 11 another 203,895 passengers were carried bringing in receipts totalling £1,156. By now 16 tramcars were operating and this increased to 25 from September 12 when the track extended from Pentre to Treherbert. Between then and September 24, the number of passengers hit 299,907 with receipts of £1,810.6s.5d. The system now covered a large part of the two valleys, but more was soon to follow. Tonypandy had become one of the most important shopping centres in the Rhondda but as yet had no trams. Rhondda Tramways put that right on November 5, 1908 when a new section from Porth to Dinas, Penygraig and Tonypandy was finished, opening up important new links for 30,000 Mid-Rhondda residents. The new loop continued to Partridge Road and this created a busy connection point with the original route. There were now 17.5 miles of track and in 1910 the tramways carried more than nine million passengers.

But there were still some parts of Rhondda without trams and Rhondda Urban District Council obtained powers to extend the system still further. In April 1912 the track was extended from Ferndale to Maerdy and

In the early days of operation, Rhondda's trams proved a constant source of fascination for the valley's inhabitants both young and old as evidenced by this view of car 50 heading along busy De Winton Street, Tonypandy, bound for Porth.

Treherbert to Tynewydd. A new mile-long spur of track was also opened from Penygraig to the council's boundary at Williamstown.

By this time, Rhondda Tramways had 54 cars to work its system and such was the demand for travel among the valley inhabitants that they were often grossly overcrowded. The mainly single track covered more than 21 miles which made it the most extensive in Wales. Cardiff's trams covered 19.5 miles of mainly double track, although its fleet was much larger.

The trams played a vital role in opening up the Rhondda Fawr and Rhondda Fach valleys which had developed rapidly in the second half of the 19th Century as thousands of people came to work in local pits. The figures continued to rise in the early years of the 20th Century. The 1901 census showed Rhondda's population to be 113,735, but the next one in 1911 recorded it as 152,798. Mining families had moved into long rows of terraced housing built as quickly as possible around the collieries and the important task was to get the coal to markets, not creating links for

Tram driver H Benham and conductor Norley with car 40 before its next run to Williamstown, early 1920s.

A group of proud drivers, conductors and depot staff line up at the depot just after the First World War.

local communities. With the arrival of the trams, people, who for many years had been largely isolated, were connected at last, but the roads remained in a terrible state of repair.

The Taff Vale Railway ran as far as Dinas by the 1840s and as new coal seams were discovered further up the Rhondda Fawr and the Rhondda Fach, the line was gradually extended. This was primarily for freight however, and it was not until January 7, 1863, that the first passengers were carried into Treherbert station and as late as 1876 into Ferndale.

Early road passenger services in the Rhondda consisted of Hansom cabs, brakes and wagonettes although by the 1860s two horse omnibuses were operating services between Treorchy and Treherbert and 10 years later this was extended to three services a day to Ystrad.

Links were a little better further down the valley, although they were hardly ideal. In 1882 the Pontypridd and Rhondda Valley Tramway Company was incorporated and the aim was to construct a horse tramway from Treherbert to Pontypridd. The scheme proved to be over ambitious and after suffering heavy financial losses it finally got going in 1888 but ran for only just over three miles from Porth to Pontypridd. The track was badly maintained and there were numerous accidents. Eventually the receivers were called in and a South Wales entrepreneur, Solomon Andrews, took over the service which ran with one horse tram every 15 minutes. It needed six cars with extra trams at busy times.

In the last years of the 19th Century the service caught the attention of a new company called British Electric Traction. This was set up in 1896 with the prime purpose of converting trams from horse power to electricity and this was what BET had in mind for the Porth to Pontypridd route.

BET quickly drew up its plans, but the reaction from Pontypridd Urban District Council was less than enthusiastic and it presented the company with a list of strict conditions which had to be met before it would allow the route to be electrified. Just to make BET feel even less welcome, it also announced proposals to run its own service.

There were many other objectors to BET's plans, not least the Taff Vale Railway. In the end the problem resolved itself as far as the company was concerned when in 1901 most of the horses caught Glanders disease, a

Rhondda trams with their crews outside the depot.

Car 41 is forced to stop for a commemorative photograph on the first day of the trams.

highly infectious bacterial infection often caused by horses consuming contaminated food or water. The only way to eradicate it at the time was to slaughter the infected animals, which was promptly done.

By now BET had exhausted its enthusiasm for operations in Rhondda and Pontypridd and opted instead to run Merthyr Tydfil's trams and complete the conversion of Swansea's horse trams. Interestingly BET returned to play a most important role in the history of Rhondda Transport but not before another 30 years had elapsed. After much haggling, Rhondda and Pontypridd councils each bought a share of the tramway with the aim of converting it to electricity in their respective districts. Pontypridd's section, from the town to its boundary at Trehafod, opened to great fanfare on March 7, 1905. Rhondda wanted to extend it up the Fach and Fawr valleys, something that was to prove a much more daunting proposition.

By now a third of the revenue on the Taff Vale Railway came from passenger receipts and the company, for whom profit was always the bottom line, saw Rhondda's proposals as a major threat. It strenuously opposed the plans, but in 1902 Rhondda Urban District Council obtained powers for the new tramways. It did not have authority to run them itself so an agreement was made with another company that was converting horse trams to electricity, the National Electric Construction Company Ltd. On December 8, 1905, the council agreed to lease the track to the Tramways Development Company as a trustee for a new company, the Rhondda Tramways Company Ltd. The date — April 14, 1906 — was a historic one for

Crowds throng tram car 1 during the opening of the extension of the system to Pentre, on September 2, 1908.

Rhondda Transport for this was when the new company was incorporated, becoming a subsidiary of the NECC. On August 2, 1907, the Rhondda Tramways Electric Supply Company Ltd was created to supply electric current for the trams and the huge task of getting things ready for the launch swung into action.

Tramcar sheds, machine shops, offices and power station buildings were needed but the question was where to locate them. Eventually an ideal site was found, at the rear of Aberrhondda Road in Porth. The entrance was where the Fach and Fawr valleys meet at Tynewydd Square and for the rest of Rhondda Transport's existence this would be its depot. It is used by Stagecoach in South Wales for its Rhondda operations to this day. The Glamorgan Free Press newspaper was delighted: "The undertaking opens out another opportunity for the development of trade in the Rhondda valleys for there will be 300 men employed and already the difficulty of finding house accommodation for them is being experienced," it said.

The tramcars were housed in two sheds at Porth depot. The smaller was called the top shed while the larger, which also housed maintenance facilities, was referred to as the bottom shed. It was situated at the Tynewydd Square entrance and consisted of four garage bays each with two tracks, or roads, making eight in total. Another track ran alongside, to the right of the shed, to reach the top shed and although the track was ripped up when the trams were scrapped in 1934, to this day it is still known as Nine Road.

Eventually all the construction issues were resolved, mostly in favour of Rhondda Tramways. But it meant the original completion date of December 31, 1907, could not be met and it was not until July 11, 1908, that Rhondda's trams were finally ready to roll.

A troubled time of touch and go

At the end of the First World War, Rhondda Tramways had 54 two axle, double deck trams operating over 21 miles of 3ft 6ins gauge track. By this time they were carrying around nine million passengers every year, but darker days lay ahead.

The system had never been immune to Rhondda's social problems. It had been hard-hit by the 1910 coal strike, which led to the Tonypandy Riots, along with another miners' strike in 1921 and for a while it was touch and go whether the service would be able to continue.

The war years had left their mark on the company with many motormen and conductors volunteering for

A lone, open-top, tram heads along High Street, Treorchy, passing workmen undertaking trackside repairs, 1920.

When the trams became too

For someone who had embarked on a career in marine transportation Ivor Kinnersley could be forgiven for being more than a little surprised to discover on his retirement in 1963 that he had spent nearly 40 years in public transport.

Times were bleak and the Rhondda Valley a very depressed area when Ivor arrived to take up a role with Rhondda Tramways during October 1925.

"Little did I know that I was joining the company as it entered into a challenging period of some significant change. When I arrived to start work with Rhondda Tramways the company operated 54 trams and only a small number of buses. The company faced a heavy financial burden with the operation of the tram system and it was eventually decided to substitute the tramways with double deck buses," he said.

"I think it was generally accepted at the time that the tramway system had to give way to the more modern, more economic operation that the internal combustion engined bus offered.

"The changeover caused quite a stir with the local travelling public and I remember the sadness felt when the last tramcar was driven into Porth depot at midnight. It was the end of an era for the valley."

A proud Rhondda Tramways Company conductor and driver with their respective tramcars.

costly to run

"It was a fascinating time to be involved in public transport which was continually developing right up to the time of my retirement. My role in the office saw the extension of Rhondda's routes, the reorganisation of the depot and offices and the introduction of modern equipment.

"To me it was always an interesting operation to be involved with but I will also remember the friendliness and comradeship of colleagues during work time and outside of it. Rhondda was that sort of company."

service. As Rhondda Tramways struggled to maintain its timetables, conductresses were taken on for the first time and some were still employed in the 1920s.

The trams had been crucial in opening up the valleys and linking communities that were formerly isolated. They helped create new sporting and cultural links as Rhondda Transport bus inspector Richard L Thomas recalled when he retired at the end of 1968.

"After the end of the First World War soccer became very popular with local teams being formed at Mid Rhondda, Ton Pentre and Pontypridd," he said. "Enthusiasm reached such a level that miners would go straight from the pit to the Mid-Rhondda ground to see their teams play. If they had to go to Ton Pentre they filled a tramcar with 120 to 150 passengers, who stood on the buffers, up the stairs and down the front stairs to the driver's platform."

The trams were a vital part of valley life. Local people even held a weekly sweep on the number of the first tram to emerge from Porth depot on Sunday morning. The last car in had to be the first out and 'nobbling' of trams on a Saturday night to delay their return to the garage was not unknown. It was illegal and there were frequent summonses in the courts. On one occasion a man and 11 boys appeared before Ystrad magistrates who were told by Police Superintendent T Edwards that the practice was rampant throughout the area.

A particular problem for Rhondda's trams was that passengers had to change at the council's boundary at Trehafod onto a Pontypridd Urban District Council tram to reach this increasingly important valley town. After

A typical early 1920s scene as a covered tramcar passses between an array of horse-drawn traffic as it heads along Bute Street, Treorchy.

Rhondda's trams played a vital role in opening up the Fach and Fawr valleys, but it was a hugely difficult system to operate. Subsidence caused by underground mine workings and appalling roads always presented the staff of the Rhondda Tramways Company with enormous problems.

Costly repairs to the track were frequently needed and it had to be carefully watched at all times for movement and instability. There were instances when ground movement caused the track to be pushed up by as much as four inches, the record was an even greater nine inches. Rails then had to be taken out to get the track back into position.

Unusually for the time Rhondda's tram track was set in a concrete base down the centre of the road. This was necessary because of the roads which were often just dirt surfaced, but it meant that when the lines needed repair or renewal the concrete had to be dug out and fresh material laid around the new section of track which made it expensive to run the service.

Rhondda's narrow roads meant its trams operated on a single track with passing loops, which also slowed down the service. There were no fewer than 52 passing loops on the Porth-Tonypandy-Tynewydd section alone.

In 1908 Rhondda Tramways was given a 42-year lease by the council at an annual rent of £2,250 to run the trams and one of the conditions was that they should operate at 10 mph every 10 minutes. In reality the combination of problems faced each day meant they rarely managed to reach those speeds which made for excessive slowness and long journey times.

Road subsidence was a continual nightmare and there were particular problems between Penygraig and Dinas, Treorchy and Ynyswen, and Tylorstown to Pontygwaith. Even though speeds were severely restricted bacause of this the trams still swayed alarmingly as they made their way along the track and derailments were not uncommon.

Such conditions made it hugely uncomfortable for passengers and there were frequent jibes in the local newspapers. One reporter wrote: "An experienced mariner says he would rather take a sea voyage in a gale from Jersey to Plymouth, when he has known the ship to rock so much that every plate was broken, than he would journey from Pandy to Porth in a tramcar."

Subsidence was not the only worry for passengers. The trams themselves, built by the Brush company of Loughborough, were all double-decked and open topped, devoid of creature comforts.

Crowds gather around a tramcar which came to grief, left the track and turned onto its side. RIGHT: The undulating conditions trams faced at Miskin Road, Trealaw. BELOW: A section of this passing loop shows exactly why early passengers could expect anything but a smooth ride.

Vital role that proved hard to accomplish

They had 48 hard, wooden seats, 26 placed longitudinally downstairs and 22 on top in the form of two plus one garden seats. Downstairs at least passengers were protected from the elements by sliding doors at each end of the car saloon, but upstairs they were at the mercy of driving rain, heavy snow, wind and freezing temperatures, as was the driver, or motorman, as he was called.

Many of the cars eventually received covered tops which made life for passengers and crews a little more tolerable, but the vestibules and platforms remained exposed right until the end.

much haggling, the two councils agreed a joint working between Porth and Pontypridd which was introduced in 1919. Now Rhondda's trams continued to Pontypridd while Pontypridd's travelled to Porth, although neither council was really at ease with the arrangement as they were concerned about the perceived loss of autonomy.

Even in the 1920s the trip by tram from Rhondda to Pontypridd was seen as a full day's excursion. Often newly-weds would get married in a Rhondda chapel and jump on a tram to spend their honeymoon at the New Inn in Pontypridd, one of the town's most prestigious hotels until it was demolished in 1982. Rhondda Transport held many of its functions there.

The 1920s were difficult times for the trams. Rhondda Tramways started to run motorbuses and while these acted as feeders for the trams rather than competition there were other operators in the Fach and Fawr valleys whose motorbuses did run in competition.

Rhondda Tramways was also affected by the recession that hit the valleys particularly hard during the 1920s. In 1913 the valley was at the height of its coal output with more than 50 deep mines and 41,000 miners. But between 1921 and 1936 mines closed as markets declined. Families were forced to leave Rhondda to search for work. In 1921 the valley's population was 162,279 but an estimated 50,000 people had left by the start of the Second World War. In 1932 Rhondda's unemployment rate was 63 per cent. Poverty and hardship hung over the valleys and the trams were not immune to the effects of this.

In the first nine months of 1925 the company had made a profit of £25,325 but this plummeted to just £355 in the same period of 1926, the year of the General Strike. In the same months of 1927 the trams lost £811. Fears about the availability of coal for the power station at Porth depot to provide electricity to run them was a serious issue in 1921 and 1926. This, together with the system's high operational costs, meant the writing was on the wall.

In 1931, Rhondda Tramways experimented with three double deck motorbuses on the tram routes. The test proved they could do the journeys quicker and at less cost.

Pontypridd Urban District Council obtained powers to operate buses and abandon trams on its section of the system in August 1931 and two years later its Rhondda counterpart obtained similar powers. The section from Maerdy to Porth closed on January 1, 1934 and the Tynewydd to Trehafod track just a month later on February 1. The last tramcar rumbled into Porth depot at 1.30 am that morning. It was car number 41, the same tram that had inaugurated the service 26 years earlier. By now it had been fitted with a roof and seems to have been the car rolled out on special occasions. It was also used to celebrate the coronation of George V in 1910. But there was sadness rather than jubilation from the crowds who watched as it was driven into the depot by Rhondda Tramways general manager TG Richardson.

A Western Mail newspaper reporter described the scene eloquently: "The day of speedier transport has dawned in the Rhondda. A modern omnibus undertaking has now succeeded the tramway system which has done service since 1908. A crowd of several hundred had gathered in the vicinity of the depot to sing the swansong. The singing of Auld Lang Syne, Farewell My Own True Love and other songs marked the finale. Residents flocked from their houses to shout a last farewell to the tram service which, despite the fact that it has now become antiquated, has served them well for over a quarter of a century."

At 4.30 that morning the first motor bus left the depot on the replacement service. Shortly after the 54 tramcars and the 21 miles of track were sold for scrap. For Rhondda, the day of the tram had ended.

Riding on the upper deck became more comfortable when the company enclosed the seating with sides and a roof as car 20 demonstrates at Porth depot.

Trams passing one another on the loop near the Cardiff Arms, Treorchy, in 1910. Car 18 is on the left and car 34, the right.

. . . and then three come along together! A busy Rhondda Valley tramway scene in the early 1920s.

The routes of Rhondda's tramways

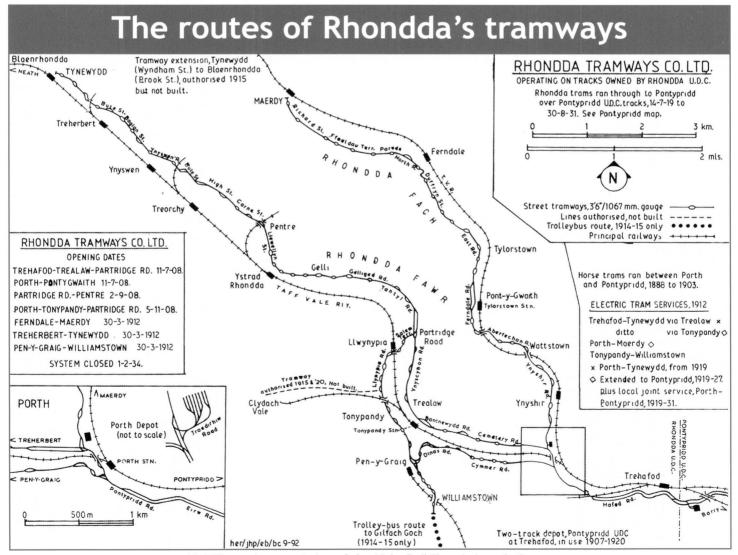

Tramway extension, Tynewydd (Wyndham St.) to Blaenrhondda (Brook St.), authorised 1915 but not built.

RHONDDA TRAMWAYS CO. LTD.
OPERATING ON TRACKS OWNED BY RHONDDA U.D.C.

Rhondda trams ran through to Pontypridd over Pontypridd U.D.C. tracks, 14-7-19 to 30-8-31. See Pontypridd map.

Street tramways, 3'6"/1067 mm. gauge	——o——
Lines authorised, not built	– – – –
Trolleybus route, 1914-15 only	●●●●●
Principal railways	+++++

Horse trams ran between Porth and Pontypridd, 1888 to 1903.

ELECTRIC TRAM SERVICES, 1912

Trehafod–Tynewydd via Trealaw x
ditto   via Tonypandy ◇
Porth–Maerdy ◇
Tonypandy–Williamstown
x Porth–Tynewydd, from 1919
◇ Extended to Pontypridd, 1919-27.
plus local joint service, Porth–Pontypridd, 1919-31.

RHONDDA TRAMWAYS CO. LTD.
OPENING DATES

TREHAFOD-TREALAW-PARTRIDGE RD. 11-7-08.
PORTH-PONTYGWAITH 11-7-08.
PARTRIDGE RD.-PENTRE 2-9-08.
PORTH-TONYPANDY-PARTRIDGE RD. 5-11-08.
FERNDALE-MAERDY 30-3-1912
TREHERBERT-TYNEWYDD 30-3-1912
PEN-Y-GRAIG - WILLIAMSTOWN 30-3-1912

SYSTEM CLOSED 1-2-34.

PORTH
Porth Depot (not to scale)

Tramway authorised 1915 & '20. Not built.

Trolley-bus route to Gilfach Goch (1914-15 only)

Two-track depot, Pontypridd UDC at Trehafod, in use 1907-1920

her/jhp/eb/bc 9-92

JC Gillham, by permission of the Light Rail Transit Association

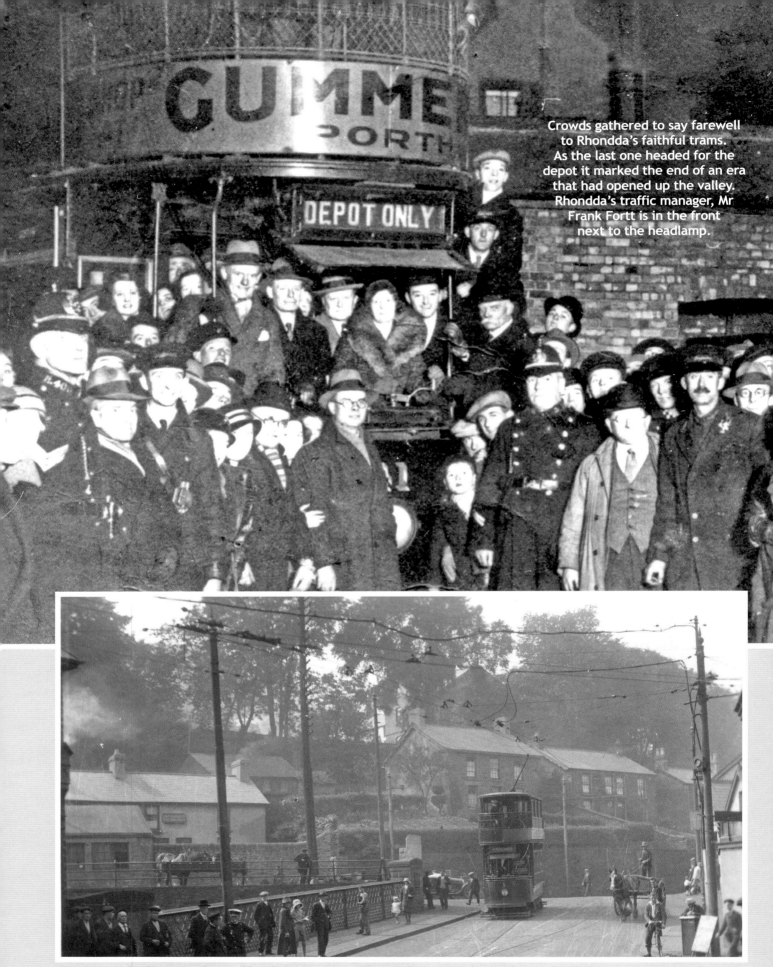

Crowds gathered to say farewell to Rhondda's faithful trams. As the last one headed for the depot it marked the end of an era that had opened up the valley. Rhondda's traffic manager, Mr Frank Fortt is in the front next to the headlamp.

Tram car 1 had acquired a roof by the time it was pictured crossing the bridge on Porth Square in the mid-1920s. There appears to have been quite a tangle of overhead wires at this point.

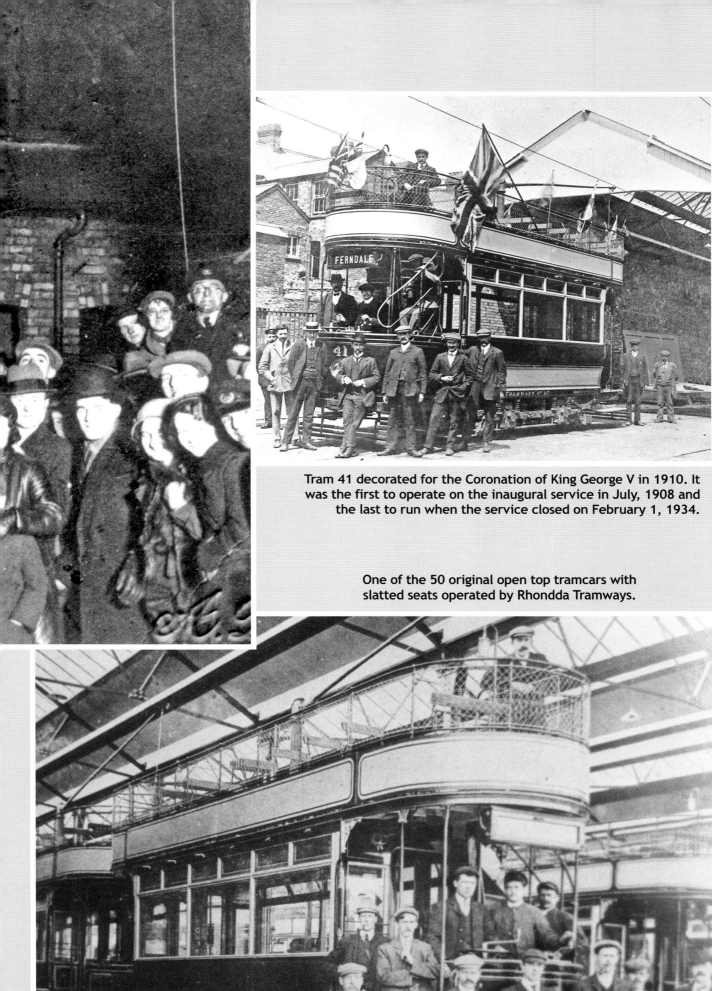

Tram 41 decorated for the Coronation of King George V in 1910. It was the first to operate on the inaugural service in July, 1908 and the last to run when the service closed on February 1, 1934.

One of the 50 original open top tramcars with slatted seats operated by Rhondda Tramways.

Trolleybus times that were a trial

Rhondda's trolleybuses were a disaster. They lasted less than three months — the shortest lived system in Britain — and came to the end of the road when one of them ran out of control down a steep hill and crashed into a terraced house.

Throughout its few short weeks of operation the system was plagued both by the appalling state of the roads and subsidence caused by underground mine workings. Rhondda Tramways had been hugely optimistic that the trolleybuses would be a resounding success and result in much needed new transport links for the valley communities. But it did not happen and passenger figures never reached the early expectations.

Rhondda's tramway system was completed in 1912 with a mile long spur connecting the main track through Penygraig up to the Golden Age Hotel in Williamstown which was Rhondda Urban District Council's boundary with the Llantrisant and Llantwit Fardre Council.

New pits had been sunk at Gilfach Goch in the adjoining valley around that time and miners living in the Rhondda had found work there. As there were no direct transport links they had to walk to work using upland trails over Mynydd Penygraig, which separated the two valleys. While this took only between 40 minutes and an hour to walk, the trails climbed to around 1,300ft, making them arduous and difficult in poor weather.

So Rhondda Tramways proposed a new U-shaped transport link running from Williamstown tram terminus, down to Tonyrefail and up to Gilfach Goch, a distance of four and a quarter miles. A plan to extend the existing tramway was quickly dropped. It would have been too expensive and the steep gradients on the route would have been difficult for trams. Motorbuses were considered but in 1912 these were primitive machines which would also have found climbing the hills extremely difficult, if not impossible.

With the words Special Car on its destination board trolleybus 58 could well have been lined up to make its first run on the ill-fated system when this photograph was taken.

CHAPTER 2

A group of children get in on the act when a passing photographer happened upon the wreckage of one of Rhondda Tramways Company's ill-fated trolleybuses. The vehicle had careered out of control before finally coming to rest against the front wall of this house.

This left just one other option, trolleybuses. To 21st Century eyes, the idea of running 'trackless trolleys' as they were known at the time, on such a route might seem astonishing. It was largely rural with steep gradients and connected villages with relatively few inhabitants. But back in 1912, electric traction was viewed as the best option and there was no-one more enthusiastic about trolleybuses than the general manager of Rhondda Tramways, Henry James Nisbett.

Even so, before the First World War, trolleybuses, like motorbuses, were at the beginning of their development. The first trolleybus schemes had only been introduced in 1911 at far more urban Leeds and Bradford, terrain that was very different from the route under consideration by Rhondda Tramways.

Then on October 3, 1912, a trolleybus system opened at Rotherham in Yorkshire which was almost identical to that being proposed for Rhondda and even connected a tram terminus to a mining area at Maltby. The length of the route was similar too, at a little under five miles. There were also steep gradients on the Rotherham route, which is recognised as Britain's first rural trolleybus operation. But whereas Rotherham's system was extended and prospered for 53 years, Rhondda's lasted just 13 weeks.

That said, Mr Nisbett was despatched to Rotherham to see its new trolleybuses in action and returned enthused, declaring: "This is the way forward!"

He succeeded in persuading Llantrisant and Llantwit Fardre Council that trolleybuses were the answer to the problem and no time was lost in submitting a Bill to Parliament which, when passed, would grant Rhondda Tramways the necessary powers to start its new trolleybus route.

It came before a committee of the House of Commons on April 23, 1913, and Mr Nisbett gave evidence. "I may say at once that it is essential that better communications should be established within the district and that the route along which it is proposed to take these trolley vehicles is the best and only practicable route within the district," he declared.

There was no direct transport link between Penygraig and Gilfach Goch and anyone tempted to use the local railways would have to travel via Llantrisant and

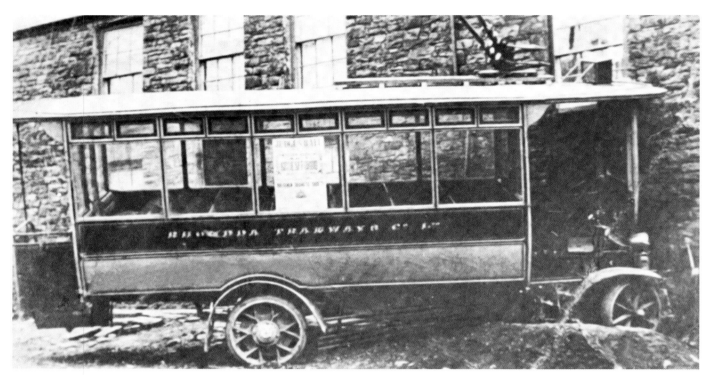

Trolleybus 56, supplied by the Brush Electrical Engineering Company, which ran out of control and crashed into a house in Penrhiwfer.

Bridgend, a journey of three hours for a distance, as the crow flies, of not more than two miles. The trolleybuses would complete the journey in half an hour, Mr Nisbett informed the committee.

He pointed out that the sinking of new mines meant the district's population was growing quickly. New houses were being built for the pitmen and generally around six people would occupy each house. All would need better transport links.

"In the next two or three years the colliery people propose to employ about 3,000 or 4,000 more hands. In my opinion, a scheme of this nature is a necessity for the district, both from the employers' and workmen's point of view," said Mr Nisbett.

He also turned his attention to the route: "There are no bad gradients and no bad corners, in fact I do not think there are any corners at all which would present any danger whatsoever. The gradients are in fact not so

bad as some we already have on parts of our existing tramway system. The surface of the road is very good and nothing wants doing to it to make it throughly suitable for trolley vehicles."

The accuracy of that statement appears questionable because as soon as the system was introduced the poor state of the roads was being blamed for damaging the trolleybuses and within a month subsidence resulted in the collapse of some sections of road.

Mr Nisbett was an engineer by profession, as were the first three general managers at Rhondda Tramways. So it is inconceivable that he was unaware of the obvious difficulties. Despite this his views were supported at the House of Commons Committee hearing by Mr Frank Stanley, chief engineer of the National Electric Construction Company, which at the time was the parent company of Rhondda Tramways.

Mr Stanley told the committee: "The route is suitable for this system of traffic and presents no difficulties in the way of sharp corners or gradients. I am convinced that the system, if started, would be of great benefit to the districts served and would put them in direct communication with Tonypandy, Porth and Pontypridd. This would undoubtedly increase the revenue of the tramways and would therefore benefit both the public of these localities and the tramways."

This, in a nutshell, appears to be the reason for the enthusiasm. Mr Stanley and Mr Nisbett were convinced that the trolleybuses would increase profits and were being "economical with the truth" to get the service under way.

The Bill to run the system received Royal Assent on August 15, 1913. MPs stipulated that Rhondda Tramways would have to contribute to the cost of adapting the roads to make them suitable for trolleybuses and make a contribution to the cost of road repairs. Fares were fixed at a maximum of 1d a mile and, although vehicle registration numbers were not legally required at the time, each trolleybus was to have a fleet number displayed at the front and back to make them distinguishable.

As the company had not expected to be asked to pay for the upkeep of the roads, it revised its expenditure estimates for the new system upwards from £15,944 to £17,277 while its profit forecasts for the first year

Two of Rhondda's early years managers — Top: Mr HJ Nisbett who served from 1908 to 1913 and Mr HH Holliday, 1913-1926.

dropped from £1,813 to £1,585. Attention then turned to the all-important job of deciding what type of trolleybuses to use on the new service. There were three systems to choose from and for two months the pros and cons of each were examined in considerable detail. The Cedes Stoll system was ruled out early on due to complex rear wheel hub motors and that left either the RET or the Lloyd-Kohler systems.

A report by the NECC came down in favour of the Lloyd-Kohler system, even though Stockport was the only place in Britain where it ran. Rhondda Tramways managers went to see it in action and concluded it was the best option for the new Williamstown to Gilfach Goch route, although a problem was that on the Stockport system the trolleybuses had to exchange trolleys to pass each other as only one pair of parallel horizontal wires had been constructed.

The company was also unhappy about the system having its trolley running on the wires with a flexible connection to the cars. It demanded that Brush Electrical Engineering, which held the patents in the UK for the Lloyd-Kohler system, modify it to resemble the RET system with two horizontally parallel wires and two trolley poles on each car.

Satisfied at last, Rhondda Tramways placed an order in November 1913 for six trolleybuses to be bodied by Brush at a cost of £740 each, although an extra £11 was added for each after the company changed its choice of wood for the mainframe of the vehicles from ash to teak. They were built on a Daimler chassis with rear entrances and are believed to have had seats for 28 passengers who would not have found it particularly easy getting on board as the height of the floor above the road meant climbing up three steps. The days of low floor buses were still many decades ahead!

Drivers did not have it easy either. They sat in a compartment open to the elements. The buses were painted with a maroon band below the windows and numbered 55-60. They were garaged in a car shed at Tonyrefail which Rhondda Tramways leased for 99 years at £20 a year.

There were delivery delays but the system finally began operation on December 22, 1914. At first, all appeared to go well. By December 31, the six vehicles had run 4,320 miles and on January 4 the Mid-Rhondda Gazette told its readers the trolleybuses were fulfilling a long felt need.
But within four weeks of their introduction into service, the company's minutes were noting the very bad state of Gilfach Road and the damage being caused to vehicles. The problems were so serious that by February 14, 1915, it was feared the service would have to stop, but amazingly it managed to soldier on.

Then disaster struck. One of the cars went out of control descending Penrhiwfer Road, towards Tonyrefail, one of the route's steepest sections, and only came to a halt after crashing into the front of a house. The driver and conductor managed to jump out of the way before impact while the only passenger on board — perhaps an indication of how poorly used the service was — escaped the experience with just bruises and shock.

If Rhondda Tramways had hoped to keep the incident quiet, it was out of luck because a photographer was passing the scene at the time and took a picture of the trolleybus firmly embedded in the front of the house.

The accident appeared to have been the final straw and on March 17, 1915, trolleybus operation was suspended, never to restart. The 'trackless cars' had operated 25,585 miles and although there was talk of resuming the service after the First World War, it never happened. In May 1920, Rhondda Tramways

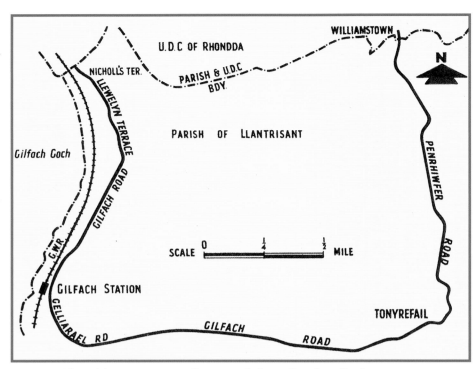

Rhondda Tramways solitary and short-lived trolleybus route.

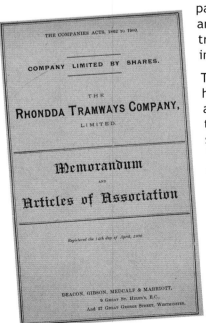

sold the trolleybuses for £2,800 and they eventually entered the fleet of Teeside Railless Traction Board at Middlesborough where they became cars 11-16 and gained registration numbers.

The car shed at Tonyrefail, only the second ever Rhondda Tramways depot, was used to house vehicles on the replacement bus service until 1931 when they were transferred to the main depot at Porth. It was sold in 1935. The poles for the trolleybus service were eventually adapted for street lighting and many were still there as recently as the 1980s.

Post war plan to extend route

Another plan for the route after the war involved extending the tramway from Williamstown to Gilfach Goch and from Tonyrefail to Pontyclun. A Light Railway Order was taken out by Llantrisant and Llantwit Fardre Council, but even though it was supported by Rhondda Tramways it was eventually abandoned for being too expensive.

The company began a motorbus service between Penygraig and Gilfach Goch in January 1921 and this continued for the rest of its existence.

After the three month debacle, both Rhondda District Council and Rhondda Tramways wanted nothing more to do with trolleybuses. Mr Nisbett never oversaw the repercussions because in 1913 he moved to run

Torquay's tramway system. His successors, Mr HH Holliday from 1913 to 1926, and then Mr TG Richardson, oversaw the introduction of motorbuses on Rhondda routes in the 1920s which, because of the steepness of the gradients, would have been better tackled at the time by electric trolleybuses. Even so, motorbuses became the order of the day and trolleybuses never got another look in as far as Rhondda Tramways was concerned.

Local opposition to trolleybuses almost scuppered a scheme to run them by neighbouring Pontypridd Urban District Council. In the late 1920s it announced plans to replace its trams running between Treforest and Cilfynydd, and on the Porth to Pontypridd tram route run jointly with Rhondda Tramways, with trolleybuses but found it had a battle on its hands.

In January 1927, Pontypridd's tramways manager, Mr JE Teasdale, had to attend a public meeting to vigorously defend the plans against powerful opponents. He told them that the town's trolleybus proposals were nothing like the failed Rhondda system.

Rhondda UDC also objected and eventually Pontypridd was forced to drop its proposals to run trolleybuses between Porth and Pontypridd and the trams were replaced by buses. But the Treforest to Cilfynydd trolleybus route was finally launched on September 18, 1930, and ran until January 31, 1957, when it was also replaced by motorbuses.

Rhondda Tramways' stance was controversial. There was strong opposition in the early 1930s when the company revealed plans to replace its tram fleet with motorbuses. Opponents said that in such a large coal producing area as Rhondda, trolleybuses powered by electricity generated by the use of coal should be the preferred option.

The South Wales area committee of the Coal Utilisation Council claimed there was no justification for local authorities changing from the use of coal to generate electricity for powering the trams to using petrol driven vehicles. It called on Rhondda UDC and Rhondda Tramways to justify their preference for motorbuses. But neither would be swayed and they seemed to have the backing of valley residents. In December 1932, a meeting of Rhondda ratepayers was held in Pentre at which a resolution was passed in favour of the council promoting a Bill to replace trams with buses.

The Rhondda Passenger Transport Bill was passed in April 1933 and the future for the valley's transport links was mapped out. In 1934 it was the motorbus, not the trolleybus, that replaced Rhondda's trams. In June of that year the company also changed its name. From then on it was known as the Rhondda Transport Company.

Welcome for the first bus

In October 1924 Rhondda Tramways began an 11.2 mile service that seems strange today, but at the time made perfect sense.

It began in Penygraig and ran to Tonyrefail, Blackmill and up the Ogmore Valley to Nantymoel which was firmly in the territory of South Wales Commercial Motors, later Western Welsh, and its route from Bridgend bus station.

Much of the route is rural and today there are no obvious reasons for such a service, but back then Rhondda's managers felt it would link two important industrial areas and prove of value to South Glamorgan agricultural districts. The service didn't last long, but at the start it was welcomed by local people who were without transport links, as the first conductor on the service, Richard L Thomas, recalled.

Richard went on to become an inspector with Rhondda Transport and was a regular at Talbot Green bus station before retiring at the end of the 1960s. He was just 20 when he conducted the first Penygraig to Nantymoel bus and remembered arriving at Glynogwr, a village between Gilfach Goch and Blackmill.

"I think all the inhabitants turned out to greet us and we became very popular with them. Previously they had to walk either to Blackmill or Gilfach Goch, both about two miles away, if they wanted to get anywhere," he said.

"Roads were rough with six inch deep ruts in places. I remember we were climbing the steep hill from Blackmill to Glynogwr one night when the driver came and sat next to me, the bus was still climbing in low gear. He had put the front wheels in the ruts and set the throttle so that the bus climbed slowly on its own. He had done this to scare me and the few passengers on board — and definitely succeeded!

"An elderly farmer, noted for being tight with his money, was a regular traveller. One December afternoon he got on my bus and tendered 6d for a 3d fare, but I didn't have any change, so he told me to keep it as a Christmas box. About nine months later he got on my bus and again I didn't have 3d change for the fare. He turned to me and said, remember that Christmas box I gave you last Christmas, take it out of that instead!"

Motorbuses really open up the valleys

The roaring twenties was one of the most exciting decades for the Rhondda Tramways Company. It launched its first motorbus service in 1920 and within 10 years it had 71 vehicles running over regular routes as far away as Porthcawl, Barry and Cardiff.

The company had truly opened up the valleys and the effect on everyone's lives was profound. Instead of being isolated in their own communities, residents were not only connected by tram to larger settlements such as Tonypandy, Treorchy, Porth and Ferndale, but they could hop on a bus for trips to the seaside or visit the metropolis that was Cardiff, at the time Wales' only city.

Rhondda Tramways, however, did not have matters all its own way. There were battles to be fought and difficulties to overcome, not least the terrain its services had to cover and the economic problems that plagued the valleys during the years of the Great Depression.

Rhondda's transport development had come to a halt during the First World War although in 1915 the district council had obtained powers to construct tramways from Tonypandy to Clydach Vale which at that time was still only being served by Hansom cabs and carts.

The area sorely needed better transport links for the collieries that had been constructed and the hundreds of new terraced homes that had been built for the miners who worked in them. The problem was that the settlements could often only be reached by roads whose gradients were as steep as 1 in 6, with the average being 1 in 12. In cases such as this, over just three-quarters of a mile, the increase in height could be as much as 323ft.

For some people walking these stiff climbs was impossible and it was discovered that many people in Clydach Vale had not ventured further than the vicinity of their own homes for as long as 10 years. Tramway

A driver and conductress with one of nine AEC YC vehicles bought from the War Department Disposals Board in 1920. They arrived with 26 seat lorry bus bodies after a period on hire to London General Omnibus Company, but Rhondda fitted 32 seat bodies.

CHAPTER 3

Bus 22, registration number BX1208, a second hand AEC YC type, in the depot yard at Porth. It was one of a pair bought from a Carmarthenshire operator, and then returned to AEC in 1932, probably as a part exchange for one of that company's newer models.

consultants were called in to survey the proposed new route but declared that gradients such as these were simply too severe to be tackled by trams. That left two options — trolleybuses or motorbuses. Neither was ideal although electric traction was a better proposition than the combustion engine at this time for such steep gradients. Rhondda remained sensitive to the disastrous failure of its Williamstown to Gilfach Goch trolleybus system six years earlier and did not want to repeat the mistake. Instead, faced with almost no option it went for motorbuses though even then it was confronted by the quandary of finding vehicles capable of overcoming such steep gradients.

At the end of the First World War, hundreds of surplus Army vehicles were coming on to the market and it was surmised that if they could carry troops across the battlefields they should be able to handle the hills of Clydach Vale. In 1920 nine former Army lorries were bought and brought to Rhondda to work the service. Two years earlier they had been carrying soldiers fighting in distant battlefields. Now, fitted with seats, they faced a peacetime task with its own difficulties.

These vehicles had AEC engines and their purchase was the start of Rhondda Transport's long association with that company. Until it was taken over at the end of 1970, it always had buses from this company in its fleet

and the last one, an AEC Regent V, was not withdrawn from Porth depot until 1979, a remarkable union that spanned nearly 60 years.

On August 5, 1920, Rhondda Tramways' first motorbus service was launched. The short 1.4 mile route stretched from Tonypandy Square to the top of Clydach Vale, near the entrance to Cambrian Colliery. Passenger seats were fitted on the back of the lorries which it is said climbed the hill at just 2 mph and descended at 4 mph. Each had a driver and conductress. In time these basic vehicles were fitted with new purpose built bus bodies seating 32 passengers. They appeared to have served the company well for it was 1932 before the last of them was withdrawn from service.

Richard L Thomas, who retired as a Rhondda bus inspector in 1968, was brought up in Blaenclydach and remembered the vehicles well: "They were very basic with wooden slatted seats, open sides and no windows. The driver sat at the wheel with a sheet of canvas coming up under his chin for protection from the

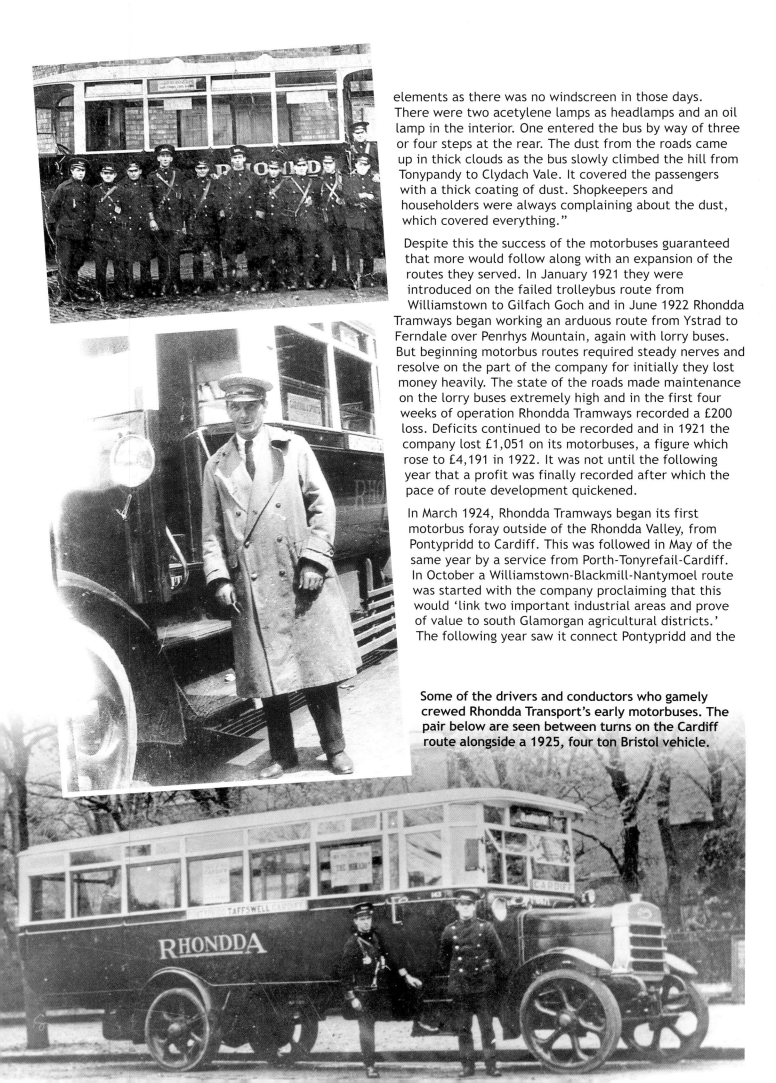

elements as there was no windscreen in those days. There were two acetylene lamps as headlamps and an oil lamp in the interior. One entered the bus by way of three or four steps at the rear. The dust from the roads came up in thick clouds as the bus slowly climbed the hill from Tonypandy to Clydach Vale. It covered the passengers with a thick coating of dust. Shopkeepers and householders were always complaining about the dust, which covered everything."

Despite this the success of the motorbuses guaranteed that more would follow along with an expansion of the routes they served. In January 1921 they were introduced on the failed trolleybus route from Williamstown to Gilfach Goch and in June 1922 Rhondda Tramways began working an arduous route from Ystrad to Ferndale over Penrhys Mountain, again with lorry buses. But beginning motorbus routes required steady nerves and resolve on the part of the company for initially they lost money heavily. The state of the roads made maintenance on the lorry buses extremely high and in the first four weeks of operation Rhondda Tramways recorded a £200 loss. Deficits continued to be recorded and in 1921 the company lost £1,051 on its motorbuses, a figure which rose to £4,191 in 1922. It was not until the following year that a profit was finally recorded after which the pace of route development quickened.

In March 1924, Rhondda Tramways began its first motorbus foray outside of the Rhondda Valley, from Pontypridd to Cardiff. This was followed in May of the same year by a service from Porth-Tonyrefail-Cardiff. In October a Williamstown-Blackmill-Nantymoel route was started with the company proclaiming that this would 'link two important industrial areas and prove of value to south Glamorgan agricultural districts.' The following year saw it connect Pontypridd and the

Some of the drivers and conductors who gamely crewed Rhondda Transport's early motorbuses. The pair below are seen between turns on the Cardiff route alongside a 1925, four ton Bristol vehicle.

These two Bristol-engined vehicles demonstrate clearly just how body styles and fashions altered in the early days of motorbus construction.

Rhondda to the seaside for the first time with routes from Pontypridd and Porth to Porthcawl. In May 1927 the upper Rhondda was linked by motorbus to Cardiff via the Ely Valley, with a service from Treorchy that was extended to Treherbert in November 1931.

Transport connections from the Rhondda were gradually improving and the late 1920s saw roads constructed over the Rhigos and Bwlch mountains. As a result, in July 1929 Rhondda Tramways launched a summer service over the Bwlch's 1,400ft summit from Treorchy to Pricetown in the Ogmore Valley.

The monthly transport trade magazine, Commercial Motor, was high in its praise of all these developments, describing them as remarkable, in an article published in its April 1925 issue.

"The Rhondda Valleys afford an instance of enterprise and fleet expansion typical of the spirit of pioneers in the past year," it stated.

All this had been achieved with very basic buses — little more than boxes on wheels — with solid tyres and speed limits of just 12 mph. Rhondda Tramways' buses in the 1920s were all single deck, slow AEC, ADC, Albion and Bristol vehicles usually seating around 32 passengers. All had tops so Rhondda residents were spared the rigours of the weather. In fact by the standards of the day, they were quite luxurious.

Commercial Motor magazine praised them because 'only the best materials are used in body construction' adding that 'seats have the best antique leather upholstery over cushion springs and that for durability, all-teak frames and aluminium panelling are utilised for the buses.'

But not everything was perfect for Rhondda Tramways. The 1920s was a time of huge competition in the bus industry as new operators tried their hand at running services. The company found itself competing against as many as 40 other firms, although most eventually fell by the wayside. Rhondda itself only ever took over two — Williams of Tynant and, in 1936, David Davies and Sons of Ynysybwl. Most small operators ran without licences, which in the 1920s were awarded by local councils, and there was little in law to stop them. The Road Traffic Act of 1930 brought some sense to the mayhem however and Traffic Commissioners were set up with powers over operators, licences, fares and timetables which benefitted respectable firms like Rhondda Tramways and frightened off the less scrupulous opposition.

With the advent of the 1930s there were also huge advances in bus design and technology. Rhondda began to acquire modern AEC Regal single deckers in 1930, a move which represented a significant step forward. In 1931 the company trialled three types of double deck vehicles and AEC again won the day with its Regent. The first 30 arrived in 1933-4 to replace the trams and, aside from the Second World War period, Rhondda Transport Company, as it was renamed in 1934, bought no other type of double decker for more than three decades, until 1968.

The abandonment of the trams in 1934 saw the arrival of replacement bus services in the Rhondda which significantly reduced journey times. Just 30 double deck AEC Regents replaced 54 trams and new backbone routes were started which continued to operate for the remainder of Rhondda Transport's life. They ran from Blaencwm/Blaenrhondda to Tonypandy and Porth, and from Tonypandy/Partridge Road to Trealaw, Porth and Maerdy.

There was also a Rhondda Tramways/Pontypridd Urban District Council joint service that had replaced the tram

An early bus crew with fleet No. 11, NY995, a 32 seat Strachan & Brown bodied Daimler Y being used between Nantymoel and Ogmore Vale, 1922.

route between Porth and Pontypridd and at one stage in 1934 there were proposals to run the 13 mile Blaenrhondda to Pontypridd service jointly. Rhondda was concerned that this would result in a loss of autonomy and eventually decided to go it alone. A private company was regarded with suspicion by some Pontypridd councillors who preferred their own municipally run transport department: "We shouldn't enter into agreements that might extend the life of private services," declared one of their councillors.

By this time Rhondda Tramways had a new owner. In 1931 British Electric Traction, which had pulled out of the area 30 years previously, took over the National Electric Construction Company which had owned Rhondda since its inauguration in April 1906.

The BET empire also owned Cardiff based Western Welsh and, not surprisingly perhaps, over the following decades a close relationship was established between these two Welsh subsidiaries.

Despite the economic hardship of the 1930s, which saw many thousands forced to leave the valleys in a desperate quest to find work, Rhondda Transport continued to build up its routes and steadily increased its fleet. By 1939 it had 137 vehicles, 120 of them built by AEC. This tally consisted of 55 double deckers and 82 single deckers. In 1938

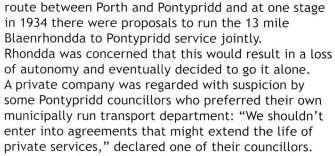

Compared to those that followed, this early bus used by Rhondda Tramways before the company was renamed would certainly have provided a harsh ride.

If an army marches on its stomach then Pat Evans was the woman who made sure Rhondda's staff were kept well fed and fuelled up.

Pat kept crews

Pat worked in the staff canteen at Porth depot for a total of 39 years, retiring in 2011.

"The staff had their own canteen, which they helped pay for with contributions of 10p a week," she said.

"The treasurer was Dai Hindler and it was managed by Arnold Owen, a driver who was an amazing character. He lived in Blackmill, which was outside Rhondda Transport's area and so it did not get a staff

bus. When he was on early shifts he had to walk, whatever the weather, from Blackmill all the way to Gilfach Goch to get the staff bus, he would have had to start off at about three in the morning! When I started work, Porth depot employed nearly 1,000 people and the canteen was available for shift times so it was open from 4.30am to 8.30pm at night. Breakfast was at five in the morning and meals were available throughout the day. I had to get up at

the company carried 21 million passengers over 4.75 million miles. But the outbreak of the Second World War confronted Rhondda Transport with many major challenges that were to test both its staff and vehicles to the limit.

A driver and conductor in front of their 32 seat, Bristol B double entrance saloon shortly before departing the Knights Arms, Porthcawl on the return journey to Pontypridd.

Clydach Vale was no easier a task

For the first motorbuses that had found their way to Rhondda from the battlefields of the First World War the task of carrying passengers up and down Clydach Vale was as difficult as that of carrying soldiers in their original role.

Numbered 1-9, they initially carried 26 passengers but in 1922-3 they were rebodied to look more like buses,

receiving 32 seat wooden frames, the work being carried out in the tram sheds at Port depot. They were AEC YC types, so heralding Rhondda's long association with AEC, and had long lives for the time. In fact they were not withdrawn until 1931-2. Some of the bodies were bought for use as sheds at the Sunny Bank allotments in Blaenclydach where they were still proudly displaying their Rhondda fleet name well into the 1950s.

fed and watered

3.30am to be at the canteen by 4am. The crews were great, I would do anything for them. If they were between duties they would sit in the canteen. We had a couple of pool tables, and they would help wash the dishes. I even met my husband Ray, a driver, at the canteen. During the coal strike, miners could get free meals there and we also gave free meals to council workers who would come to clear the snow around Porth depot in bad weather."

The staff canteen at Porth where tasty, reasonably priced meals were always on the menu.

No new buses were bought in 1921 but the following year Rhondda Tramways acquired its first real motorbuses. They were three Daimler YC vehicles with Strachan and Brown 32 seat bodies, numbered 10-12, and they were withdrawn between 1929 and 1932. Also in 1922, the company received two more AEC YC types which had been running with Devon General. One, numbered 13, with a bus body but the second, numbered 16, arrived as a lorry bus but is believed to have been rebodied later. Both ended up as lorries with the Hendy Quarry Company in Pontyclun where they lasted until just before the Second World War.

In 1923, the first of one of the most successful motorbuses of the 1920s arrived at Porth depot. It was a Bristol, bodied by Brislington Body Works, usually known as BBW, a four-ton, front entrance vehicle seating 32 passengers which Rhondda Tramways numbered 14. It was followed by two similar vehicles in 1924, another six in 1925. Three B types arrived in 1927 and five in 1928 with six of the updated Bristol D model arriving in 1931. All had been withdrawn by 1939.

Rhondda continued to buy the AEC YC type and in 1924 bought a charabanc for tours and private hires.

The only Dennis Lance II to join the fleet was 78, TG2119, one of the 1931 intake. Its specification was identical to that of the London General DL class, and it was fitted with a 48 seat body by MCW.

Rhondda Tramways found itself facing formidable opposition when it tried to run buses into Cardiff city centre in the late 1920s and early 1930s. It seemed that this intrusion from the valley was regarded as most unwelcome by the transport watchdogs of Wales' biggest urban sprawl.

The company started a service from Pontypridd to Cardiff in March 1924 and the following May began another from Porth-Tonyrefail-Cardiff, but Cardiff Watch Committee, the body that looked after transport matters in the city, did not want Rhondda vehicles in the city centre.

The committee refused to let Rhondda Tramways pick up or set down passengers within Cardiff's boundaries and would not allow the company's buses further into the city than the tram terminus in Cathedral Road, Llandaff. Rhondda also wanted to run double deckers but the watch committee insisted on single deckers only, even though Cardiff Corporation used double deckers.

It meant Rhondda Tramways buses were relegated to the position of feeder services for Cardiff's trams. Eventually the company decided to launch a battle to get the restrictions lifted. It appealed to the Ministry of Transport which held an inquiry on September 5, 1927.

Lined up against Rhondda were the watch committee, Cardiff Corporation and the city's chief constable, who contended that the number of accidents would rise if the company's buses were allowed into the centre. Rhondda Tramways wanted its vehicles to be allowed to terminate in Westgate Street and the company's barrister, Mr E Kirkhouse Jenkins, claimed the corporation was "reducing a first-class bus service to the level of feeding its trams."

The company's general manager, Mr TG Richardson, rejected the chief constable's claim about accidents and he called for Rhondda to be allowed to use the same size vehicles as Cardiff Corporation was operating.

The inquiry eventually ended with Rhondda's buses being allowed further into the city centre, although only as far as Fitzhamon Embankment. It was eventually allowed to use double deckers, but the restriction on picking up passengers within Cardiff's boundaries remained.

It was hardly satisfactory from Rhondda Tramways' viewpoint and in 1933 it appealed to the South Wales Traffic Commissioners after they had taken over bus licensing functions. Once again the chief constable warned of a rise in accidents if the company's buses were allowed to use Westgate Street as a terminus. But after a three-

Park Royal bodied Daimler 206, FTG119 near its terminus on a run into Cardiff.

Cardiff route was a ticket to trouble

day hearing, the chairman, Mr AT James KC, said the police had greatly exaggerated the evidence. "We are unable to accept the traffic statistics in Westgate Street submitted by the police," said Mr James, who gave the go-ahead to its use as a terminus for Rhondda's buses. He described Fitzhamon Embankment as "a bleak, unsheltered spot, far from the centre of the city."

But Cardiff Corporation was still not done and in March the following year appealed against the decision. Eventually Rhondda's buses were allowed into the city centre, although the restriction on picking up and setting down passengers was to remain until the Thatcher government de-regulated bus services in 1986. Rhondda Transport began running double deckers on its Treorchy to Cardiff route in 1937, but without a bus station services were forced to terminate at different streets in the city centre.

It was not until 1954, the year before Cardiff became the capital of Wales, that the city's central bus station opened and all Rhondda Transport's services to Cardiff terminated there.

Driver Ben Evans stands proudly in front of his Leyland TD1 double decker in Ferndale, 1935. The vehicle was one of the first double deckers to be operated by the Rhondda Tramways Company whose initials can be seen above the cab.

It was another one bought from the War Department and had a detachable roof with doors for passengers to get on and off fitted all along the vehicle. There were seats for 35 passengers but it was a tight squeeze! The company numbered the bus 19 and it was sold in 1928.

In 1926, AEC and Daimler merged their bus production activities to form ADC and the following year Rhondda Tramways bought four ADC 415A models which were bodied by Hall, Lewis & Company. One of the Rhondda vehicles appeared in a company

One of two Albion PMB28 models with six cylinder engines and 32 seat bodies, which Rhondda acquired in 1930. This vehicle, yet to be registered, is already displaying Upper Boat as its intended destination.

advertisement which proclaimed: 'New methods of seating, both in the springing and upholstery, have been adopted to provide the highest degree of ease and comfort.' The buses had two entrances, one at the front, the other at the rear and seated 32 passengers. Numbered 43-46, they were withdrawn in 1935-6.

Rhondda bought yet another different model in 1929. The first of these, two Albion PMB28s, numbered 56 and 57 were followed by seven more in 1930, numbered 58, 59, and 61-65. Albion was a Scottish bus builder and enjoyed significant sales with the Red & White bus company, which acted as one of its agents. The first four of Rhondda's vehicles had six cylinder engines, the last five had four cylinders, but all had 32 seat bodies.

Rhondda Tramways buses were single deck in the 1920s and were slow, often uncomfortable machines with the earliest running on solid tyres. But towards the end of the decade significant advances had been made in bus technology which would bring public transport into a new age. The company would be at the forefront of those changes.

Terrain proved a tough test for all

The Rhondda valleys suffered immense hardship and deprivation during the years of the Great Depression that gripped the country in the late 1920s and early 1930s and this had a huge impact on the Rhondda Tramways Company.

It had developed bus services to serve the valley collieries, but as coal markets declined many pits closed and between the General Strike of 1926 and the end of 1931 the number of miners plummeted from 48,700 to 29,530. In 1931, around 12,000 people left the Rhondda in a desperate bid to find work and this had a sobering effect on the company's bus receipts.

In 1923, receipts per mile on Rhondda's buses were just over £1 but during the 1926 strike they fell to just over 12 shillings. By 1931 this was down to 10 shillings, but remarkably Rhondda Tramways not only managed to keep services going, it continued to increase them and saw passenger totals rise. In 1921 the company's buses ran 114,475 miles but 10 years later this had risen to 2,267,206. Over the same period the number of passengers carried rose from 541,058 to 6,671,988, a remarkable achievement given the limited number of

Some of Rhondda's earliest double deck vehicles. FAR LEFT: Weymann bodied AEC Regent No.129 TG6329 at the depot. This high bridge vehicle with seating for 52 arrived in 1934. CENTRE: left to right a 1933 Weymann bodied AEC Regent; a 1943 Guy Arab II with Park Royal body; a 1934 AEC Regent, again Weymann bodied and finally another of the 1943 intake of Guy Arab IIs. ABOVE: The piano-style front of this Leyland TD1 with lowbridge 51 seat body dated very quickly with the advent of more modern design in the 1930s. Registered as TG2120 and unusually for the time, it received a new Weymann highbridge body in 1938. It was withdrawn in 1945, and was eventually sold to a showman.

buses and routes being operated. Not least among the difficulties was the tortuous terrain over which the buses ran. The only level route on the system was that from Cardiff to Pontypridd, which rose 180ft in 12 miles. Between Porth and Tonyrefail, for example, the route rose 480ft in just three-quarters of a mile with two short stretches as severe as 1 in 4.

Tough at the best of times, the routes were even more of a nightmare during wintertime and there were occasions when icy conditions resulted in two or three buses being stranded overnight. Once in the harsh winter of 1931-2 a severe frost resulted in around 30 vehicles being unable to complete their journeys, either to Porth depot or their destinations.

All this meant that drivers had to be especially proficient and as more bus routes developed the company inaugurated its own training school in which tram drivers received what were described as sound theoretical and practical instructions in the control of petrol-engine vehicles. Conductors were generally promoted from cleaners at the depot and inspectors

Rhondda Tramways Company employees with vehicles used for a poor children's outing to Porthcawl, 1933.

were chosen from the staff, a procedure followed for many years.

By 1932, Rhondda Tramways had 560 employees, most of them at this time tram drivers or conductors. Many were retrained for the buses which replaced the trams in 1934. After the lorry buses and the primitive single deck ADC, Albion and Bristol buses of the early years, more modern AEC vehicles were entering the fleet. The first single deck Regals arrived in 1930 by which time the bus fleet stood at 71, and in 1933-4, a fleet of 30 double deck AEC Regents replaced the trams.

By this time, most bus routes had a frequency of between 30 minutes and one hour and peak traffic, outside travel to and from work, was on Thursday afternoons and Saturdays. Thursday was always half-day closing in the Rhondda and it saw a big exodus on the buses to Cardiff. In the summer months Barry Island and Porthcawl were the favourite travel hotspots. Evening trips to the coast were popular and regularly needed as many as 20 buses.

Rhondda Tramways was meticulous about vehicle maintenance. Buses were brought in after 6,000 miles and engines examined with minor work, such as decarbonising and valve grinding, undertaken. Engines and chassis were overhauled at 30,000 miles with a complete dock, which involved stripping the chassis down to the last nut, at 60,000 miles. Tyres lasted for

around 35,000 miles and apart from a nightly wash each bus was thoroughly cleaned with soap and water once a week. Porth depot in 1932 had a well-equipped machine shop, a bay for overhauls, and oil and tyre stores. There was a smith's shop, an upholstery shop for making bus seats, a paint shop and a body repair shop.

Rhondda Tramways was a thriving, professionally run operation that served 160,000 people in an area covering 360 square miles.

Missing out on a trick or two

Rhondda Tramways faced much competition as it began to extend its motorbus operation in the 1920s. At one time there were as many as 40 small operators in the area all trying to run services and one entrepreneur in particular was a real thorn in the company's side.

His name was David Morgan and in 1921 he came up with the idea of running a bus between Ferndale in the Rhondda Fach, over Penrhys Mountain, to Ystrad in the Rhondda Fawr, a tall order given the route's severe gradients and the primitive vehicles available to him.

From Ystrad to the mountain top was a climb of 451ft in three-quarters of a mile, while from Tylorstown the

route climbed 328ft in a similar distance. But Mr Morgan used an ex-Army lorry bus which could manage the gradient, although very slowly, and the service got underway, much to the consternation of Rhondda Tramways. The main reason for this was that the route was a much quicker way of connecting the Fach and Fawr valleys. Previously the only way had been to catch a tram from either valley to Porth and change to a connecting tram service up the other side.

Rhondda Tramways had clearly missed a trick and Mr Morgan's bus proved popular. He was given a licence by Rhondda Urban District Council, but in June 1922 Rhondda Tramways started a similar service and when the time came for Mr Morgan's licence to be renewed, it objected claiming it had a monopoly agreement as it paid the council £2,250 a year to lease the tramways.

The council then refused Mr Morgan a licence and gave one instead to Rhondda Tramways. The decision caused uproar. Ferndale and Blaenllechau ratepayers met and passed a strongly worded resolution calling on the council to renew Mr Morgan's licence. Ferndale Chamber of Commerce protested that it was against the public interest that a monopoly should be created for the tramways company. "There is considerable public feeling that an injustice has been done to this bus operator," said its spokesman.

The council stood firm and continued its refusal to renew Mr Morgan's licence, but agreed he could run unlicensed and eventually the two sides came to an agreement over timings and schedules so that both services could run. But then Rhondda Tramways missed another trick. In 1928 a controlling interest in Mr Morgan's company, Rhondda Motor Services (Ferndale) Ltd, was obtained by Aberdare Motor Services based in the adjoining Cynon Valley. This company later became part of the Red & White bus group which extended Mr Morgan's service into the marathon 36-mile long Aberdare to Porthcawl route which continues up to the

present day.

Rhondda Tramways pressed on with its service over Penrhys and in July 1932 extended it to Blaenllechau. In the beginning the company used lorry buses on the route which it is said took all day to climb Penrhys Mountain. Drivers were instructed to descend either side in first gear. From the 1930s the route was run by 34 seat AEC Regals until work to improve a turning circle was carried out at Blaenllechau in 1958. Their place was taken by larger 44 seat vehicles.

Double deckers weren't allowed on the climb which was shared by Rhondda and Red & White. The AEC Regal's 7.7 litre engines of the 1940s were no match for Red & White's 8.4 litre Albion single deckers and were often overtaken on the straight run up from Ystrad. But in 1948 the tables were turned when Rhondda allocated its 9.6 litre AEC saloons to the route.

Later Rhondda's route was extended from Ystrad to Treorchy and Cwmparc and when a housing estate was built at the top of Penrhys in the late 1960s a new service from Tonypandy was added. But in the major cutbacks of the late 1970s and early 1980s the original route was dropped entirely. Stagecoach in South Wales runs the Tonypandy-Penrhys-Rhondda Fach service to this day.

With steamed up windows it appears that this Brush bodied Daimler, 212, FTG206 had just discharged its passengers after arriving at Cardiff.

Stepping forward to serve the nation

The people of Rhondda played an immensely important role in the effort to repel Hitler's forces during the Second World War and much of that was only made possible by the Rhondda Transport Company and the services it provided in conveying people to their places of work.

Although the valley largely escaped the aerial bombardments that brought misery to Cardiff and Swansea during the hostilities, its residents made a huge contribution through their round-the-clock work in factories and pits engaged in vital production for the war effort. It was Rhondda Transport's buses that took them to their workplaces and it tested the company to the limit. The fact that the operation succeeded so well is a huge tribute to the crews, engineers and managers.

As the dark clouds of war slowly gathered during the late 1930s, the company had continued to build up its services despite the Great Depression which saw around 50,000 people forced to leave the Rhondda to find work. The 1930s became known as the Devil's Decade but despite this Rhondda Transport kept growing. It carried 17.5 million passengers in 1935, the year after the trams were withdrawn, and the buses ran a total of 3,835,000 miles.

The core routes were the tram replacement services from Blaenrhondda/Blaencwm-Porth, which ran every 15 minutes in the morning and then every 10 minutes in the afternoons, and Tonypandy/Partridge Road-Porth-Maerdy, which ran every 15 minutes.

But there were also regular services from the Fach and Fawr valleys to Cardiff and evening tours to Porthcawl for two shillings return (10p) or half-day excursions to Barry for 2s 6d, or half a crown (12.5p). Cheap day returns could be bought from Ferndale to Cardiff for 10p and between Porth and Pontypridd on Wednesdays and Saturdays, which were market days, for just sixpence (2.5p).

This Weymann bodied AEC Regent on the Pontypridd to Cardiff run was one of a batch of 10 delivered during 1940 complete with a grey roof as wartime camouflage.

CHAPTER 4

The company produced timetables for all its routes with this stern warning: "The times shown in this timetable are only an indication that vehicles will not leave the scheduled points before such times, and the company do not undertake that the omnibuses shall start or arrive at the exact times specified."

An express parcels service was operated with agents across the company's area and it was possible to advertise on buses for as little as 7.5p (1s 6d in old money) a week. The company's own advertising proclaimed that this was 'positively the finest advertising medium in the Rhondda valleys and surrounding districts.'

All of this was being achieved despite Rhondda's huge unemployment problem which was a crisis that needed to be tackled urgently. To ease matters the Government decided to build factories on huge new industrial estates which were eventually to become of extreme importance to the war effort. The first of these in Wales opened in 1937 on 165 acres of land near Nantgarw, north of Cardiff, which became known as the Treforest Industrial Estate.

Rhondda Transport found itself with new works services to the estate, although initially little thought was given to creating a bus station on the site and factory workers had to queue up at the roadside without

This 56 seat double deck Daimler, FNY809, picking up passengers on its journey between Porth and Blaencwm would have been a familiar sight on Rhondda's roads during wartime. By the time this picture was taken in the early 1950s it had been rebuilt.

shelter whatever the weather. New factories were also being opened in Rhondda itself and Rhondda Transport was called upon to take the employees to and from work. They included a clothing factory started by Alfred Polikoff at Ynyswen, near Treorchy, on March 6, 1939, just months before the start of the Second World War in September that year.

Within three months the workforce rose to 1,000 and then 1,500 as the factory gained substantial contracts with the War Department which continued for many years after the war. Later Rhondda Transport rewarded the custom by giving Polikoff's the contract to make its employees' uniforms.

Another factory that contracted Rhondda Transport to carry its staff to and from work was EMI at Treorchy which was built in 1940 to produce thermionic valves for aircraft radar sets and continued with Ministry of Defence contracts until the late 1950s when it diversified. Sadly, Polikoff's closed in March 2007 and EMI in the late 1990s.

More Rhondda people were employed at a new industrial estate at Bridgend and at the outset of the Second World War the RAF's St Athan and Llandow airfields required an expanded civilian labour force. It all meant extra services for Rhondda Transport which by 1940 was carrying 400 passengers a day to the RAF stations and this figure doubled after the Dunkirk operation in 1941.

Two Royal Ordnance factories had been built at Bridgend in the late 1930s and by 1940 they were in full production with nearly 40,000 people working on the sites at Waterton and Brackla. There were no fewer than 1,000 buildings serviced by 60 miles of roads and the plants became known as the Bridgend Arsenal. Rhondda Transport was called on to take workers to and from the sites on a round the clock, three shift basis.

Every day by April 1940 Rhondda buses were carrying 700 passengers to the Bridgend Arsenal, 1,300 to Treforest Industrial Estate and 800 to Polikoff's factory. It was also taking hundreds of miners to 18 local pits which were producing coal day and night for the war effort. After 1941, these figures approximately doubled.

Such an increase in passenger numbers and services placed a huge demand on Rhondda Transport's crews and buses. The situation was made more critical because many of the company's staff were called up

A wartime utility double decker at Porth Square. The toilet block on the left acted as a roundabout for buses on the Maerdy service.

for military duties and the training school swung into full action to train new drivers, conductors and garage staff from the ranks of the unemployed.

Such was Rhondda's unemployment crisis in the 1930s that the company found little difficulty recruiting labour during the Second World War and, unlike many other bus companies, found it did not have to take on women as conductresses so Rhondda Transport's vehicles continued to be an all-male affair. Rhondda's long term unemployment rate in 1932 had been 63 per cent. By the start of the war it was just one per cent in Treorchy and 3.7 per cent in Tonypandy.

All this put an enormous strain on Rhondda's buses which during the war were massively overworked and minimally maintained. They were in use around the clock and there was only time for bare essential maintenance for which there was a shortage of parts and skilled manpower.

Some services were reduced or even cut, the Merthyr to Cardiff route was suspended during the war, and Rhondda was loaned 11 single deck buses and coaches from its sister companies, Western Welsh and South Wales Transport, as well as less familiar vehicles from London Transport which was dispersing some of its buses to the provinces to avoid the ravages of the Blitz. Rhondda's came from the famous ST class and, with their open staircases at the rear and huge bulb horns attached to the outside of the cab, looked ancient alongside the company's modern vehicles.

Then in 1941 the Ministry of War Transport allocated 43 new wartime utility buses to the fleet. These were

vehicles devoid of any refinements and many arrived in all-over camouflage grey. It was an unusually high number for a fleet in the provinces during the war and Rhondda Transport even received what it asked for, 56 seat, highbridge double deckers. It was obvious that huge importance was placed on the vital task the company was performing for the war effort.

Rhondda largely escaped the Luftwaffe's bombs during the war apart from one terrible night in April 1941, when a German aircraft ditched its bombs on Cwmparc. As many as 27 people died, including three children who only months before had been evacuated from their home in London believing the valley was a safe haven.

Although falling bombs were rare, air raid sirens were still heard across the valley and when they were, passengers and crews on the buses would leave their vehicles and rush to public air raid shelters.

One such shelter was built at Tonypandy Square, next to the local fire station, as Lyndon Rees, who began work as a trainee with Rhondda Transport in the late 1950s, recalled:

"Whenever the air raid warning siren was sounded the queue of waiting passengers, drivers and conductors would disappear in a flash into the adjacent, damp air raid shelter, emerging only when the all clear siren sounded," he said.

At Treforest Industrial Estate with a good load of passengers and heading for Ferndale in 1952 is Weymann bodied Regent 167, ETG745. The 1940 bus has drop down windows which was usual for Rhondda's pre-war Regents, and it was obviously a warm day because they all appear to have been opened.

"While the intending passengers were 'trapped' inside the shelter, the section inspector would insist on conductors taking the opportunity to collect fares and issue tickets with the aid of flashlights. As kids, the retreat into the air raid shelter was considered great fun!"

Rhondda Transport took the threat of air raids very seriously. A couple of well-aimed Luftwaffe bombs on Porth depot would have decimated the fleet and badly affected Rhondda's war effort. To lessen any impact, buses were parked up on various sites throughout the Fach and Fawr valleys, including empty land behind St Andrew's Church in Tonypandy which was used by travelling fairs. In more recent times it has been occupied by a health centre. The company also used Talbot Green bus station, which it bought in June 1938, as a bus park.

When peace was finally declared in 1945, Rhondda Transport's fleet was in a sorry state and required large-scale investment and rebuilding. The war years had placed a tremendous strain on the company and all that would have to be put right. But Rhondda Transport

emerged with its reputation greatly enhanced, as an article in the AEC Magazine acknowledged in 1956 when the company was celebrating its golden jubilee.

"Neither blackouts, war weariness, nor any other obstacle prevented drivers from delivering their passengers promptly and regularly even under the worst possible conditions. Perhaps it was in those war days that the company's value to the valleys, and the whole nation, was fully realised," stated the magazine's salute to the proud Rhondda busmen.

Guy Arab I, 179, FNY60, which was new in 1943 is seen at Porth during the mid-1950s.

Passengers lose comfort factor

Spartan bodywork, wooden seats and painted in an all-over drab grey. Rhondda Transport's wartime new double deckers were hardly inspiring.

They must also have come as a complete shock to the company's passengers who had been spoiled by the pre-war AEC Regents with their comfortable sofa-type seats and powerful engines.

But this was war and Rhondda, like all provincial bus operators, had to be grateful for what it could get its

Front and back views of some wartime vehicles, including a 1941 Park Royal bodied AEC Regent, a 1944 Duple bodied Daimler CWA6 and a 1945 Daimler CWA6 Park Royal bodied vehicle.

hands on. At the beginning of hostilities in 1939 the Ministry of War Transport set strict standards about the type of bus that could be built and all had to be produced as cheaply as possible, devoid of any frills.

Rhondda Transport had built up a strong relationship with AEC and its Regal single deck and Regent double deck vehicles during the 1930s but during the war AEC and Leyland, the more popular bus chassis producers,

A sad view of 115 which suffered accident damage at Furnace Road, Pontygwaith, during the Second World War.

Crews would always help

Rhondda Transport's drivers and conductors got to know their passengers well and always went that little bit further to make sure they were looked after, recalled former miner, Bill Richards.

Every morning in the 1950s, Bill would leave his Tonypandy home to catch the 6.25 am works service to Cambrian Colliery, at the top of Clydach Vale. He always caught the single decker at Tonypandy Square, rather than his nearest stop which was close to the Empire Theatre in the middle of Tonypandy. "It was 5d return from the Empire to the top of Clydach but only 3d from the square and I was one of many who preferred to save 2d a day by walking the distance, whatever the weather!

"Even today the drivers and conductors who crewed the Clydach Vale route are remembered with affection. Passengers always called them by their first names and they contributed much to the fabric of the community with their friendly ways."

He remembered two in particular, conductor Arthur Hunt and his regular driver partner, George Thorne. "They knew their passengers well and George would stop the bus outside a passenger's front door if they were laden with shopping while Arthur would get out on to the pavement to help someone elderly or infirm to get on or off the bus.

"The bus would turn just outside the entrance to the colliery and there were many times when I ran out of the pithead baths to see it inching away from the stop. But Arthur would be looking through the windows at the back of the vehicle for any latecomers and when he saw me he would shout to George to stop so that I could run to catch the bus."

Bill, who later opened a carpet shop in Tonypandy, remembered that Arthur walked with a slight limp because he lost one of his legs below the knee during the Second World War. "One day he complained his artifical limb was annoying him by squeaking as he walked. His driver watched in amazement as he went to the aluminium case where conductors kept spare ticket rolls and so on, took a can of oil out and lubricated it to stop the problem!"

were ordered to turn their expertise to armoured personnel carriers, tanks and the famous AEC Militant and Matador military trucks.

So bus companies had to borrow what they could and accept new vehicles which were totally alien to them. For Rhondda Transport that meant 28 buses on loan, 17 from the London Passenger Transport Board, nine from Western Welsh and two from South Wales Transport. Alongside these were 40 new Guy and Daimler utility double deckers. Bedford supplied wartime single deckers but Rhondda was spared these and even managed to get its preferred type of double decker — 56 seat, normal height vehicles.

The first of these arrived in 1942 and were three Guy Arab 1s with Gardner 6LW engines, a completely alien bus type for Rhondda Transport. They took fleet numbers 176-178, ETX832-ETX834, but the second two were

A rear view of 115, TG6315, the longest serving of a batch of Weymann bodied Regents delivered in 1934. It was eventually withdrawn in 1955 after completing an amazing 21 years of daily service.

Rhondda was once one of the most important coal producing areas in the world and this created a host of challenges for Rhondda Transport.

After the Second World War, the company operated buses to 18 collieries and 60 vehicles were needed for miners' services, about a quarter of the fleet. There were three shifts and thousands of miners would be taken to and from their pits each day.

Miners also travelled on normal service buses and that gave the company another problem in the days before pithead baths. Older buses, with easily cleaned wooden slatted seats, were usually allocated to colliery services which solved the difficulties of miners returning home covered in coal dust after a hard shift down the mines. But Rhondda Transport did not want them sitting on moquette seats fitted in newer buses used by other passengers. Yet to refuse miners a ride home was unthinkable, however blackened they were.

So conductors allowed them on service buses but they were not allowed beyond the rear open platform. The difficulty was that this added significantly to overload at the back of the bus and, over time, vehicles would develop a near-side sag at the rear which sometimes resulted in cracked chassis that needed welding.

Dust disease is a cruel illness caused by exposure underground and many miners suffered. It was not uncommon for male passengers to cough up congealed dust on to the floors of buses. In the 1940s and 1950s, Rhondda buses carried 'Spitting Prohibited' signs while cleaning staff were employed at Porth Square to pour cans filled with strong smelling disinfectant around the floors of both decks of each bus at least twice daily.

A major dispute broke out between Rhondda Transport and the miners' union in 1950 when the company, along with others in South Wales, announced it wanted to abolish workmen's fares. These were cheaper than ordinary fares charged to the general public and the company said this meant its mining services were losing £14,121 a year and had to be subsidised by other passengers. But the NUM said miners only took home £5 15s 0d a week, and it would cause hardship.

At one point the miners threatened to strike over the issue and the dispute was heard by the South Wales Traffic Commissioners. Local councils also objected and their lawyer, Mr Meurig Evans, told the hearing: "It's a revolutionary step in proposing to abolish workmen's fares and all the local authorities in Wales are up in arms against it."

The driver of this 1956 Weymann bodied AEC Regent 418, TTX996 would have had little chance to 'open her up' on the 13 mile journey the full length of the Rhondda Fawr from Pontypridd to Blaencwm, except perhaps between Hopkinstown and Trehafod, where he was seen in the late 1960s passing Ty Mawr Colliery.

Coal created a host of challenges

But the Traffic Commissioners approved the move saying any profits made by Rhondda Transport should be used to reduce fares for all passengers, some of whom were worse off financially than the miners.

The company's drivers and conductors were sympathetic to the miners, particularly as many of them were former miners themselves. Many colliers left their jobs underground for a career on the buses and this trend increased as a growing number of pits closed in the 1960s.

As the years went on and pit closures quickened, Rhondda Transport's colliery contracts became less important. Yet Porth depot, by now part of National Welsh, still suffered financially during the year long miners' strike in 1984-5. Rhondda's last pit, Mardy Colliery, closed in 1990.

CLYDACH VALE COLLIERY—	
Penrhiwfer	W.13
Porth (via Trealaw)	W.14
Porth (via Penygraig)	W.15
COEDCAE COLLIERY—	
Coedely (via Trebanog)	W.32
Maerdy	W.33
Treorchy (via Tonypandy)	W.31
COEDELY COLLIERY—	
Gilfach Goch	W.26
Porth (via Pretoria Road)	W.25
Tonypandy	W.28
Porth (via Tynybryn)	W.27
CWM COLLIERY—	
Maesycoed	W. 2
Porth (via Pontypridd)	W. 1
Rhydyfelin	W. 3
Talbot Green	W. 4
Tonypandy (via Talbot Green)	W. 5
CWMPARC COLLIERY—	
Blaencwm	W.17
Porth (via Tonypandy and Gelli)	W.16
Ystrad (Station)	W.92
TRANE COLLIERY—TRINITY or PARTRIDGE ROAD	W.90
TREFOREST ESTATE or NANTGARW COLLIERY—	
Blaencwm (via Trealaw)	W.41
Blaencwm (via Tonypandy)	W.43
Blaenrhondda (via Trealaw)	W.40
Blaenrhondda (via Tonypandy)	W.42
Clydach Vale (via Tonypandy)	W.38
Clydach Vale (via Trealaw)	W.39
Coedely (via Trebanog)	W.37
Cwmparc	W.36
Gilfach Goch (via Penygraig)	W.44
Maerdy	W.34
Porth	W.29
Tonypandy (via Trealaw)	W.66
Ynysybwl	W.35
TYMAWR COLLIERY—	
Penrhiwfer	W.91
Porth	W.93
YNYSYBWL (LADY WINDSOR COLLIERY)—	
Porth	W.12
Tonyrefail (via Edmundstown)	W.11
Ystrad	W.10
LLANHARAN COLLIERY—	
Pontypridd	W. 6
Porth (via Trealaw)	W. 8
Pencoed	W. 9

Just some of the many collieries served by Rhondda Transport during its heyday.

The austere lines of its utility body can clearly be seen as 1943 Mk I Guy Arab 6LW with its 56 seat highbridge Park Royal body languishes in the depot awaiting repairs to a seriously damaged roof.

Rhondda Transport Company, Limited.

Fare Schedules
and
Season Tickets Rates
1937.

T. G. RICHARDSON, M.Inst.T.,
General Manager.

exchanged in 1944 for two even odder Devon General double deckers, utility Daimlers with Gardner 5LW engines and pre-selector gearboxes. These were given fleet numbers 193/194, HTA881-882, and it isn't exactly clear why the exchange took place, although Rhondda's later wartime arrivals were Daimlers.

Worse was to come in 1943 with the arrival of utility Guy Arab I double deckers, 179-180, FNY60-FNY61, and Guy Arab IIs 181-192, FNY390-FNY395 and FNY530-FNY535, the last of which did not enter service until January 1944. They had Park Royal bodywork to the absolute bare minimum wartime specification painted in all-over camouflage grey. The masked headlamps, no rear destination display and dreaded wooden slatted seats which could be compared to the hard pews in Rhondda's many chapels helped complete buses that were heartily disliked by passengers, especially when they were used on long journeys to Cardiff. On the other hand, their Gardner 6LW, 8.4 litre engines were impressive performers and easily climbed the steepest of hills in second gear, even with standing loads.

Drivers also disliked them and found changing gears on the crash gearbox and the slow revving Gardner engine much more difficult than on the AEC Regents with their faster revving engines and quicker gear changes. The cab could also become unbearably hot in summer because of the position of the exhaust manifold and drivers often found their left trouser leg being scorched. But the

One of the 10 Weymann bodied AEC Regents delivered in 1940 heads for Cardiff via Pontypridd with a healthy contingent of passengers.

engineers liked the reliable engine with its frugal fuel consumption even though it did tend to drip oil.

Many of these vehicles were rebuilt after the war although the entire contingent of Guys was withdrawn between 1955 and 1958 and most went for scrap. Rhondda Transport never bought any more Guys, although the type became popular with municipal operators like Pontypridd Urban District Council and Cardiff Corporation, which bought a large batch of Guy Arab Vs as late as 1966.

R hondda's Daimlers arrived in the summer of 1944 and as the war was nearing its end these came in red fleet livery. The first five had wooden seats but on the following examples passengers once more enjoyed the luxury of upholstered green leather lightweight seats, light shades and better ventilation on both decks.

They received fleet numbers 195-214, FNY809-FNY814, FTG114-FTG120, FTG202-FTG208 and all were CWA6 double deckers, the designation standing for Commercial, Wartime AEC 7.7 litre engine.

This smaller engine made them less suitable for Rhondda's difficult, hilly routes and although drivers generally liked them, finding them easier to drive than the Guy Arabs, the clutch pedal had a tendency to 'kick like a mule' and some drivers even suffered sprained ankles. There was just one more wartime vehicle supplied to Rhondda Transport and this did not arrive until 1946. It was a Daimler CWD6, standing for

Park Royal bodied wartime Guy Arab II, No. 183, FNY392 of 1943 vintage, seen picking up miners after their shift, in 1946.

Commercial, Wartime Daimler 8.6 litre engine, with a Duple 56 seat body, rebuilt by Longwell Green in 1950. This saw the return of the rear route destination indicator and was liked by the drivers because of its more powerful engine. It had a fine turn of speed, particularly on hills, and was nicknamed 'the greyhound' by the crews, but it suffered a broken crankshaft in 1955 and was never used again before being sold to a dealer in 1958.

The earlier Daimlers were reconditioned or rebuilt in the late 1940s but all were scrapped between 1955 and 1958. The era of Rhondda's war time utility buses had ended. And no one at the time would have been happier than the company's passengers.

Good times roll as peace returns

Rhondda Transport had come through the war years and triumphed. But as the guns fell silent across Europe, the company faced new challenges that would again test the ingenuity of all its staff. Demand for travel surged after the conflict and millions more people began travelling by bus.

In 1947 Rhondda carried 40,592,004 passengers and the figure was rising every month. That was good news for the company, but it brought with it a major problem. Many of its buses were in a shocking state after the rigours of the war years when they were called upon to run around the clock. Vehicles desperately needed replacing, but there was a post war shortage of new buses and it became clear that if Rhondda Transport was to meet its commitments then urgent action would be required.

After much thought the company decided to take the bull by the horns and adopted drastic measures. This resulted in a scheme aimed at a rolling reconditioning of the entire fleet, part of which included a major programme of bus body re-building.

Vehicles dating back as far as 1933-34 were sent off to be rebuilt by Welsh Metal Industries of Caerphilly as well as Bence and Longwell Green, both of Bristol. The wartime utility buses were also despatched for similar treatment and they returned as good as new. The result of this was that some of the early AEC Regents served no less than 22 years with Rhondda. This in itself was a remarkable achievement given that their life xpectancy when new was only eight years. Even some of the no frills, utility buses, for all their faults, managed to soldier on until 1958.

Thankfully, between 1946 and 1949 Rhondda received 45 new double deck Regent IIIs which formed the backbone of its post-war fleet modernisation quest. The size of the deliveries is significant given the huge

One of Rhondda's faithful Regent Vs, 402, STG873 a 1956 Weymann bodied, vehicle with exposed radiator, waits at Porth depot for its next tour of duty on the R28 run to Cwmparc.

One of 18 Weymann bodied AEC Regent IIIs bought in 1949, fleet No. 257, JTG948 drops off passengers in a busy Pontypridd shopping street in the early 1950s.

demand for new buses from companies all over the UK at the time. It was seen as Rhondda Transport's reward for the huge wartime effort put in by the entire company to carry thousands of workpeople to the mines, factories and ordnance establishments which was so vital in support of the war effort.

These buses were certainly needed as passenger demand soared. In 1948 Rhondda and Western Welsh were given permission by the traffic commissioners to double the frequency of their jointly operated Ferndale to Cardiff route. Rhondda's traffic manager, Mr Frank Fortt, said the companies had to run as many as five extra buses at busy times and during March that year 509 relief vehicles were put into operation on 400 scheduled services.

Extra buses also had to be laid on for other routes, especially the Treorchy-Cardiff service which saw overwhelming demand on Saturdays when Cardiff City Football Club was playing a home fixture at Ninian Park or if there was an international rugby match at Cardiff Arms Park.

Rhondda people also began demanding more trips to the seaside and the summer months saw many extra double deck journeys running to Porthcawl. Occasionally, Rhondda Transport found it could not

meet the demand. In September 1948 it was told by the traffic commissioners to run more excursions and tours from Ynysybwl after protests from the local miners' lodge that although the town had 4,000 residents there was no facility for pitmen and their families to get away for a day or two. Mr Fortt said the company had not run Ynysybwl tours since 1939 because of fuel shortages.

As the war years slowly faded into history, the situation steadily improved and Rhondda Transport's passenger figures reached heights never before or since seen. In 1938 the company had carried 21 million passengers more than 4.75 million miles. It had 138 vehicles, 56 double and 82 single deckers. In 1952 it had 214 buses, 142 double and 72 single deckers, carried 43,300,000 passengers and covered 7.4 million miles.

The company now operated 40 routes totalling 532 miles. There were local services in the Rhondda Fach and Rhondda Fawr together with others to Cardiff, Merthyr, Cowbridge and Porthcawl. There were six seasonal express services, one from Ferndale to Barry Island and five special miners' services from the valleys to Ninian Park for Cardiff City's home games. Each weekend during the summer Rhondda Transport's double deckers carried families from the valley's chapels, mines and social clubs on day trips to places such as Barry Island, Porthcawl and Aberavon Beach.

All this was achieved against a background of enormous challenges. Miners were being carried to 18 collieries and workers to new factories that had opened as far as 20 miles away from Porth depot. The trouble was that the roads to them were often in extremely poor condition, even as late as 1952. It also meant that many buses were only needed during peak times, the requirement being for 70 off-peak buses, but this soared to an amazing 178 at starting and finishing times for work people and schoolchildren.

This all required careful planning with vehicles, and crews, having nothing to do during off-peak periods. The collieries worked three shifts with the early shift using buses at about 5.45 am. Factory workers travelled from 7 am and children were carried between 8 am and 9 am. Miners became the main traffic again at 2 pm and 3 pm, school children between 4 pm and 5 pm, and factory workers from 5 pm to 7.30 pm. Looking back it is abundantly clear that Rhondda Transport had a vital role to play in the daily lives of everyone living in the Fach and Fawr valleys.

An article in Commercial Motor magazine in March 1953 summed up the situation admirably: "Transport is life in the Rhondda valleys. Without

The cover of the Golden Jubilee celebration brochure produced by Rhondda in 1956.

it, the terrible years of the depression would have caused the area to be deserted and much of the country's mineral wealth would have virtually been lost. If Rhondda Transport has contributed to the economic and social stability of the area it serves, it has also contributed to the solution of some of Britain's major problems."

But to make that contribution, Rhondda Transport had to ensure that it had got the basic essentials of running a bus company absolutely right. With 1,000 staff, that was no easy task. Management had to be efficient and understand the area's needs. Vehicles had to be properly maintained and until a major rebuilding project got underway in the mid-1950s, that was difficult to achieve at a bus depot originally built to accommodate 54 trams. The fleet by this time totalled more than 200 buses which meant many vehicles had to stand outside in all

Welsh Metal Industries of Caerphilly rebodied 1933 Rhondda Regent 111, TG6311 and for some time it was used as a demonstrator.

One of the 1937 Weymann bodied examples, 151, CTG428, heads up a pair of AEC Regents some time after it had been rebodied by Longwell Green in 1949.

weathers, yet this didn't stop it earning a deserved reputation for smartness.

The period between 1945 and 1955 was undoubtedly Rhondda Transport's golden age and there was immense pride in the fleet, not only on the part of its managers and crews, but also the community that the buses served. It was a much envied transport operation and respected by other bus companies across the UK.

Days that were golden indeed

Rhondda Transport celebrated a very special event in April 1956 — its golden jubilee! All the stops were pulled out to make sure the commemoration was as memorable as possible.

The company decorated one of its newest double deckers in a special eye-catching livery and operated it on routes during the golden jubilee week issuing souvenir tickets which were particularly popular with local children. So popular in fact that one mother wrote to Rhondda's managers asking them to take the vehicle away as her children had travelled on it four times, spending the money she usually kept for them to visit the cinema. The vehicle chosen to serve as the

anniversary bus was one of Rhondda's first AEC Regent Vs, fleet number 400, STG871, a Weymann Orion bodied example that had been delivered only a short time before.

In true celebration mode, the company also organised three staff dinners and concerts at the British Legion Club in Pentre along with a special commemorative dinner at the New Inn in Pontypridd. This was attended by Rhondda Transport's board of directors and Rhondda's Mayor, Councillor JG Elias, who praised the company for its growth over the years. In return, the company's chairman, Mr WT James, paid tribute to the co-operation he said Rhondda Transport had always been fortunate to receive from the council.

Amid this mutual back-slapping, a blind eye seems to have been turned to one uncomfortable fact. In 1952 the company had carried more than 43 million passengers, but just three years later, in 1955 the figure was down to 38,100,000. It was a significant drop and Rhondda Transport would surely have been aware that month after month fewer and fewer people were electing to travel on its buses.

But that wasn't allowed to dim the sparkle of the celebrations. Those first 50 years had brought with them much to salute. A company called Rhondda Tramways that had been running an antiquated tram system had been transformed in 1934 into a modern bus company known as Rhondda Transport. That year it had run 106 motorbuses but by 1956 this figure had almost doubled to 207.

In 1950 work started on expanding the company's depot and in May 1955 a modern central workshop and stores were opened followed in March 1956 by new administrative offices. From this date the company's legal address changed from Rheola Road, Porth to Aberrhondda Road, Porth.

New, modern buses replaced the tired vehicles of the 1930s and 1940s and Rhondda Transport had a smart fleet, including some new coaches, for private hire work. There was innovation too, such as the decision in February 1953 to base its fares on mileage. It was the first bus company to do so. For journeys of up to half a mile, passengers paid 1d; for journeys of up to five miles, 1.8d per mile; for journeys between five miles and 7.5 miles, 1.7d per mile; and down to a minimum of 1.3d per mile for 20 miles.

In 1954 Rhondda stole a march on its larger sister company, Western Welsh, when it started using route numbers which appeared on bus destination blinds. This was at the instigation of general manager, Tom Strange. Valley routes were prefixed R while services to Cardiff or Porthcawl were numbered from 100 up. Schools services were prefixed S and works buses W. Route numbers started appearing on Western Welsh vehicles in 1958, but the route numbering system simply never caught on with people in the Rhondda who invariably described the services they intended to catch as 'the Cardiff bus' or 'the Maerdy bus.' Conductors had the job of ensuring the correct route number was carried, but they were rather cavalier

about the whole system. There were, for example, four derivatives for the Rhondda Fawr-Pontypridd route but invariably only R20 was used.

The crews must have wondered why their company bothered with destination indicators at all as valley folk never seemed to look at them. Conductors on the Cardiff service were well used to their bus being stopped by an intending passenger who would ask: "Is this the Ponty bus?" If they had worked for a different

One of the buses that would have carried Jim Simmonds on his regular route around the valleys calling on customers.

Jim Simmonds' first encounter with Rhondda Transport came in 1947 as a 10 year old when he became friendly with another boy who lived on a farm near what is now Pentrebane, Cardiff.

"It is very much a suburb now, but in those far off post-Second World War days Pentrebane was really out in the wilds," said Jim.

"There was no nearby bus service so getting into the centre of Cardiff was an expedition for us youngsters. We'd have to trek across the fields to the road at Radyr Cheyne crossroads. Once there we would wait patiently for the welcome sight of the red Rhondda double decker which came from the Tonypandy area. On its arrival we would excitedly

The specially decorated AEC Jubilee bus that commemorated a remarkable 50 years of progress during the reigns of five monarchs. OPPOSITE: a group of the company's staff admire the sign on the front of the vehicle which proved popular with passengers.

company they might have replied: "No, what does it say on the front?" But Rhondda crews were of a different calibre and would reply with infinite patience: "No, it's the Cardiff bus."

THE RHONDDA TRANSPORT CO. LTD.
1906 ——— 1956
FIFTY YEARS OF SERVICE
Souvenir Ticket
1/- SINGLE
APRIL, 1956

1298

| 1906—1934 TRAMWAYS | 1914—1915 RAILLESS BUSES | 1920—1956 MOTOR BUSES |

ISSUED SUBJECT TO THE COMPANY'S REGULATIONS AND ROAD TRAFFIC ACT, 1930

Over the fields and far away

take our seats and enjoy the run into Cardiff. This would take us along Llantrisant Road, Cardiff Road, Penhill, Cathedral Road, Tudor Street and finally Wood Street and the terminus.

"This seems a grand title for what was simply a tract of open, derelict land on which Thomson House, the nerve centre of the Western Mail and South Wales Echo, was later built. Between 1953 and 1960, I worked as an office machine engineer with no luxuries such as a van or company car. The only way

to accomplish many journeys to the Rhondda valleys was by bus and once again Rhondda Transport came to my rescue.

"I would often start my day by boarding a double decker going to Ystrad Rhondda (Star Hotel) from where I would head off on other routes as I went around the valleys calling on my customers.

"It's strange, but those places seemed far away then and yet they are just a short drive today. I have many happy memories of those journeys though."

Conductors would often sing out 'Cardiff service' as their vehicle pulled up at stops but passengers getting on the wrong bus was not uncommon.

Rhondda Transport had meatier matters on its mind as the 1950s progressed. As television became more popular and the car started to enter people's lives, passenger figures continued to fall. It was not helped by rising fuel prices and the Government's tax on fuel which saw the company's costs increase. So almost annually the company was forced to seek fare increases from the traffic commissioners which invariably were opposed by the local councils.

The hearings became increasingly acrimonious and in June 1958 Rhondda Transport was accused by barrister, Alun T Davies, of 'feathering its own nest' by releasing inaccurate figures that had grossly underestimated profits. In March 1955 the company expected receipts to be £811,000 and profits £103,000 but the actual figures were £839,000 and £130,000. The fares inquiries continued right through the 1960s until Rhondda was taken over by Western Welsh at the end of 1970.

By the end of the 1950s, Rhondda Transport's expansive days were coming to an end. The 1960s would be a very different decade of fewer services and passengers and increasingly painful cost cutting.

Courtesy and care mattered

People are the most important part of any organisation and that was always recognised by Rhondda Transport which did all it could to promote harmonious relationships, both among its staff and with the travelling public.

'Courtesy costs nothing' and 'Courtesy aids service,' were among the many slogans that were promoted by the company throughout its existence.

Salesmanship was the requirement of all members of staff, according to Rhondda's general manager between 1948 and 1952, Mr TG Davies.

"This is in our own interests," he wrote in the Staff News in March 1950. "Every employee can help, particularly the conductors, drivers and inspectors (I have intentionally put them in that order) who are in such close touch with our customers.

"It is evident from letters received and remarks which are made to me that we enjoy a very high reputation for service and courtesy, which are the most important factors in salesmanship."

A contented, satisfied workforce would be much more likely to make passengers feel welcome on Rhondda's buses than an unhappy one and as a result they would probably use the services more frequently, thereby boosting profits. As passenger figures began to fall from the mid-1950s this message became an increasingly important one.

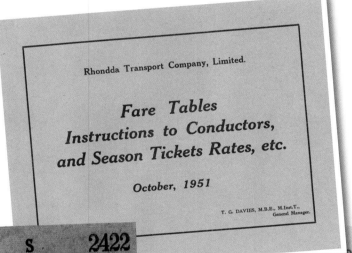

Rhondda Transport recognised the need for an enthused workforce right from the beginning. As early as 1910 employees had their own football team and sport was always encouraged by the company.

An article in the Electric Railway, Bus and Tram Journal in February 1936 warmly praised the company's longest serving general manager, Mr TG Richardson, who it said "believes that employees, both administrative and traffic, do better work when their environment is agreeable." The feature went on to praise Porth depot offices for being "beautifully light and airy and equipped with many up-to-date appliances for reducing the drudgery and routine work."

It also observed that traffic staff were similarly well catered for: "Every consideration is shown to the men in the way of canteen and rest room accommodation, and there is in existence on the Rhondda system, one of the best employees' clubs of which we have any knowledge. Every kind of indoor and outdoor recreation appears to be encouraged, and it was obvious to us that this club plays a large part in solving many of the social problems of this important little transport community."

The journal certainly wasn't reserved in its observations. The praise continued: "The social club opened in the late 1920s in remarkably spacious premises." By 1932 Rhondda Transport's 560 employees had use of a 250 seater hall for concerts, a billiards room with three tables, a full-size skittle alley, a fully licensed canteen, a card room, lounge and library. A radio gramophone was also installed.

Fully laden with passengers, 1954 Weymann bodied Tiger Cub 337, PNY374 leaves Bridgend bus station on its way to Porthcawl.

The club was built on the opposite side of the river to the depot and could be reached by a bridge that later employees remember as being distinctly shaky. The steward was Harry Hayward who appeared to have been a very genial character.

The social club, run by an employees' committee, continued throughout Rhondda Transport's existence and was home for the various social activities. The football team was always active, thanks in part to the hard work put in over many years by driver Len Williams, an affable character with white hair parted in the middle, a moustache and always smoking a pipe, unless he was busy giving the team a pep talk.

At the start of the 1963 season the team played an annual friendly match against Glamorgan Police at Porth and was beaten 6-1, but there were no hard feelings as both teams were entertained to tea, followed by a concert in the evening.

Similarly hard work by staff men Gerald Lynch and Glyn Jones kept the rugby team going while Islwyn Davies saw to the success of the cricket side. Employees also set up a motor club, a bowling club, an ex-servicemen's social association and a horticultural society which, each August or September, held one of South Wales' most successful flower and vegetable shows at the depot's bottom garage.

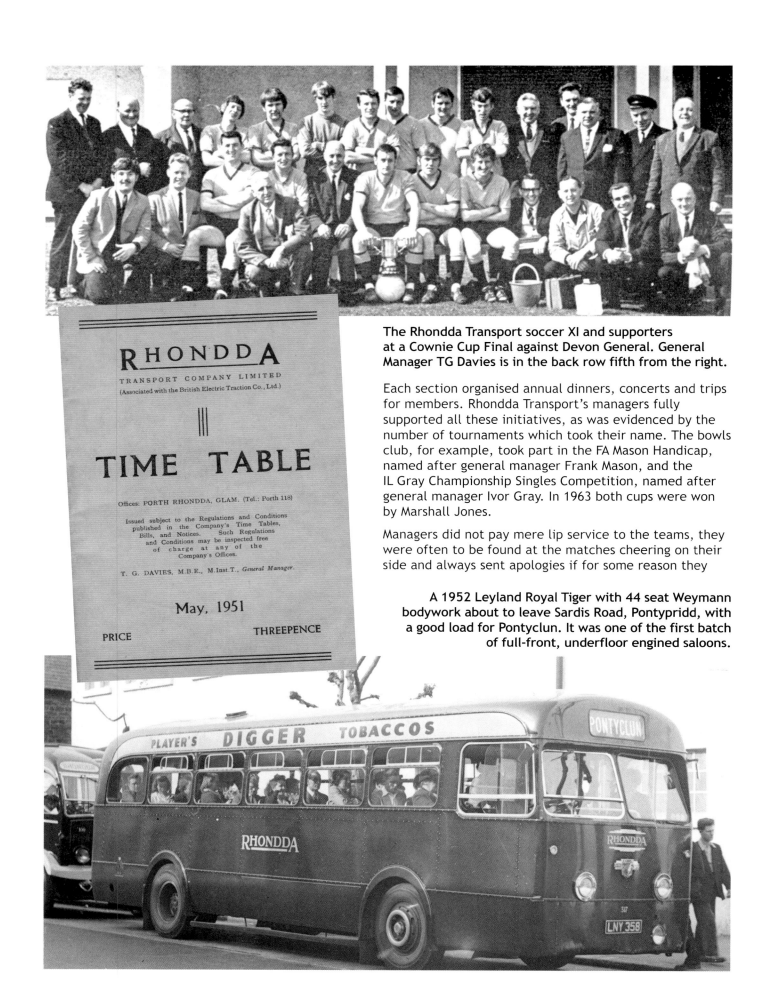

RHONDDA

TRANSPORT COMPANY LIMITED

(Associated with the British Electric Traction Co., Ltd.)

‖

TIME TABLE

Offices: PORTH RHONDDA, GLAM. (Tel.: Porth 118)

Issued subject to the Regulations and Conditions published in the Company's Time Tables, Bills, and Notices. Such Regulations and Conditions may be inspected free of charge at any of the Company's Offices.

T. G. DAVIES, M.B.E., M.Inst.T., *General Manager.*

May, 1951

PRICE   THREEPENCE

The Rhondda Transport soccer XI and supporters at a Cownie Cup Final against Devon General. General Manager TG Davies is in the back row fifth from the right.

Each section organised annual dinners, concerts and trips for members. Rhondda Transport's managers fully supported all these initiatives, as was evidenced by the number of tournaments which took their name. The bowls club, for example, took part in the FA Mason Handicap, named after general manager Frank Mason, and the IL Gray Championship Singles Competition, named after general manager Ivor Gray. In 1963 both cups were won by Marshall Jones.

Managers did not pay mere lip service to the teams, they were often to be found at the matches cheering on their side and always sent apologies if for some reason they

A 1952 Leyland Royal Tiger with 44 seat Weymann bodywork about to leave Sardis Road, Pontypridd, with a good load for Pontyclun. It was one of the first batch of full-front, underfloor engined saloons.

A queue of passengers waits to board as an inspector guides the driver of this 1949 AEC Regent as he reverses on busy Taff Street, Pontypridd, during the early 1950s.

were unable to attend. It was this happy atmosphere that gave Rhondda Transport such a good record when it came to long service employees. The company was immensely proud of the number of long serving staff on its books and held presentation ceremonies each January, when awards were presented by the chairman for terms of 25, 40 and 50 years' service. Between 1948 and 1967, 357 awards were presented, including 11 for 50 years' service and 117 for 40 years' service.

The company also believed in letting employees know what was happening within the company and supported the setting up of a regular magazine called Staff News which contained details of arrivals, illnesses, retirements and general gossip, put together for many years by Ivor Kinnersley.

It loved to publish letters of praise for staff received from passengers, including the one below that appeared in the September 1950 edition from Mr EP Hardwidge of London who had been a passenger on the Cardiff to Tonyrefail service:

"On the way my wife suffered an attack of giddiness. It gives me the utmost pleasure to bring to your notice the exemplary conduct of your conductor (Mr AJ O'Leary). He rendered all possible assistance, was courteous in his manner, and indeed made me thank my lucky stars that we were on that particular vehicle."

This investment in promoting courtesy and so many activities paid real dividends when it came to staff loyalty. Whether it was the sports matches, the regular staff dances at Bindles in Barry, the annual Christmas parties for staff and children or just a post-shift pint at the Rhondda Transport club, employees had a real sense of belonging. Even today surviving staff warmly remember the family atmosphere that existed within the company that made their jobs so much easier and more enjoyable.

They treated the bosses like gods

They were treated like gods and ruled Rhondda Tramways and Rhondda Transport with rods of iron. Always addressed as sir, they were the nine general managers who led the company over its 65-year history, from the early tram days until its takeover by Western Welsh at the end of 1970.

The first was Henry James Nisbett, who oversaw the introduction of the trams in 1908. Mr Nisbett was an engineer by profession, which was seen as a pre-requisite in the early days. It was largely through his efforts that the go-ahead was given to the ill-fated trolley bus system in 1914. Perhaps fortunately, Mr Nisbett was not around when the system collapsed within three months as he left the company in 1913 to run Torquay's trams.

His place was taken by Mr HH Holliday, another engineer, who was at the helm when the company introduced its first motorbuses in 1920. It was Mr Holliday's ethos to have frequent meetings to discuss bus and tram developments with Rhondda Urban District Council from whom the company leased the tramways. The early 1920s were exciting times for transport in the valleys and there was much to do and much to talk about. Unfortunately, Mr Holliday found it increasingly difficult. He suffered deteriorating health and spent time recuperating in Switzerland before leaving the company in 1926.

His replacement was Rhondda Transport's longest serving general manager, also an engineer, Mr TG Richardson. He is remembered as being genial and

It's all smiles from this group of Rhondda staff during a private hire to Barry Island.

TG Richardson, General Manager 1926-1948

TG Davies MBE, General Manager 1948-1952

affable, a smoker who always had his beloved pipe close at hand.

It fell to Mr Richardson, ably supported by the company's traffic manager, Mr Frank Fortt, to phase out the trams, introduce replacement motorbus services and cope with the huge increase in demand for bus travel during the years of the Second World War.

Under Mr Richardson, whose son John H Richardson became Rhondda Transport's chairman in the 1960s, the buses won a reputation for being well kept and presented, despite the arduous operating conditions. He was well-liked by the employees because he took their welfare seriously.

Mr Richardson encouraged the setting up of the company's various social sections, including the bowls, football, rugby and cricket teams and the gardening club. His opinion was that if an employee enjoyed the job, he would perform it better.

Rhondda Tramways had 42 buses when Mr Richardson became general manager in 1926 and when he retired 22 years later the fleet had grown to around 200

vehicles carrying more than 40 million passengers a year. He foresaw a huge increase in demand for bus travel but warned in 1948: "Roads will be the greatest problem. The valley roads are narrow, winding and hilly, and at present it is out of the question to give local inhabitants the increased comfort of 8ft wide buses. When new factories go into production and traffic increases, the roads will become saturated."

Mr Richardson was right about road congestion, but wrong about the width of vehicles. Rhondda Transport took delivery of its first 8ft wide buses just four years later in 1952. He was succeeded at Porth by Mr TG Davies who, along with Mr Fortt, was awarded the MBE for services to transport, largely because of the sterling service given by the company to the wartime effort. Mr Davies stayed for four years before moving on to become general manager of Rhondda's sister company, Western Welsh.

He was succeeded in his role by Mr Tom Strange, who declared the company faced unusual problems for a transport concern. "Subsidence threatens most of the roads, the valley's dogs and children run all over the place, and the sheep, unable to find sufficient grazing on the hillsides, come into the towns and villages looking for scraps of food. So the average speed of our vehicles is far too low," he told Comercial Motor magazine in 1953. It was on his watch that major redevelopment work was carried out at Porth, which saw new fitting shops replace out of date facilities.

Mr Strange was succeeded in August 1957 by Mr Ivor Gray who was highly regarded in the transport industry. His father, Mr Albert Gray, was general manager of South Wales Commercial Motors and became the first general manager of Western Welsh when South Wales Commercial Motors and the bus operations of the Great Western Railway were merged in 1929. His brother Leslie was WW's assistant chief engineer.

Lyndon Rees, a trainee at Porth in the late 1950s, remembered seeing Ivor Gray for the first time:

"I had only been at Rhondda for a few months before he arrived and remember the shock I had upon first sight of him in the top office car port, he was as dark skinned as you could get and had obviously done his fair share of sun worshipping!"

The tan was down to the fact that Mr Gray had arrived at Porth after a stint with the Jamaica Omnibus Company, which at the time was, like Rhondda and Western Welsh, owned by British Electric Traction. "He was an extremely business minded general manager," recalled Lyndon.

"He was a cost cutter with a keen eye on the bottom line and developed a reputation as an outstanding after dinner speaker at the many transport related functions that were held in those days.

Called up for tobacco trip

It happened over 70 years ago, but Don James remembered clearly the day he was summoned by Rhondda Transport's legendary general manager, TG Richardson.

It was 1944 and Don, a fresh faced 14 year old just out of school, had only recently started with the company after succeeding his brother, Doug, as an office boy.

"My job was to do anything that needed doing, I was at the beck and call of everyone," he recalled. "One day I was told to go upstairs to the general manager's office. I was shocked that someone so important wanted to see me and knocked on his office door with trepidation.

"He called me in, said he had run out of tobacco for his pipe, and asked if I would fetch some. I was so relieved. Although he was strict everyone respected him.

"I became a junior clerk in the general office afterwards. It was a busy place with a good atmosphere and friendly colleagues. I did my National Service in 1948 and returned to the company, eventually rising to become its chief clerk.

"In the 1950s Rhondda needed all the staff they could get and some drivers and conductors were kept on to the age of 70. Many had started on the trams. We called them the 'sick and tired,' and they were put on lighter duties. For example, we used to send five work buses down to RAF St Athan and to save fuel the crews returned on just one bus, the other vehicles remained on site. The crews returned to St Athan on the same bus in the afternoon to pick up the other vehicles and bring the workers home.

"It was sad when Rhondda Transport was taken over by Western Welsh on January 1, 1971. We were all against it. We had our own way of doing things and it was different to Western Welsh. I stayed when it became National Welsh in 1978, but it was never the same. I did 48 years service altogether and I was relieved to leave in 1992. But I will always have happy memories of Rhondda Transport."

Weymann bodied AEC Regent 137, TG9556 which arrived at Rhondda in 1935 gamely ploughs through flooding at Trehafod, a regular occurrence at this location for many years.

Tom Strange, General Manager 1952-1957.

Ivor Gray, General Manager 1957-1962.

At the beginning of 1962, Mr Gray was appointed general manager of Western Welsh, succeeding Mr TG Davies who had retired on medical grounds. His place at Porth was taken by WW's assistant general manager, also usually seen puffing on his pipe, Mr Frank Mason, another engineer.

He stayed until November 1965 when he was succeeded by Mr DP Drew, who had been secretary/accountant of South Wales Transport and Thomas Bros of Port Talbot, also BET companies. Mr Drew was an accountant and his appointment is indicative of the financial concerns being felt at the time. Like other bus companies, Rhondda Transport was making less money and losing passengers annually. Mr Drew was with Rhondda for a very short time. He left to take over as manager with Llynfi Motors at Maesteg and was replaced by Bill Cooper, who had arrived at Porth as Rhondda Transport's new traffic manager in 1964. By this time financial concerns were catching up with the company and in June 1966 it was announced that its future management would be taken over by Western Welsh. Ivor Gray became general manager at both Rhondda and WW, while David Cherry, who had been chief engineer at Porth, assumed that role at both companies.

The general manager's role at Rhondda was downgraded to manager only, with Mr Cooper reporting to Mr Gray, although Rhondda continued to be run as a separate company.

"He arranged for Keith Holmes, who was chief schedules officer with Northern General, another BET company, to be seconded to Porth in 1959 to review the bus and crew duty schedules and I was instructed to work alongside him as part of my training. We ended up reducing the fleet by 20 buses. Previously the entire scheduling system was in the head of the depot's chief inspector and it fell to me to prise it out of him. It's all done by computer these days, but it was a terrible strain on the eyes and probably as a result, I'm now seriously visually impaired."

Mr Gray's business-minded approach led to the ethos 'let the assets sweat.' He insisted that only five per cent of the fleet was reserved for engineering maintenance each day while the rest had to be available for service at peak periods on Mondays to Fridays. This meant that fewer buses were needed in the fleet and turned Rhondda Transport into a highly efficient bus company.

Falling passengers and fewer profits continued to affect the industry and in 1967, BET sold its transport interests to the state and the National Bus Company was born two years later. In January 1971 Rhondda was taken over by Western Welsh and Mr Cooper became manager of the Rhondda area. Just a month later he replaced Fred Pengelly at WW as traffic manager. His place at Porth was taken by Mr Derek Price, who was WW's assistant area manager at Haverfordwest. He had joined the company in 1954 as a conductor at Pontypool depot.

Mr Gray retired at the end of April 1971, ending a family association with Western Welsh that stretched back more than 50 years. His place was taken by Mr Keith Holmes, who had been seconded to Porth depot back in 1959. Mr Cooper eventually retired as planning manager with National Welsh, the company formed out of a merger between Western Welsh and Red & White, in May 1981 after 47 years in the bus industry.

Rhondda's general managers were lucky in having the support of some of the most able traffic managers and engineers in the bus industry. Mr Frank Fortt began his long career with the company as a conductor on the trams in September 1908 and ended it in June 1956 as traffic manager. The company news letter said he had "created a bond of mutual trust in his dealings with the public which greatly contributed to the happy state of good public relations which this company enjoys."

Chief engineer from the early days until the 1950s, Mr A Graham Slee was an innovator. He developed experimental exhaust brakes for use when buses descended long gradients, ideal for Rhondda's hilly routes. Mr Slee was also an enthusiastic supporter of AEC

engines and it is largely down to him and general manager, Mr TG Richardson, that the company turned to this make in the early 1930s.

Lyndon also recalled CM Williams, who was Rhondda Transport's secretary/accountant in the late 1950s before moving to a similar position with WW.

"He was very much a gentleman. He had been taken prisoner by the Japanese in the Second World War and suffered very badly. He was a distinguished and popular executive," said Lyndon.

Everyone deferred to the general managers back then it seems. "Everyone, including senior managers, addressed the GM as sir, they were treated like Gods in those days," said Lyndon.

A 25-year, long service award presented to Glyndwr Isaac on December 9, 1965.

Glyn entertained them all

Driver Glyn Isaac was always a popular personality at Rhondda Transport's Porth depot, remembered his granddaughter Karen Rees.

"He was an accomplished pianist and often entertained the staff and their families at various functions held at the Rhondda Transport Social Club," said Karen.

"For many years he drove a double decker bus for the company and would always give us a wave when he passed us near our home in Trealaw. It made me so proud.

"One of Glyn's proudest moments however, was when he was presented with his 25-year service certificate by the company."

Glyn's two sons, Gareth and Allan, also worked at Porth depot. Sadly, Allan, Karen's father, who had started as an apprentice in the paintshop, died at the early age of 34. In 1966, at the age of 60, Glyn had a heart operation and thought his working days were over. But then he was asked to drive the depot's bus inspectors around by car.

Tragically, he died a few months later, aged 61.

It's over the hills and far away

Every summer weekend in the 1950s and 1960s, long convoys of red double deck Rhondda Transport buses carrying thousands of excited families left the valleys for the seaside. Porthcawl, Barry Island or Aberavon Beach were the favourite destinations and for the trippers this was the highlight of the year and perhaps their only chance to see the sea.

These day trips were the famous chapel, colliery and social club outings which were unique in the UK and only possible because Rhondda Transport had such a large fleet of double deckers available for private hire. The first mass outing was in August 1934 when Penygraig Labour Club hired 16 new buses for a trip to Barry Island. The AEC Regents had only recently entered the fleet as replacements for the trams and for many years a magnificent framed photograph of the convoy between Williamstown and Trebanog took pride of place in the traffic office at Porth depot.

Rhondda Transport's private hire service actually started much earlier, in the early days of the trams which could be privately reserved for special occasions such as school outings, chapel choir competitions and Cymanfa Ganu events up and down the valleys. Trams could even be hired for wedding parties with the New Inn Hotel in Pontypridd a favourite location.

The company's chief inspector in the 1950s, WJ Evans, recalled the days of private tram hire in long conversations with Lyndon Rees, a Rhondda Transport traffic trainee from 1958-60. Mr Evans was known as Billy Wire from his days as overhead line superintendent in the company's tramway era. Lyndon recalled him explaining how it was necessary for groups who hired trams to assemble at the pick-up point 30 minutes before the pre-arranged time. Rhondda's system was single tracked with passing loops and crossover points and it was necessary to leave on time to avoid delaying the scheduled service. But it didn't always work. There

Private hire duty was the order of the day for 1958 Weymann bodied Regent V, VTX440, seen in a lay-by alongside Cardiff Castle loaded with school children during the mid-1960s.

CHAPTER 6

It wasn't all about the destination — the excitement of the journey there in an open top charabanc with the wind in your hair, often made for wonderful memories for Rhondda's early day trippers.

were often stragglers who were late, and the tram motorman would be forced to shunt his car back and fore across a junction to allow a service tram to pass, much to the amusement of local schoolchildren!

Rhondda's first motorbuses arrived in 1920. After that, instead of being confined to where the valley's tramway tracks ran, trips could go much further afield, albeit slowly and on often appalling roads. The company bought what was called a 'chara-bus' in 1924 which was little more than a lorry fitted with seats but was used on private hires until its withdrawal in 1928. This made it possible for valley people to make day visits to the seaside although a trip to Porthcawl at a maximum speed of 12 mph would have taken three to four hours. The chara-bus, sometimes called a charabanc, had a detachable bus top to protect the 35 passengers during inclement weather. Vehicles such as this were often unreliable and there were frequent breakdowns, but that was all part of the fun!

Private hires took off in the 1930s as Rhondda Transport received its first double deckers but the real explosion in demand did not come until after the Second World War. Demand for leisure travel soared after the tough years of depression in the valleys and the rigours of the hostilities. Trips from the valleys went further afield as vehicles became more reliable and one of the first

'long haul' mass outings was in 1946 when a fleet of new single deckers went on a day trip to Ascot Races, a favourite destination for many years.

From the 1930s, Rhondda Transport always had a small contingent of no more than six single deck coaches for longer distance journeys. They included three Windover-bodied AEC coaches delivered in 1948. These 32 seat luxury vehicles made frequent trips to London, one of which conveyed the Cory Workmen's Band to a competition held at Olympia.

Club, church and chapel summer outings from the valleys to the coast became increasingly popular with Penygraig Labour Club, Tynewydd Social Club and Cwm Colliery laying claim to some of the biggest expeditions. They would each hire 40 or more buses. This all needed careful planning by Rhondda's private hire and tours department and its manager at the time, Horace Purcell.

It was his job to secure the contracts for the trips and that was no easy matter as the railway was a major competitor and the pits, churches and workingmen's

EXCURSIONS & TOURS

OPERATING FROM THE RHONDDA VALLEYS,

as agreed upon for 1934 by the under-mentioned operators:—

CHARLIE MORGAN, Berw Road, Tonypandy,
J. HENDERSON & SONS, Tylacelyn Road, Penygraig,
SYDNEY DAVIES, Railway Street, Penygraig,
A. J. BRYANT & Co. Llewellyn Street, Pentre,
The RHONDDA TRAMWAYS Co., Ltd., Porth.

DESTINATION.	ROUTE FORWARD. Via	ROUTE RETURN. Via	Fare s. d.	Journey Time Hours.	Miles
Aberystwyth	Rhayader	Aberayron	9 0	10	202
Aberayron	Merthyr and Lampeter	same route	8 0	9	182
Abergavenny	Pontypool	same route	4 0	5	70
Abergavenny, Monmouth, Chepstow and Newport (circular)		same route	6 0	8	125
Aberavon	Bridgend	same route	3 6	4	70
Aberdare	Pontypridd and Abercynon	same route	2 6	3	40
Aldershot	Monmouth, Gloucester and Reading	same route	17 6		
Ascot	Monmouth, Gloucester and Reading	same route	17 6		
Builth Wells	Treherbert, Hirwaun and Brecon	same route	5 9	6	106
Bristol	Monmouth, Gloucester and Filton	same route	10 0	10	212
Birmingham	Monmouth and Worcester	same route	10 0	12	224
Brecon	Hirwaun	same route	3 9	4	65
Barry, starting from	Treherbert, Treorchy, Ystrad, and Ferndale Day Trip	via Cowbridge Out and In	3 0	4	60
Do. do.	do. do. Half-day Trip	same route	2 6		
Do. do.	do. do. Evening Trip	same route	2 0		
Barry, from Tonypandy and Porth, Day Trip		same route	2 6	3½	50
Do. do.	Evening Trip	same route	2 0	3½	50
Bath	Gloucester and Stroud	same route	10 0	10	228
Carmarthen	Bridgend and Pontardulais	same route	6 9	7	144
Cardigan	Carmarthen	same route	9 0	10	204
Cheddar Caves, including Rock of Ages and Heaven Gate		(circular tour)	14 0		
Cheltenham	Monmouth	Chepstow and Newport	8 6	8	166
Chepstow	Newport	same route	4 9	6	100
Cardiff (Pier Head)	Pontypridd	same route	2 6	2	40
Caerphilly	Pontypridd	same route	2 6	2	35
Epsom	Monmouth, Gloucester and Reading	same route	17 6		
Evesham	Monmouth and Cheltenham	Chepstow and Newport	9 0	9	198
Gloucester	Monmouth	Chepstow, Newport & Cardiff	7 6	8	146
Hereford	Pontypool	same route	7 6	8	130
London	Gloucester, Northleach and Uxbridge	same route	17 6	14	356
Llandrindod Wells	Brecon and Builth	same route	6 3	9	135
Llangorse Lakes	Brecon	Abergavenny and Pontypool	5 0	5	95
Llantwit Major	Cowbridge	same route	3 0	3	50
Llantwit Major	Cowbridge (short coast trip)	Aberthaw and Barry	3 6	5	74
Llantwit Major	Porthcawl and Marcross (do.)	Cowbridge	3 9	5	70
Llandovery	Brecon and Senny Bridge	same route	6 0	6	120
Machynlleth	Brecon, Builth and Newton	same route	10 0	9	200
Mumbles	Bridgend and Neath	same route	5 0	6	100
Mountain Ash	Pontypridd	same route	2 0	2	28
Merthyr	Pontypridd	same route	2 6	3	42
Malvern	Monmouth and Ledbury	same route	7 3	8	152
Neath	Bridgend	same route	4 0	4	76
Swansea	Treherbert and Glyn-Neath	Bridgend	4 3	5	86
Porthcawl	Bridgend	same route	2 6	3	52
Penarth	Cardiff	same route	2 9	2½	48
Pontypool	Newbridge	same route	3 0	4	58
Stratford-on-Avon	Monmouth, Glo'ster and Cheltenham	same route	10 6		226
Worcester	Monmouth and Malvern	Tewkesbury, Glo'ster, N'port	8 9		182
Tenby	Neath, Carmarthen and Red Roses	same route	8 9	9	200
Tintern and Wye Tour	via Monmouth, Chepstow & Newport		5 6	6	107
Symonds Yat	Monmouth	Monmouth, Chepstow, N'port	6 0	6½	119
Port Eynon	Neath and Swansea	same route	6 0	6	110
Circular Tour via Treherbert, Neath, P'thcawl, Southerndn.		Barry and Cowbridge	5 6	6	96
Circular Tour—Barry, St. Athan's, Llantwit, Southerndown,		Ogmore-by-Sea and Porthcawl	4 6	6	86
Shrewsbury	Hereford and Leominster	same route	11 0	11	222
Afternoon Trips and	Sunday Afternoon Trips to Porthcawl	Llantwit Major, Marcross or Rhoose	2 6		
Newport	Cardiff	same route	3 6	3	60

Weston (Coach & Boat), 5/6.   Bristol (Coach & Boat), 6/6.   Evening Trips to Seaside, 2/-

These women were enjoying an outing to the popular South Wales seaside resort of Barry Island, courtesy of Rhondda Transport. Their driver can be seen on the left.

clubs had to be convinced that Rhondda Transport's buses offered the best deal.

Lyndon Rees remembered the effort it took: "Horace's duties included visiting the numerous workingmen's clubs and these often became long drinking sessions! He was ably supported by Cled Jones, who handled claims at the office, and it was always obvious when a big deal had been negotiated because of the hangovers they suffered the next morning."

The clubs and colliery lodges cut a tough deal, but with both sides satisfied, the trips would be arranged for the required date. The big day would finally dawn and families would be up early making sandwiches and packing swimsuits. There would be anxious looks at the sky as the weather was all important in helping make the trip a success.

At about 8.30 am, excitement would mount as the roar of AEC engines announced the arrival of the buses. Many valley clubs were built on steep hills but that was no problem for the Regents which climbed them in their stride. They parked up in long rows outside the assembly point and at 9am, with every seat filled, they set off. Soon the valley streets were left far behind and youngsters on the top deck were competing to be the first to see the sea.

Aberavon, Barry Island and Porthcawl were at the height of their popularity in the 1950s and 1960s and thousands of people packed the sands on fine summer

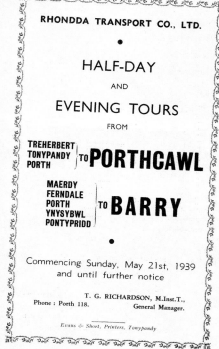

RHONDDA TRANSPORT CO., LTD.

•

HALF-DAY

AND

EVENING TOURS

FROM

TREHERBERT TONYPANDY PORTH } TO **PORTHCAWL**

MAERDY FERNDALE PORTH YNYSYBWL PONTYPRIDD } TO **BARRY**

•

Commencing Sunday, May 21st, 1939 and until further notice

T. G. RICHARDSON, M.Inst.T., General Manager.
Phone : Porth 118.

Evans & Short, Printers, Tonypandy

days. Many came on a Rhondda double decker and the company's buses lined up every Saturday and Sunday in June, July and August at one of the resorts' main parking areas, usually Sandy Bay in Porthcawl and behind the railway station in Barry Island.

Hopefully the weather would be fine and mothers and children would walk the short distance to the beach and sea, which always tended to be grey rather than sparkling blue. The dads, meanwhile, would make their way to the nearest watering hole and families would not get back together again until home time. If the rain

The term 'full up' would certainly have been true on this occasion, when one of four new vehicles purchased in 1924, fleet No. 19, a chara-bus, prepares to set off on an excursion.

came, it was unfortunate and mam and youngsters might have their picnic on the bus before heading off to the fair to spend the money that had been given to them earlier by the club committee.

At around 6 pm, tired and happy, families would clamber back on board the buses for the long trek home, already looking forward to the following year's trip, which would usually be to a different resort.

Private hire became more of a problem for Rhondda Transport towards the end of the 1950s as its double deck fleet shrank along with the decline in passenger numbers. It was becoming more difficult to provide buses both for the large convoys and scheduled services. In its heyday, the company's summer season private hire commitment was 60 buses a day and the fact it fulfilled its other bus service requirements to the full was no mean feat.

It required careful pre-planning, a task allocated to Lyndon Rees who said that bus allocations had to be carefully juggled to ensure a smooth operation and that all bus duties were met. "Single deckers were sometimes used as substitutes for double deckers on local services and the engineering department played its part by turning out the entire fleet, which they never failed to do," said Lyndon.

It wasn't uncommon to see buses in service in a partially repainted and patched up state on those rare

occasions when this became neccesary. At normal times this would have been unthinkable.

"Porth depot, on a full turnout on a summer Saturday morning, presented a ghostly spectacle of emptiness and gave us all a wonderful sense of achievement once the last bus had been despatched. While the engineering department staff had a quiet day, special provision had to be made for the returning bus convoys at night to be quickly washed and refuelled to prevent queuing on the approach roads to the depot, which was sometimes impossible to avoid. Buses usually returned with sand covered floors and even the remnants of tummy upsets, all of which had to be thoroughly cleaned, ready for the next morning's service."

Despite these problems, Rhondda Transport's private hires became more adventurous. It received its first 70 seat double deck Regent Vs in 1958 and these were sent as far away as Chepstow races and Weston-super-Mare, always a popular destination for valley people. The vehicles had to reach fast speeds and were fitted with high speed specification tyres for safety.

But by 1959, it had become obvious that Rhondda Transport would struggle that summer to maintain its private hire commitments. It was a real challenge which prompted a decision to ask other bus companies if Rhondda could hire their double deckers but most said no. Cardiff Corporation, with most double deckers, cited 'fleet insurance limitations' for its refusal. Western Welsh and South Wales Transport, despite being Rhondda's sister companies all under British Electric Traction ownership, also responded negatively. United Welsh agreed to consider specific requests and in 1959 and 1960 provided double deckers which were sent empty over the Bwlch mountain to take up duties at Treorchy and Treherbert.

It was Pontypridd Urban District Council's transport department that eventually came to the rescue. The general manager of the transport undertaking, George Ludlow, agreed to offer six double deckers at a time, although he stipulated that they had to be sandwiched in the convoy to ensure there was no off-route wandering, a necessary precaution given the large number of low railway bridges in the area.

"The arrangements lasted successfully for many years with PUDC buses regular summer visitors to Barry Island and Porthcawl," recalled Lyndon Rees. "The newest Pontypridd Guy Arab buses were, initially, exclusively allocated to these hires, but since they were significantly slower than Rhondda's faster AEC buses, they were positioned towards the rear of the convoy followed by a minimum of two Rhondda buses with strict instructions to resist the temptation to overtake," said Lyndon.

"We felt a strong sense of responsibility for the safety of our Pontypridd colleagues who enjoyed being released from the drudgery of a busy Saturday shift on the Treforest to Cilfynydd route. Later, Merthyr Corporation also agreed to help out and provided buses for several hires from Abercynon to Barry Island."

A low railway bridge was a particular problem for Rhondda's private hires to Aberavon beach. It carried the main Swansea to Paddington line over Water Street in Port Talbot. This was the most direct route to Aberavon Beach, and the company could not risk a double decker going the wrong way and having its roof ripped off, even though drivers were always carefully pre-briefed about the route they should take. So the convoy was always supervised by a mobile team of two inspectors who would remain on point duty until the last bus had cleared the safer route around the sprawling Sandfields housing estate.

Tina's double deck fun run

Tina Simpson of Talbot Green clearly recalled the excitement of summer trips to the seaside, on top of a Rhondda Transport double deck bus:

"We lived in Tonyrefail in the 1960s, me and my eight brothers and sisters and our dad, Gwilym Edwards," said Tina. "Everyone called him Ginger and he was a member of Gilfach Social Club in Gilfach Goch.

"At the end of July every year — always on a Saturday — the club would run its annual outing to the seaside. Where we went varied. Sometimes it was Aberavon, sometimes Barry Island or Porthcawl, it didn't matter to us because it was one of the most exciting days of the year. This was our holiday in those days and we might not see the sea again that year.

"Rhondda Transport always provided double deckers that would line up in a long row outside the social club. We'd rush to climb on to the top deck to get the best seats and there was nothing more thrilling than when we finally pulled away at nine o'clock, clutching our half-crown (12.5p) spending money that we had been given by the club committee. It didn't really matter if it rained, although it was always better when the sun shone and the bus ride was a treat in itself."

Aberavon Beach was the destination for many, when the sun shone.

A summertime convoy lines up at Porthcawl to await the return run.

Changing times and new leisure trends heralded the end of the long double deck convoys to the seaside, although they continued well into the 1970s. Today, Porth depot has no double deckers but there are many valley people who remember with great fondness those annual outings to the seaside.

Rhondda Transport's service buses were also familiar sights in South Wales's coastal resorts with Porthcawl and Barry Island becoming destinations early on. The company had started services from Porth and Pontypridd to Porthcawl in July 1925 and applied to Porthcawl Urban District Council for licences for six buses for a summer service. It might have been thought that councillors would eagerly welcome any move to bring visitors and their spending power to the town, but while they granted the request they warned the company to be careful that the 'plums' of the summer trade were not taken by firms which left the 'stones' of the winter season to other companies.

By the mid-1930s Rhondda Transport was offering cheap daily return tickets to both resorts. The charge from Treherbert was 2s 6d (12.5p) to Porthcawl and

3s (15p) to Barry Island. Every Thursday and Sunday from May the company ran half-day pre-booked tours to Barry that left Maerdy at 1.40pm and Ynysybwl at 2pm.

Thursday was always early closing day in the valleys and if passengers were a little late in the day getting to the seaside then this was made up for by a late departure home from Barry Island at 9pm.

Leisure buses to the seaside were suspended during the war but in the 1940s and 1950s demand for services to Porthcawl soared. Rhondda Transport ran the 160, which started at Porth and took 93 minutes, and the 161 which departed from Treorchy and took 101 minutes.

Both services ran via Tonyrefail, Gilfach Goch and Bridgend and were co-ordinated and jointly worked with Red & White's marathon 36-mile Aberdare-Tonypandy-Porthcawl route which went over Maerdy and Penrhys mountains. During the summer extra vehicles were required and Red & White, which could not run double deckers because of the mountainous nature of the route and the existence of some low bridges, might need five or six buses for one journey

RHONDDA TRANSPORT COMPANY LIMITED

LUXURY
Sun-Saloon Coaches
FOR PRIVATE HIRE

FOR SUGGESTIONS AND QUOTATIONS APPLY

Rhondda Transport Company, Limited, Rheola Road, Porth

Tel.: Porth 118.   Evans & Short, Printers, Tonypandy   T. G. RICHARDSON, M.Inst.T., General Manager.

One of three, 31 seat Weymann bodied AEC Regal coaches which the company took delivery of shortly before the outbreak of war, in 1939.

A smartly liveried front entrance AEC Regal III half cab, 32 seater coach, one of three that arrived in 1948.

This Willowbrook bodied Dennis Lancet II coach would have been the height of luxury along with its sister vehicle when they were delivered in 1937.

alone. Tonypandy Square was always the point of greatest demand and Rhondda Transport's Pandy section inspector was told to pay special attention to the Porthcawl service.

A gentleman's agreement meant Rhondda did not run a bus until after the Red & White convoy left the square, but that did not prevent some underhand trickery. The inspector would often have a double decker lined up at the square with the destination indicator tantalisingly set for Porthcawl.

Canny passengers would know that once the Red & White buses had gone, the Regent would depart and do the journey more quickly as it was limited stop and avoided Bridgend. So they would hang back for the Red & White buses to go, then jump on the Regent.

The trick always worked and caused endless rows between the two companies, which Rhondda, in true fashion, simply ignored.

The double deckers were well used during the 1950s. On Bank Holidays as many as 16 of them were needed at the end of the day to clear the queues at Porthcawl. These fast buses did not pick up or set down passengers before or after Tonyrefail and would leave Porthcawl at 10 minute intervals between 6.35pm and 7.55pm. If there were still passengers waiting, as was often the case, more buses would run and it could be as late as 9.45pm before the queues were finally cleared.

Ploy to earn extra wages

Passengers welcomed the arrival of new, modern double deckers at Porth depot in 1958, but the drivers were much less keen, remembered Gwyn Jones.

"They were the first front entrance double deckers and the first to carry 70 passengers but they didn't have power steering and were incredibly heavy to drive," said Gwyn who believed there was no doubt that they affected the health of some of the older drivers who found they made their job more difficult.

"I joined Rhondda Transport in 1958 as a bus conductor. You had to work six years as a conductor before you could become a driver in those days and while some of the men stayed conducting many wanted to move on to driving even though the pay differential between the two jobs was not that great.

"I preferred driving and well remember a ploy by crews to add a little extra to their take home pay. There was a rule that if a bus came into the depot after midnight, the driver and conductor got an extra 1s 6d.

"So it was not unknown for a driver to park his bus a little way from the depot and then bring it in at a minute after midnight. Everyone knew it was going on but it seems to have been accepted by the company."

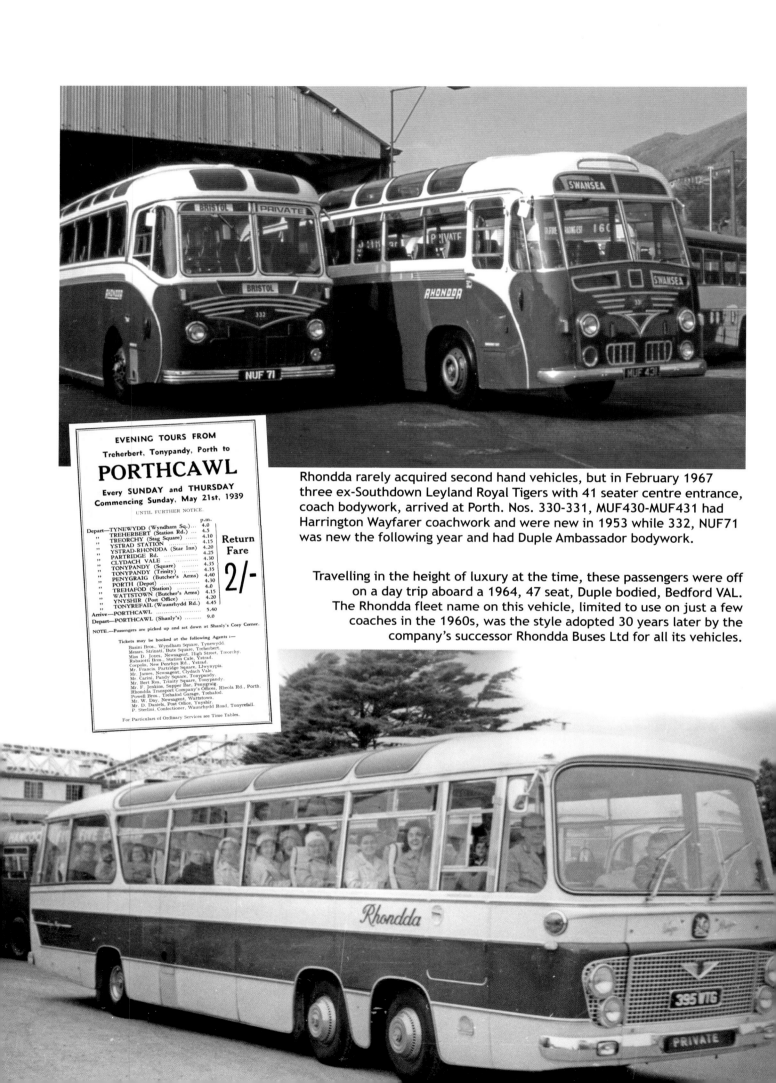

Rhondda rarely acquired second hand vehicles, but in February 1967 three ex-Southdown Leyland Royal Tigers with 41 seater centre entrance, coach bodywork, arrived at Porth. Nos. 330-331, MUF430-MUF431 had Harrington Wayfarer coachwork and were new in 1953 while 332, NUF71 was new the following year and had Duple Ambassador bodywork.

Travelling in the height of luxury at the time, these passengers were off on a day trip aboard a 1964, 47 seat, Duple bodied, Bedford VAL. The Rhondda fleet name on this vehicle, limited to use on just a few coaches in the 1960s, was the style adopted 30 years later by the company's successor Rhondda Buses Ltd for all its vehicles.

The services arrived and departed from outside the Knights Arms Hotel in Porthcawl, which was known as the terminus, but it was a small turning area and just not large enough at busy times for the number of passengers using the buses. So after 4.30pm on summer weekends passengers were told to catch their bus from the long Eastern Promenade, opposite Coney Beach. Unfortunately, like Rhondda's other services, the Porthcawl route suffered from declining passenger numbers during the late 1960s and in 1970 it was converted to driver-only operation. The drop in demand continued and after Western Welsh took over Rhondda Transport in 1971 the route was dropped entirely apart from one college journey which started at Bridgend bus station at 9.17am. Red & White's 172 service took over the operation on a basic two hourly frequency and it continues to this day, operated by Stagecoach from its Aberdare depot.

By the early 1960s Rhondda was running summer weekend expresses further afield. An X1 Maerdy to Barry Island service had started in the 1950s and was later joined by summer service X6, Trethomas-Caerphilly-Saundersfoot-Tenby; X7, Trehafod-Treorchy-Tenby; X8, Maerdy-Tonypandy-Aberavon; and X9, Ynysybwl-Pontypridd-Talbot Green-Aberavon Beach. Unfortunately, the growth in car ownership meant these services were not used as

Working a private hire to Aintree Racecourse, No. 328, LTG268, was one of three Leyland Royal Tigers bought by Rhondda in 1952. They remained with the company for eight years before being withdrawn and sold.

much as they might have been in the early 1950s while another problem was that they were highly dependent on the weather. Sunny days might mean packed buses, but rainy days brought with them far fewer passengers.

Rhondda's private hires went further afield when the Severn Bridge opened on September 8, 1966. Each Saturday coaches left Rhondda for Bristol, 12 were needed on the first trip. The company received licences to run to Bath, Longleat House and Weston Super Mare, among other West Country destinations.

Busy times in the private hire office.

One of three Weymann Fanfare bodied Leyland 41 seater coaches which arrived in 1959.

Unusually, when the Strachan bodied Tiger Cubs Nos. 357-9 became due for replacement in 1964, Rhondda chose Bedford VALs with Duple coachwork. Although lacking power and braking capabilities they gave passengers a very comfortable ride. Cream and maroon when new they soon received green relief. No. 397 is seen at Porth depot in spotless condition. It was sold in 1970.

This impressive line-up of drivers with their 1946, 1947 and 1948 AEC Regals, appear to have been engaged in a large scale private hire.

A close look at one of the last buses with coach seats ordered by Rhondda Transport, this dual purpose 1968 Leyland Leopard was the first vehicle of its type delivered to the company.

Routes reach out around the valley

Rhondda Tramways began the 1920s without a single bus route, but by the end of the decade it was running motorbuses as far away as Cardiff, Barry, Bridgend and Porthcawl. Initially the company was slow to enter the age of the bus although circumstances would change that and within just a few years it was vying to become one of South Wales' major operators.

At the start of 1920 it was still only running trams in the Rhondda Fach and Rhondda Fawr on lines that it leased from Rhondda Urban District Council. Little had changed since the system had started in 1908, although an extension was opened to Williamstown in March 1912 and in July 1919 through trams from the Rhondda to Pontypridd began operating. Previously, passengers were required to change from a Rhondda tram to a Pontypridd Urban District Council tram at Trehafod. From this time there was a joint service through from Porth to Pontypridd, an arrangement that would continue right through the bus days until PUDC brought it to an end in 1969.

Rhondda Tramways' first bus route only came about because the valley's council wanted better transport links to and from Clydach Vale. The steepness of the 1.4 mile route made it impossible for trams and so the company was asked to provide motorbuses which eventually began running in August 1920.

Motorbus service development for Rhondda Tramways continued at a slow pace. It started running buses to Gilfach Goch in January 1921 to replace the trolleybus system that had ended so disastrously in March 1914. In June 1922 the company began the short Treorchy to Cwmparc service after local residents complained about the inadequacies of their transport links and the same month it started a route from Ystrad in the Rhondda Fawr over Penrhys Mountain to Ferndale in the Rhondda Fach after a similar service had been started by independent operator, David Morgan.

Waiting for its driver — and a run to Treorchy — at Cardiff central bus station 448GTX was one of a batch of Regent Vs with Metro Cammell Weymann bodywork, delivered to Rhondda Transport in 1961.

CHAPTER 7

In fact it was entrepreneurs of his ilk that forced Rhondda Tramways to buck up its ideas. These people started services across the company's area and towards the end of the 1920s with around 40 of them in existence, it became clear to Rhondda that if it was to survive and grow, then it would need to join in.

Major bus expansion began with a Pontypridd to Cardiff route which Rhondda Tramways started in March 1924, even though there were a number of operators already running a similar service. In July the following year two 24 mile routes to Porthcawl — one from Porth and Blackmill, the other from Pontypridd and Talbot Green — got under way. These were followed in August by a 26 mile service from Pontypridd to Beddau, Pontyclun and Cowbridge, extended in the summer months to Barry. May 1927 saw the company begin a 24 mile service from Treorchy to Cardiff which was extended to Treherbert in November 1931.

But Rhondda Tramways' had even more ambitious plans which, if they had materialised, would have seen its operating area extend much further. In June 1928 the company announced it wanted to run services from Merthyr to Cardiff; Aberdare to Cardiff; Pontypridd-Caerphilly-Newport; and Pontypridd to Newbridge via Nelson and Ystrad Mynach. After a major battle with Merthyr Council, the 24 mile Merthyr service finally

If Rhondda Transport was in decline in the late 1960s then so too, was the valley it had served for so long. This telling scene at Ferndale, complete with a Leyland Tiger Cub depicts some of the feeling and atmosphere of the decaying times.

started in November 1931 but the others fell at the first hurdle.

In the 1920s bus companies had to apply to local councils for licences to run services and there was a reluctance to allow private concerns such as Rhondda Tramways to operate routes. Local authorities like Merthyr, Caerphilly, Pontypridd and Cardiff thought they could do a better job on behalf of their ratepayers and wanted to run their own buses. Rhondda Council was different. It enjoyed good relations with the tramways company to which it leased the valley tram services and saw the benefits of allowing a private company to take the financial risks of running buses.

Rhondda Tramways' major expansion into buses came in 1934 following the decision to withdraw the valley's trams and replace them with motorbuses. Beginning in January that year what were called the backbone routes from Blaenrhondda and Blaencwm down the Rhondda Fawr to Pontypridd and from Tonypandy and Partridge Road to Porth and up the Rhondda Fach to

Maerdy were being operated by faster and more flexible buses and the company changed its name to Rhondda Transport.

With this fresh impetus it set about improving its services with gusto, particularly on routes outside the Rhondda, and there was a good reason for this. Despite its amicable relations with Rhondda Urban District Council, the local authority retained an option to take over bus services within its area. Fortunately, it could see the losses being made on local bus operations by other South Wales authorities and had no desire to suffer similar problems. Even so, it was always a risk as far as Rhondda Transport was concerned so developing routes outside the valleys was a strategy for survival.

Rhondda later introduced a system to differentiate its routes. Services operating within the Rhondda were prefixed with the letter R, while routes that went outside the valley were numbered from 100 up. Meanwhile, workmen's services were prefixed with the letter W, while express routes were prefixed with the letter X.

The most important bus route for people living in the Rhondda Fawr was the backbone 10.5 mile service from Blaenrhondda and Blaencwm at the top of the valley down to Porth, where the Fawr and Fach valleys meet.

For many years, if passengers wanted to continue their journeys to Pontypridd, they had to change at Porth onto another service run jointly by Rhondda Transport and Pontypridd Urban District Council, Rhondda's dark red livery providing a stark contrast to the navy blue PUDC used for its buses. Later the arrangement changed and Rhondda buses ran straight through although the Pontypridd authority was refused permission to run any further than Pontypridd-Porth.

The Blaencwm/Blaenrhondda-Porth/Pontypridd service was sometimes called 'the ordinary service bus' to set it apart from the more prestigious Treorchy-Cardiff route which charged higher fares. But to most people in the Rhondda Fawr it was simply 'the Ponty bus.' Eventually there were four variations, numbered R20-R23, while the joint service continued and was numbered R24, and together they provided a five minute frequency from Porth to Pontypridd. But at busy times, particularly on Wednesday and Saturday market days in Pontypridd the vehicles, always double deckers, would be jam-packed and even this wasn't enough.

There were problems running extra buses, despite the demand, because like the trams before them the buses entered Pontypridd town centre via Mill Street and turned right into Taff Street. Passengers would be unloaded outside the Marks and Spencer store and the bus would then have to reverse down to the stop to start the return journey by the same route. Before making the manoeuvre the previous bus had to leave the stand and this slowed the operation considerably

One of the last Rhondda Transport conductors with his driver and their Regent V at Blaenrhondda before setting of for Pontypridd.

with long queues of passengers commonplace. The route was equally busy between Blaencwm/Blaenrhondda and Porth. It connected the large shopping centres of Treorchy, Tonypandy and Porth with villages like Gelli and Penygraig and the smaller shopping centres between them. After the Second World War, and until the late 1960s — before the advent of out of town stores — these were busy and customers were brought to them by Rhondda's buses.

Tonypandy was always a hive of activity, particularly on Friday afternoons and Saturdays when, for nearly a mile from the start of De Winton Street at Tonypandy Square down through Dunraven Street to the start of Tylacelyn Road, the pavements would be packed with shoppers.

Between larger establishments including Woolworth's, furniture and clothes stores there were numerous independent greengrocers, butchers and bakers as well as pubs and the legendary Italian cafes, known as Bracchis. This was originally the name of one Italian family which opened cafes in the Rhondda but it became a generic term for the others as well. There were two cinemas, the Picturedrome at Tonypandy Square and the Plaza in lower Dunraven Street as well as the famous Empire Theatre which became a Woolworth's store and later an Iceland store.

With so few people owning cars in the 1940s and 1950s, particularly in the Rhondda where car ownership was even lower than the national average, it was the bus that people used to get to these centres and they were always full, from early in the morning for workers, through the day and late at night to take people home from the pubs and social clubs. Cinema patrons often filled the late buses home, to bursting point.

Buses were so full on Saturdays in the 1940s and 1950s that Rhondda Transport employed 'jumpers' — these were conductors who would wait at stops along busy sections and jump on a bus to help collect fares. They would take fares on the upper deck while the regular conductor would continue to collect them on the lower deck and take charge of passengers getting on and off the vehicle. Sundays were also busy for although Rhondda Transport did not begin services until midday the buses were packed in the evening to take people to and from churches and chapels.

The Blaenrhondda/Blaencwm-Porth services replaced the trams in February 1934 and followed the same route down the valley. The buses were much faster than the trams but it was never a quick service, passenger loads and the narrow roads saw to that. In 1951 the 10.5 mile journey took around 53 minutes and the later three-mile extension to Pontypridd another 16, although there was often a long wait at Porth for a changeover of crews.

The journey began at the head of the Rhondda Fawr, in the small mining villages of Blaencwm and Blaenrhondda whose long strings of terraced homes nestled below the steep crags of Mynydd Blaenrhondda and Mynydd Tynewydd. From here the route ran past allotments to Treherbert, the first station on the Rhondda Fawr rail line to Cardiff and the buses ran parallel to the railway down the valley until the terminus at Porth or Pontypridd.

Treorchy was the first major stop, another important centre from where Rhondda's flagship service to Talbot Green and Cardiff began, although it took a different route down the valley to Tonypandy. The 'Ponty bus' would continue its slow progress to Ton Pentre and originally followed the former tram track that ran parallel to the railway between Pentre and Ystrad. In the mid-1950s the route was diverted around Gelli

which previously had been served by a limited supplementary service between Treherbert and Porth which was known as the 'Ystrad shuttle.' After the diversion it operated on Saturdays only which provided a service frequency of a bus every five minutes.

Tonypandy was the next major stop and an important transport hub. Here the 'Ponty bus' connected with the Porthcawl, Cardiff, Clydach Vale and Maerdy services at what was always known as Pandy Square. The route then continued to Penygraig, itself a thriving shopping centre, and on to Dinas and Porth, another major bus connection point for services up to Rhiwgarn, Tonyrefail and Maerdy in the Rhondda Fach. At this point the Porth only service would negotiate around the public conveniences at Porth Square to turn back for the return journey up the valley while the Pontypridd buses would stop behind a navy blue PUDC bus which parked outside the Porth Hotel ready to operate the joint service. Passengers waiting on the council vehicle would then transfer to the Rhondda bus and then it was off for the three miles to Pontypridd and journey's end.

Important service was slow one too!

The most important bus route for people living in the Rhondda Fach was from Maerdy to Porth which continued to either Tonypandy or Partridge Road in the Rhondda Fawr. It was the second backbone service and like the Blaencwm/Blaenrhondda-Porth journey replaced the trams in 1934.

This was also a slow service and took 50 minutes to complete the seven miles from the top of the Fach at Maerdy down to Porth and then for just under three miles to Tonypandy or Partridge Road. It was never as busy a route as its counterpart in the Rhondda Fawr but

One of four 34 seat, 1946 Burlingham bodied AEC Regals at Porth Square before making the steep climb up Cymmer Hill.

it still ran every 15 minutes and was always double decker operated, requiring eight vehicles. It split at the Miskin Hotel in Trealaw with the R31 variation continuing to Tonypandy Square while the R30 made its way along Ynyscynon Road, terminating in Llwynypia, just below Rhondda's main hospital.

For most of its existence the R30 carried Partridge Road on its destination blind but later this was changed to Llwynypia. This terminus was an important changeover point during the tram days when the service from Porth via Dinas and Tonypandy connected with the route up from Porth via Trealaw. The R30 bus also connected with the R20-23 set of services but passenger transfers in the days of the bus became fewer. The Partridge Road section, where many mining families lived, became less important with the closure of local collieries.

Even so, the R30 and R31 continued to be run by double deckers throughout Rhondda Transport's existence, not becoming single decked, one person operated until as late as 1975 when the company was part of the National Bus Company. By then passenger figures were way down on the 1940s and 1950s when many extra vehicles had to be brought in to cope with peak period demand between Porth Square and Ferndale and Porth Square and Pandy Square.

Ferndale was the most important village in the Rhondda Fach and while not having as many shops as the larger centres in the Fawr it was always busy, particularly on Friday afternoons and Saturdays. The R30 and R31 were the main means of bringing in shoppers and after the Rhondda Fach passenger railway closed in 1964 the services became more important for getting people down the valley to Porth.

Rhondda Transport's flagship was undoubtedly the service that ran from Treorchy, down to Tonypandy and on to Talbot Green and Cardiff. It was the

Rhondda Inspector Frank Reed.

Inspector's mistake renamed

Rhondda Transport's Frank Reed had an unusual claim to fame: it is said he renamed a district where he worked as an inspector.

For many years Frank was one of the inspectors at Talbot Green bus station, which was owned by the company. The district was originally known as Green Talbot however and it seems one day Frank made a mistake when writing out a fare list and called it Talbot Green. The name stuck and that is still what it is called today.

The story, although disputed by some local historians was retold in Rhondda Transport's Christmas 1963 Staff News which reported that Frank had decided to hang up his inspector's hat after a half-century on the buses. His career began as a tram conductor in 1913 and in 1915

A mixed line up of Rhondda Transport vehicles at Talbot Green bus station, on June 12, 1971. INSET: similar scenes at the same location in earlier years.

a community

he was promoted to tram driver, eventually becoming an inspector. During the First World War and in the 1920s, Rhondda Transport employed women conductors and that is how Frank met the woman who became his wife.

"I have enjoyed my work and having completed 50 years service it is time I called it a day," said Frank in the Staff News article.

company's most profitable route and was always allocated the newest buses. Introduced in May 1924 to operate between Porth, Tonyrefail and Cardiff, in May 1927 it was amended to run from Treorchy and Cardiff. In November 1931 it was extended to Treherbert, although this was withdrawn during the war years and for the rest of Rhondda Transport's existence, apart from a short time in the mid-1950s when it was extended on Saturdays to Blaenrhondda, it was the popular Treorchy-Talbot Green-Cardiff service.

Initially the route was allocated single deck AEC Regal buses, but demand grew and double deckers running at 30-minute intervals were introduced in 1937. The service was so well used that after the war Rhondda Transport introduced a variant that ran from Ystrad down to Trealaw, meeting up with the original service in lower Tonypandy, to provide a 15-minute frequency to Cardiff. Even this was not enough in the 1950s and early 1960s when large numbers of relief buses had to be brought in to cope with passenger numbers at weekday peak times and on Saturdays, particularly for rugby internationals or when Cardiff City Football Club were playing at Ninian Park.

Staff at the newly opened ticket office near the entrance to Porth depot, September 10, 1967.

Most journeys at busy times were supplemented by one or two relief buses at Tonypandy Square with a third usually standing by at Tonyrefail and a fourth at Talbot Green. These extra buses would park up at Western Welsh's Cardiff depot in Penarth Road, ready for the exodus home. Often there were too many vehicles for the depot and these had to be parked along the Fitzhamon Embankment.

Rhondda Transport decided to introduce route numbers in 1954 and the Treorchy-Cardiff service became the 120 while the Ystrad variant was numbered 121.

From Treorchy it was just under 25 miles to Cardiff, a journey that took the 120 a total of 95 minutes, while Cardiff was 23 miles from Ystrad which took the 121 a slightly quicker 80 minutes. Both services left the Rhondda from pubs. The 120 departed from the Cardiff Arms Hotel, which still exists, while the 121 went from the Star Hotel in Ystrad, now a supermarket. On its return journey the 121 always carried Ystrad Rhondda (Star Hotel) on its destination blind to ensure passengers would not confuse it with the municipal 36 Cardiff-Ystrad Mynach-Tredegar service.

Premium fares were charged on the 120 and 121 and so that passengers would not mix them up with the local R20 to R23 services, conductors would call out 'Cardiff service' at bus stops. They provided an alternative route to Cardiff for people living in the Rhondda Fawr. While the train went via Pontypridd, Treforest and Taffs Well, the buses went to Tonyrefail, Talbot Green and on to Llandaff and Cardiff.

The journey made its way initially through ribbons of terraced houses and along Rhondda's narrow roads to Trebanog before descending more than a mile to Tonyrefail, one of the steepest hills on the Rhondda Transport network. But the AEC Regents used on the route for many years coped admirably with the return climb, even with full or standing loads. By now, the Rhondda had been left behind and the bus entered the Ely Valley, but the coal industry was still evident as the bus passed Coedely coke works with all its fumes and flames. If there is a hell, this was surely it but at least one or two Rhondda Transport buses would usually be seen parked there waiting to take workers home at the end of their shifts.

From here the route became more rural before arrival at Talbot Green bus station which Rhondda Transport bought in June 1938. During the company's existence, Talbot Green was little more than a large village overlooked by Llantrisant old town which had been built on the hill above. It had yet to become a major commuter town for people working in Cardiff and its large shopping centre, industrial estate, the Royal Mint and hospital were yet to be built. Despite this the bus station was always a busy and important interchange

About to leave the depot for a turn on route R20 to Blaenrhondda is one of 27 AEC Regent Vs delivered in 1956. The Lady Lewis Colliery can be seen in the background.

point, manned by a Rhondda Transport inspector even if its facilities for passengers were basic, amounting to just a concrete shelter.

The bus to Cardiff would meet up with the returning service to the Rhondda and they would connect with Rhondda Transport's service to Cowbridge and the company's joint service with Western Welsh's Bridgend depot between Pontypridd and Porthcawl which, because of low bridges en route, was always single deck operated. As the crews chatted, transferring passengers would pick their way through the buses, taking care to get on the right vehicle. After Talbot Green and Pontyclun, the driver could put his foot down through the rural parts of the Vale of Glamorgan passing through Groesfaen, Creigiau Cross and Capel Llanilltern before arriving at Llandaff on the outskirts of Cardiff. Now the route started to become built up once more and soon Llandaff Fields were reached. When the 120 service first started, this was as far as Rhondda's buses were allowed to come as this was Cardiff's tram terminus and the council was concerned about competition with its trams. So passengers wanting to get to the city centre had to change here. Eventually, a long battle by Rhondda Transport resulted in its vehicles being allowed into the city centre albeit with restrictions on picking up and letting down passengers. This was also the turning point for the number 24 Cardiff trolleybus service until 1970.

The 120 and 121 continued along Cathedral Road before passing Cardiff Arms Park, now the Millennium Stadium, and finally arriving at the city's central bus station which opened in 1954. Here Rhondda's buses would mingle with vehicles run by its sister companies, Western Welsh and N&C Luxury Coaches, with Red &

White Services and the South Wales municipal buses all dominated by the crimson and cream displayed on Cardiff Corporation vehicles.

As the 1960s progressed and car ownership soared, passenger figures plummeted on the 120 and 121 and in the mid-1960s the frequency was cut to 20 minutes on weekdays although there were still four buses an hour on Saturdays. The 121 was also extended to Treorchy and the well-known and unusual Ystrad Rhondda (Star Hotel) destination blind became a thing of the past.

Three year battle for route rights

Rhondda Tramways' bid to run buses between Merthyr Tydfil and Cardiff turned into a three year battle with Merthyr Tydfil Corporation. In June 1928 the company announced plans to run the route, but when it applied to the corporation for a licence it was immediately blocked.

At the time local authorities issued licences for bus services and Merthyr didn't want Rhondda running on the same route as the Cardiff service it proposed for its own municipal buses. Cardiff Corporation also planned to run the route and the two local authorities were happy to accept each other's tickets on their buses. But when Rhondda Tramways applied for a licence on the same terms, Merthyr Corporation objected.

The town's mayor explained: "We objected to this because Cardiff allowed Merthyr municipal buses to pick up passengers in the Cardiff area with a similar

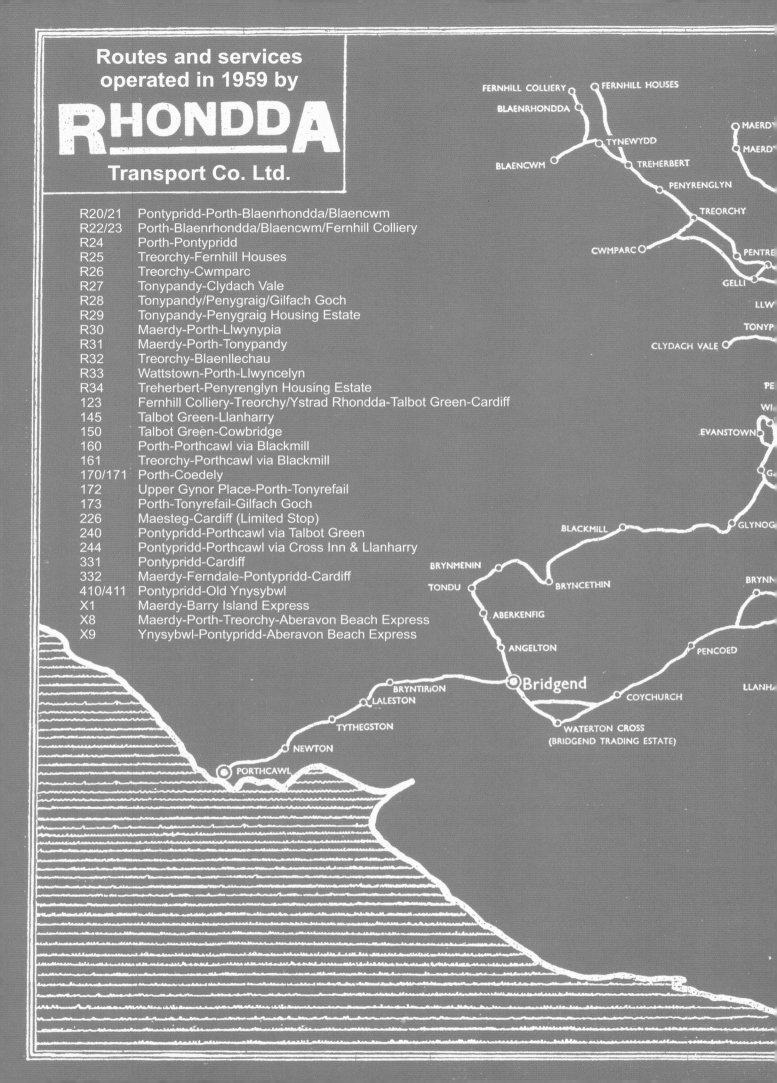

Routes and services operated in 1959 by

RHONDDA

Transport Co. Ltd.

R20/21	Pontypridd-Porth-Blaenrhondda/Blaencwm
R22/23	Porth-Blaenrhondda/Blaencwm/Fernhill Colliery
R24	Porth-Pontypridd
R25	Treorchy-Fernhill Houses
R26	Treorchy-Cwmparc
R27	Tonypandy-Clydach Vale
R28	Tonypandy/Penygraig/Gilfach Goch
R29	Tonypandy-Penygraig Housing Estate
R30	Maerdy-Porth-Llwynypia
R31	Maerdy-Porth-Tonypandy
R32	Treorchy-Blaenllechau
R33	Wattstown-Porth-Llwyncelyn
R34	Treherbert-Penyrenglyn Housing Estate
123	Fernhill Colliery-Treorchy/Ystrad Rhondda-Talbot Green-Cardiff
145	Talbot Green-Llanharry
150	Talbot Green-Cowbridge
160	Porth-Porthcawl via Blackmill
161	Treorchy-Porthcawl via Blackmill
170/171	Porth-Coedely
172	Upper Gynor Place-Porth-Tonyrefail
173	Porth-Tonyrefail-Gilfach Goch
226	Maesteg-Cardiff (Limited Stop)
240	Pontypridd-Porthcawl via Talbot Green
244	Pontypridd-Porthcawl via Cross Inn & Llanharry
331	Pontypridd-Cardiff
332	Maerdy-Ferndale-Pontypridd-Cardiff
410/411	Pontypridd-Old Ynysybwl
X1	Maerdy-Barry Island Express
X8	Maerdy-Porth-Treorchy-Aberavon Beach Express
X9	Ynysybwl-Pontypridd-Aberavon Beach Express

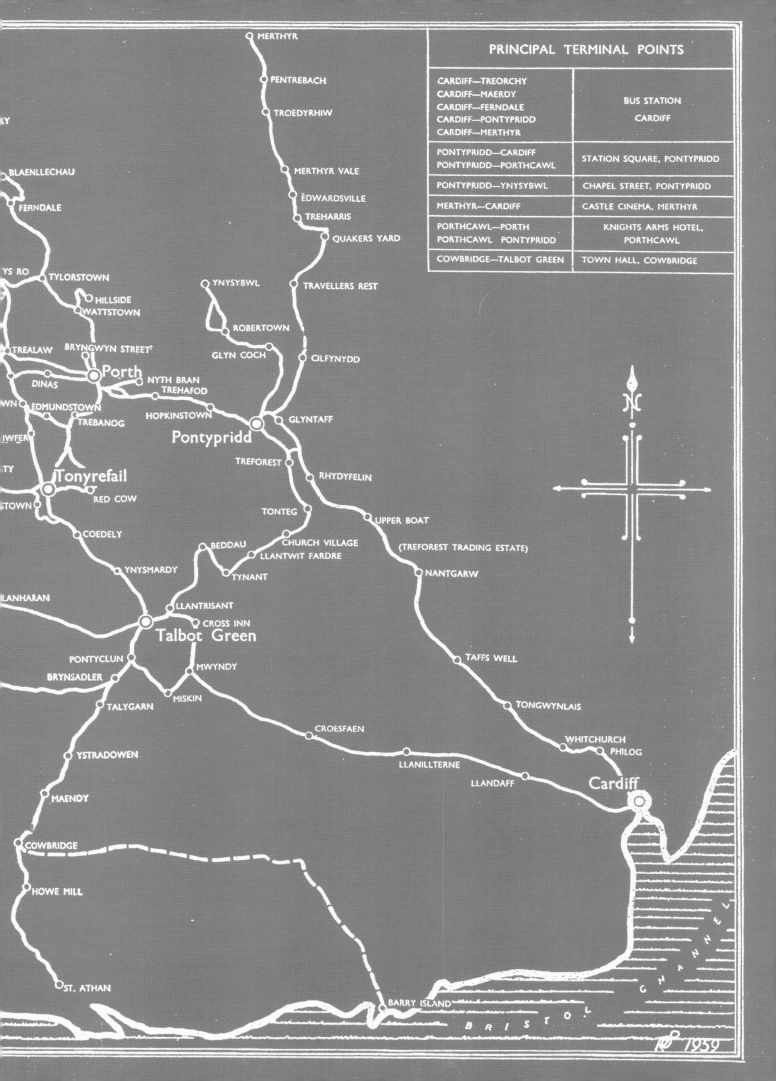

PRINCIPAL TERMINAL POINTS

CARDIFF—TREORCHY CARDIFF—MAERDY CARDIFF—FERNDALE CARDIFF—PONTYPRIDD CARDIFF—MERTHYR	BUS STATION CARDIFF
PONTYPRIDD—CARDIFF PONTYPRIDD—PORTHCAWL	STATION SQUARE, PONTYPRIDD
PONTYPRIDD—YNYSYBWL	CHAPEL STREET, PONTYPRIDD
MERTHYR—CARDIFF	CASTLE CINEMA, MERTHYR
PORTHCAWL—PORTH PORTHCAWL PONTYPRIDD	KNIGHTS ARMS HOTEL, PORTHCAWL
COWBRIDGE—TALBOT GREEN	TOWN HALL, COWBRIDGE

MERTHYR
PENTREBACH
TROEDYRHIW
MERTHYR VALE
EDWARDSVILLE
TREHARRIS
QUAKERS YARD
BLAENLLECHAU
FERNDALE
YNYSYBWL
TRAVELLERS REST
YS RO
TYLORSTOWN
HILLSIDE
WATTSTOWN
ROBERTOWN
TREALAW
BRYNGWYN STREET
GLYN COCH
CILFYNYDD
Porth
NYTH BRAN
DINAS
TREHAFOD
WN
EDMUNDSTOWN
HOPKINSTOWN
GLYNTAFF
TREBANOG
IWFER
Pontypridd
TY
TREFOREST
Tonyrefail
RHYDYFELIN
TOWN
RED COW
TONTEG
UPPER BOAT
COEDELY
(TREFOREST TRADING ESTATE)
BEDDAU
CHURCH VILLAGE
YNYSMARDY
LLANTWIT FARDRE
NANTGARW
TYNANT
LANHARAN
LLANTRISANT
CROSS INN
Talbot Green
PONTYCLUN
MWYNDY
TAFFS WELL
BRYNSADLER
MISKIN
TALYGARN
TONGWYNLAIS
CROESFAEN
WHITCHURCH
PHILOG
YSTRADOWEN
LLANILLTERNE
LLANDAFF
Cardiff
MAENDY
COWBRIDGE
HOWE MILL
ST. ATHAN
BARRY ISLAND
BRISTOL CHANNEL

1959

facility being granted to Cardiff buses in Merthyr but we cannot allow the company such a concession because it has nothing to offer us in return."

Rhondda refused to take the decision lying down and appealed to the Ministry of Transport which in September 1930 sided with the company. It ordered Merthyr Tydfil Corporation to issue a licence to Rhondda Tramways on equal terms with its own and Cardiff Corporation's services, but still Merthyr prevaricated. It adjourned a decision to comply with the order for talks with the ministry.

Finally, in November 1931, agreement was reached and Rhondda began its service from Merthyr to Cardiff. It meant the two councils and the company each running one bus on a joint hourly service on the 24-mile journey which took 80 minutes. This was many years before the A470 trunk road was built and the service ran from Merthyr down the valley to Troedyrhiw, Treharris and Cilfynydd. It by-passed Pontypridd town centre and continued to Treforest, Nantgarw and on to Cardiff.

Return tickets were inter-changeable between the three operators, fares were the same and the timetable was co-ordinated. But later, when route numbers were introduced, Rhondda numbered its service 100, Cardiff used 41 and later 20 while Merthyr's was 7, which must have confused passengers.

Initially single deck buses were used but after the war, as passenger loads began to climb, the three operators ran double deckers. The now renamed Rhondda Transport ran the busiest trip of the day, the 8am journey from Merthyr which until the mid-1950s was duplicated with a second double decker, as were most of the company's Saturday journeys with passengers travelling to Cardiff for shopping and major sporting events. There was also an hourly train service from Merthyr to Cardiff, but the rail competition didn't seem to have any effect on passenger numbers

using the bus service. One pre-Christmas shopping Saturday in 1962, the 5.30 pm bus from Cardiff operated by Merthyr Corporation left with a full load, but there was still a very long queue waiting to be taken home. Passengers were furious that they would have to wait up to an hour for the next bus, but Rhondda came to the rescue by transferring one of the vehicles it had on standby for the Treorchy service. This was just one small example of the co-operative attitude of Rhondda Transport crews.

Despite all this, the Merthyr route was never a goldmine for Rhondda Transport. One of the problems was its distance from Porth depot. To run the 8am working from Merthyr, the Rhondda bus had to leave the depot at 6.55am and take up the journey at 7.12am from Treforest. Rhondda also ran the last bus of the day from Cardiff at 9.30pm which left Merthyr at 10.50pm, running to Treforest and then to the depot, not getting back until 11.53pm. The crews changed at Pontypridd and had to get there to take up their duties on the company's other services which was described as 'travelling passenger.'

There were also severe restrictions on picking up and unloading passengers. No-one could be conveyed locally within the Merthyr Tydfil or Cardiff council areas or between Pontypridd and Cardiff to protect the service run jointly by Rhondda and Western Welsh. This meant the journey time was shorter and the crews called the 100 the Merthyr Flier. But it reduced the number of passengers and at the same time the service's viability.

By the end of the 1960s passenger numbers had dropped to such an extent that Rhondda converted the route to one person operation, apart from the still busy 8am working. Now, instead of the AEC Regents and the occasional Atlantean on the route most workings were operated by single deck vehicles including the green and cream dual purpose Leyland Leopards of 1968. After the Western Welsh takeover of the Rhondda Transport Company in 1971, the Merthyr route was renumbered 327 but it was withdrawn on November 27 that year. Cardiff Corporation also pulled out leaving Merthyr Tydfil Corporation to run the service on its own.

A pair of different generation AEC Regent vehicles at Porth depot during the mid-1960s. They were however delivered just 2 years apart the first in 1956 and the second in 1958.

Queuing workmen prepare to board a 1946 AEC Regent III, 219, GNY371, with low built RT style bonnet and Weymann bodywork, outside the Lewis Merthyr Colliery, Trehafod, in the 1950s.

The first Rhondda Transport route to be converted to one person operation was the rural service between the communities of Talbot Green and Cowbridge.

The 150, as it became when route numbers were introduced in 1954, was one of the company's oldest services. It was started by Rhondda Tramways in August 1925 and originally ran from Pontypridd to Beddau, Talbot Green, Pontyclun and Cowbridge. However, in July 1932 the company saw the growing popularity of Barry Island resort and extended the route to Barry during the summer months.

Initially it competed with the Llantrisant-Cowbridge branch rail line until it closed on November 26, 1951. The train had served the students of Cowbridge Grammar School who then became the responsibility of the bus service. Amazingly, by current standards, Rhondda Transport provided three double deckers for the route, one running on the hourly service and the other two for morning and afternoon school trips. Between the peaks, the two school buses parked up at Talbot Green bus station and their crews were used to cover for colleagues on the Pontypridd and Cardiff routes during meal breaks.

The rural nature of the route, which took 23 minutes, is evident from some of the names of the 24 bus stops along the way which included Rhiw Talog Farm, Forest Farm, Llwynwyntog Farm and The Manse. Despite this it ran all day, the first bus leaving Talbot Green bus station at 7.22 am, the last at 9.30 pm on weekdays and 10.30 pm on Saturdays. The last bus back from Cowbridge was 10.55 pm. There was even a Sunday service which started at 1.30 pm from Talbot Green with the last bus back from Cowbridge at 10.05 pm. Trees lined the route and they frequently damaged the roofs of the double deckers which had to be repaired at Porth depot. Eventually the service became single deck operated, but it was still running hourly as late as 1965. By then passenger figures were dropping alarmingly and in 1967 it became the first service to be converted entirely to driver only operation. As the decade proceeded and after the Western Welsh takeover in 1971, there were timetable cutbacks and by 1974 the last bus from Talbot Green was 6.32 pm and from Cowbridge at 7.05 pm. By now the service had been renumbered 502 and eventually it became part of the Village Bus minibus network, later a Bustler service, run by National Welsh.

Rhondda's shortest bus route took just eight minutes and in the 1950s there were just six stops. It ran from the Parc and Dare Hall in Treorchy for 1.2 miles to the top of Cwmparc with its long strings of terraced houses below Mynydd Tyle-Coch and Mynydd Maendy.

The service began in June 1922 after the company responded to the complaints of local residents about the paucity of their transport links. Initially operated by single deckers, the route became double decker operated in the 1930s and was so busy that it was allocated two vehicles with a third added exclusively to cater for miners at the Parc and Dare Colliery. Its timetable was unusual. The first vehicle didn't run until 8.08am from the Parc and Dare and the frequency was every 24 minutes until 12.10pm when it became every 15 minutes until 7.58pm, reverting to every 24 minutes until 10.46pm.

Most people got on the service, which was numbered R26 after 1954, at the Parc and Dare, probably after shopping in Treorchy, one of the Rhondda Fawr's main shopping centres. There was a long layover for the crews here and conductors were instructed to collect fares before the bus departed. This was because the route was so busy but so short that the company was concerned they wouldn't have time to collect all the fares on the way and valuable revenue would be lost.

By the 1960s three more stops were added to the route and it was later integrated with the Treorchy-Ferndale service and renumbered 532.

Extension bid became a battle

Rhondda Tramways found it had a real fight on its hands when it announced plans in November 1928 to run through buses from the Rhondda Fach to Cardiff. It had started a service from Pontypridd to the Welsh capital in March 1924 where it competed with a number of operators, notably South Wales Commercial Motors and White's of Cardiff and Barry.

Now it wanted to extend the route to Ferndale and applied for licences to Rhondda, Pontypridd and Caerphilly councils and to the two Cardiff local authorities, the city and rural district councils. The company was turned down several months later by all but the Rhondda authority because of concern that the extension would take passengers from existing services.

Before the decision was announced, Thomas White & Co. (Cardiff and Barry) had made a similar application to begin a Ferndale-Cardiff service in March 1929 and this was also rejected. The following September, Rhondda Tramways renewed its application pointing out that its proposed service 'would not interfere with any of the local services,' and was meant for longer distance passengers. It was refused once more and the company appealed to the Ministry of Transport.

In February 1930 an inquiry was held into both the Rhondda Tramways and White's applications and it resulted in an agreement being reached for both operators to run a joint service from Ferndale to Cardiff which began in August 1930 and was co-ordinated with the Pontypridd-Cardiff timetable.

The section from Cardiff to Pontypridd was operated jointly by Rhondda Tramways, White's and Western

Rhondda's first bus route from Tonypandy Square to Clydach Vale was just 1.4 miles long but it was an immensely difficult one to operate and, as a result, gave the company headaches for more than 50 years.

Originally planned to be tram operated, the gradients were simply too severe and instead it was launched on August 5, 1920, with converted Army lorries that themselves could only climb sections of the hill at 2 mph. But they were an immediate success and packed with passengers for every journey. By December that year the 'buses' had run 22,996 miles and for every mile operated the receipts were as high as 26s.79d.

Demand for the service was high from the 1920s right through to the 1960s and long queues would build up at the Pandy Square stop. Often passengers would have to wait for two or three full departures to leave before they finally managed to board for a journey of just 10 minutes but this was infinitely preferable to climbing the very steep hill.

There were just nine stops on the way up and eight on the way down as the buses went up Berw Road and Thomas Street and came down Court Street. Five of them were outside pubs, the Royal, Central, Bush and Clydach Vale hotels both up and down and the Court Hotel on the journey down, which took nine minutes.

Originally the buses used on the route had rear entrances but in 1946 Rhondda took four Burlingham bodied AEC Regals with front entrances which sometimes found themselves on the Clydach route.

Late one evening a somewhat inebriated regular at the Bush Hotel ran out to catch the last bus and made his usual blind leap at what he thought was the rear entrance. But it was one of the new vehicles and he knocked himself flat out cold on the pavement!

Single deck vehicles were the regular performers on this service because of the steep gradients. There was a rise of 323ft in just three-quarters of a mile between Pandy Square and the top of Clydach Vale with an average of 1 in 12.26, although the steepest sections were as tough as 1 in 6.8.

This made it difficult to operate Rhondda's double deckers on the route because of problems with brake fade caused by brake drums overheating when heavy vehicles were used intensely on severe and long downhill gradients. But at peak times double deckers were used on single journeys up the hill, particularly at school and factory work times. That however could lead to a

Having been fitted with a new Strachan and Brown body in 1922, a Rhondda AEC YC vehicle negotiates the junction of Thomas Street and Berw Road, Tonypandy. INSET: a similar vehicle before its body conversion.

Popular first route was a real challenge

different set of problems. Rhondda Transport's all-powerful employees' union, the General and Municipal Workers' Union, stipulated that no more than 48 passengers could be carried on double deck buses on the hill but this was frequently ignored by the crews who knew which of their vehicles could handle the strain of a full or even standing load. The problem was when less powerful buses, such as the wartime 7.6 litre Daimlers, found their way on to the route. Then the fun could really begin!

One of the steepest sections of the climb was right at the start, in lower Berw Road, and sometimes a

double decker with a full complement of school children on board would stall part of the way up. That either meant offloading lower deck passengers or reversing the vehicle back down the hill to have another go. To loud cheers from the children, the bus would slowly crawl back up and make the awkward turn left up into Thomas Street, a manoeuvre so tight that the bus would lean over to such an extent that its tyres would rub against the mudguards!

Buses ran from 5am until nearly midnight and were well used for shopping trips to Tonypandy and for visits to the area's many pubs and clubs. They were also used by miners working three shifts at Cambrian Colliery which was the last stop right at the very top.

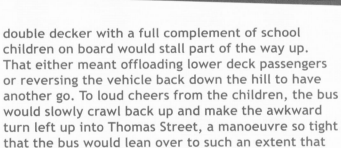

Passengers aboard one of the company's early solid tyred vehicles.

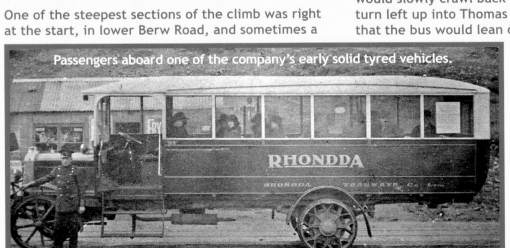

85

Queuing up at Porth Square to board a 1959 Weymann Hermes bodied Leyland Tiger Cub for the journey to Nythbran — despite the destination blind.

Welsh, which had formed in 1929 after South Wales Commercial Motors merged with the bus operations of the Great Western Railway. The Cardiff-Porth-Ferndale route was run jointly by Rhondda and White's, which allowed the tramways company to set up the timetable and fares. There were strict rules over where passengers could be picked up or set down but it meant that for the first time people living in the Rhondda Fach had a direct bus to Cardiff instead of having to change on to the railway at Porth or the bus at Pontypridd. The service was hourly from Ferndale to Cardiff but ran up to six times an hour between Pontypridd and Cardiff.

Then in July 1935 Western Welsh took over White's and its depot in Penarth Road and the service was shared by WW and Rhondda Transport. The joint working continued for the next 46 years until 1981 when what had become National Welsh closed the Penarth Road depot and the service was run entirely from Porth.

The route was always a busy one and frequent duplication was needed, especially at peak times. It was Rhondda's first route to be operated by double deckers which arrived in 1931, the first three for evaluation before the company decided to purchase AEC Regents which were the main performers on the route for nearly 40 years. Even so, the Pontypridd to Cardiff section suffered from keen end to end competition from the railways. The branch line up from Porth to Maerdy closed in 1964 but by then its passenger figures had dropped to such an extent that Rhondda Transport's competing bus service saw little benefit. There were two buses an hour from Cardiff to Ferndale and eventually one of these was extended to

run to Maerdy but, just as at the beginning, these did not pick up local passengers in the Rhondda Fach.

The services gained route numbers and, after some changes, buses on the Pontypridd to Cardiff section eventually carried 331, those between Maerdy/Ferndale-Cardiff 332. These fitted in with the Western Welsh numbering system. Services from its Cardiff depot were always in the 3XX series. There were also limited stop, commuter journeys after the closure of the Rhondda Fach railway. They ran at 6.33am from Ferndale and 7.27am from Maerdy and took just 73 mins to complete the 24 mile journey from Maerdy compared with 88 minutes for all-stop journeys.

During the 1950s and 1960s, Western Welsh provided eight vehicles for the services while Rhondda Transport ran six, but despite WW's strong involvement people in the Fach valley preferred their local crews — 'they're more friendly than the Western Welsh conductors,' they would say. The Cardiff crews for their part disliked the service with its narrow valley roads and steep climbs. It began among terraced houses and colliery workings before making its way to Pontypridd, one of the busiest valley towns which lays claim to being the capital of the South Wales valleys.

From here the 331 and 332 joined up on a co-ordinated timetable running to Treforest Industrial Estate which opened in 1937 to help ease the valleys' chronic unemployment levels as local collieries closed. As well as the 331 and 332, Rhondda Transport provided the estate with numerous works services alongside buses from Red & White's Aberdare depot, Western Welsh and the various council undertakings. The 331/332 buses were always busy here and duplication was often needed which was looked after by WW and its Penarth Road depot traffic superintendent, Bert Hill.

Next came the Nantgarw coke ovens before Taffs Well was reached with the fairy tale castle, Castell Coch, perched on the hillside above. Finally the 331 and 332 went through Whitchurch on the outskirts of Cardiff and into the city centre, passing the historic civic centre and Cardiff Castle on the way. Before the central bus station was built in 1954, the services terminated in Park Place. As the 1960s progressed, passenger totals on the 331 and 332 dropped and eventually the 331 from Pontypridd to Cardiff was withdrawn while both 332 journeys went on to Maerdy. The route continues largely unchanged as the 132, 85 years after that historic first journey.

Company finally reached the sea

Rhondda Tramways reached the seaside for the first time in July 1925 when the company launched two new services to Porthcawl.

One ran from Porth, the other started in Pontypridd and they took completely different routes until they arrived at Bridgend where South Wales Commercial Motors had opened the first bus station in Wales three years previously.

The Porth route, 24.7 miles long, ran via Tonyrefail and Blackmill to Bridgend while the 24.2 miles service from Pontypridd went via Beddau and Talbot Green. Both services then continued on the same route from Bridgend to Newton and Porthcawl. All Rhondda's services were single deck operated in the 1920s, but while passenger demand saw most of the others convert to double deck operation the Porthcawl routes continued with single deckers due to the existence of low railway bridges.

These services played an important role in opening up the valleys. For the first time it was possible for families to go on day trips to the seaside and the buses proved popular. Unfortunately Rhondda had to use its single deck AEC Regals which only seated 34 passengers and this meant crowded vehicles and duplication which a double deck, 56 seat AEC Regent would have solved. However, things became easier in 1952 when the company introduced front entrance Leyland Royal Tiger 44 seat single deckers.

The service from Porth, which took 1hr 43 minutes, became the 160 when route numbering was introduced

in 1954 by which time Rhondda Transport had also started a Treorchy to Porthcawl service, the 161, which took 1 hour 53 minutes. They joined up at Tonypandy, although the 161 later ran during the summer only.

Rhondda's original Pontypridd to Porthcawl service was later joined by a Pontypridd-Beddau-Talbot Green-Pontyclun service and another that took a different route to Pontyclun from Llantwit Fardre via Cross Inn. South Wales Commercial Motors, which became Western Welsh in 1929 when it merged with the bus operations run by the Great Western Railway, also had a Porthcawl to Pontypridd service operated by its Bridgend depot. There were also three main independent operators running from Pontypridd to Beddau: Edwards, Maisey and Bebb who joined up to form Amalgamated Bus Services.

That meant much competition on the section from Pontypridd to Beddau so Rhondda and Western Welsh agreed to co-ordinate the timetable with ABS but relations were not harmonious. Crews would delay their buses to pick up the competitors' passengers while overtaking and racing was not unknown. It began to get out of hand so Bundy clocks were installed at Church Village and Tonteg and conductors ordered to record their arrival and departure times. These were checked every week and fines levied for early or late running, although the crews soon learned it was fairly easy to sabotage the recordings and the clocks were eventually phased out.

Later Edwards and Maisey pulled out of ABS and the route was left to Bebb's which ran from Pontypridd to Beddau. Western Welsh and Rhondda began to operate their services jointly and eventually they were rationalised into two routes. One operated from Pontypridd-Beddau-Talbot Green-Bridgend-Porthcawl, which took 1 hour 38 minutes, while the other ran from Pontypridd to Cross Inn, Llanharry, Brynna and Bridgend to Porthcawl, taking 1 hr 43 minutes. When Rhondda introduced route numbers, the Talbot Green service became the 140 and the Cross Inn route the 144, although these were changed to 240 and 244, when Western Welsh began to put route numbers on its buses in 1958, to fit in with Bridgend depot services which ran in the 2XX series.

From 1953 right through to the end of the 1970s, Western Welsh and Rhondda operated the Porthcawl services with Leyland Tiger Cub single deck buses, the Weymann bodied version with three windows at the rear to accommodate the emergency exit the most common in the 1950s and early 1960s.

In 1972, a year after Rhondda Transport was taken over by Western Welsh, as passenger figures fell, the 160 and 161 services were withdrawn. The 240 and 244 continued to be operated jointly by Porth and Bridgend depots right through the 1970s, eventually becoming one-person operated.

Gradient proved a test for buses

The route up from Porth to Trebanog and down to Tonyrefail had one of the steepest gradients on the Rhondda Transport network. For more than a mile it was as severe as 1 in 6 while in two particular sections it was as much as 1 in 4.5. Yet the buses coped with these challenges magnificently.

The journey began in Porth Square at the bottom of Cymmer Road where buses parked on the right hand side of the road facing up the hill. It meant passengers had to walk out into the road to board, at the rear of the vehicle in the 1930s and 1940s when AEC Regals were the order of the day. This would certainly be banned on safety grounds today!

Then with the AEC, and from the 1950s the Leyland engines, straining to the maximum, the slow ascent up the hill would begin. There were five stops along the way and at each the buses would have to climb from a standing start. Finally they would arrive at the Trebanog Arms on the hilltop but the problems would not be over because from here the steep descent into Tonyrefail began. The destination was Coedely, a journey of around 22 or 23 minutes, where there was just a minute layover time before the bus would turn around and make its equally difficult return.

Later the service was split into four sub-routes but none of them could avoid that steep hill. One journey an hour started at Upper Gynor Place, reached by similarly steep gradients, which took six minutes to get to Porth Square from where the 170 would leave for Tonyrefail via Pretoria Road, the 171 via Collena Road and the 172 to Glynfach. On Saturdays only there was a 173 service which was extended to Gilfach Goch.

Double deckers were never used on the route because of a low railway bridge at Tonyrefail. But they did climb Cymmer Road on private hire journeys between the Rhondda Fach and Porthcawl, although depot staff ensured only the most powerful, with 8.8 or 9.6 litre engines capable of making the steepest part of the climb in first gear, were used.

One interesting route was that from Pontypridd to Old Ynysybwl which only took 15 minutes but was jointly run by three operators: Rhondda Transport, Red & White Services from its Aberdare depot, and Pontypridd Urban District Council. Rhondda and PUDC used double deckers but R&W's Aberdare depot allocation was solely single deck due to low railway bridges. Rhondda's share of the route was split into two, the 410, which went via the Windsor Hotel, and the 411 which served the Ynysybwl housing estate. Red & White numbered its service 183. The same operators also jointly worked the 10 minute Pontypridd to Glyncoch route which ran half hourly, Rhondda numbering its service the 412 while R&W's was 191. In 1969 Rhondda gave up its share of the 412 to PUDC in exchange for the council's share of the jointly worked R24 between Porth and Pontypridd.

The ill-fated trolleybus service was replaced by the R28 and was only the second of Rhondda's bus routes. Introduced in January 1921, it ran from Woolworth's store in Penygraig to Tonyrefail and Gilfach Goch every 30 minutes, a journey of 6.2 miles which took 25 minutes. One journey went clockwise from Garden City to Evanstown and Gilfach Goch, the other travelled anti-clockwise, but both had the same route number. The service required two vehicles, which in later years were always double deckers despite the journey's largely rural nature. A third vehicle was needed on Saturdays when the service was extended to Tonypandy Square. Shortly after Rhondda became part of Western Welsh in 1971, it became one-person operated and was reduced in frequency to every 40 minutes.

The R33 had 24 stops but the journey only took 25 minutes. It ran from Wattstown in the Rhondda Fach to Llwyncelyn in Porth. It ran hourly on Mondays to Thursdays and every 30 minutes on Fridays and Saturdays. There was even a Sunday service which did not begin until after 1 pm but like the rest of the week continued until late.

The last bus didn't leave Wattstown until 10.45pm and from Llwyncelyn at 10.42pm. Many of its stops didn't have names, just the street numbers of houses, indicating that much of the journey was away from main roads. Up the valley the service carried the destination Wattstown (Heol-y-Twyn), which is the housing estate on the hillside overlooking Wattstown. Nythbran was carried by Porth-bound vehicles, short for Nythbran Terrace which is on the hill overlooking Rhondda's railway line. Introduced in the mid-1930s, this was a loss maker and always single deck operated.

Meanwhile, one AEC Regal single decker operated R25, a short journey between Station Road in Treherbert and Fernhill Houses which had been built on the hillside overlooking Blaenrhondda. It took 10 minutes and was loss-making. The houses were eventually demolished and the service was withdrawn in the late 1950s.

Rhondda Transport's three hospital routes were lifelines for the people of the valleys. They connected them directly with East Glamorgan Hospital at Church Village, a difficult place to get to for those relying on public transport, even if it was the area's major general hospital before the Royal Glamorgan Hospital was built at Talbot Green. There were three services: the 140 which ran from Evanstown and Gilfach Goch; the 220 linking Treherbert and the Rhondda Fawr, and the 230 from Maerdy in the Rhondda Fach. They provided direct links for people wanting to see sick relatives or friends and coincided with hospital visiting times which were between 7pm and 8pm on weekdays and from 2 pm to 3 pm on Sundays. But visitors could not afford to hang about if they wanted to catch the return journey as the buses left smartly at either 7.55pm or 3.10pm and there was no waiting for stragglers!

Rail cutbacks and station closures led to Rhondda Transport and Western Welsh introducing a fast service from Maesteg to Cardiff.

The companies each ran one vehicle on the 1 hour 23 minute journey for which Rhondda usually allocated one of its single deck buses with coach seats. This was long before the M4 was built in South Wales and the route, numbered 226, took in the old road from Aberkenfig to Bryncethin, Pencoed, Llanharry and then through the Vale of Glamorgan to Cardiff. It was limited stop and passengers were not picked up or set down before or after Llanharry, 33 minutes away from Cardiff Central Bus Station. There were similar restrictions between Maesteg and Aberkenfig. Despite expectations, the service was not a success. Passenger loadings proved disappointing and Rhondda withdrew its vehicle leaving WW's Bridgend depot to run the service itself, which it continued to do into the 1970s.

This unique way of keeping alive the spirit of Rhondda Transport was created in matchsticks by Graham House. The long time Rhondda employee patiently crafted three of the intricate models.

Livestock travelled too

The day a fire drill at Porth depot went wrong was one of the most frequently told tales of Rhondda Transport employee Graham House, recalled his widow June.

"He used to tell how they grabbed a hose, turned on the water and pointed it at the 'fire' only to find nothing came out of the nozzle. Apparently the hose was so full of holes that the water shot up in fountains all along its length, so it was a good thing it wasn't a real fire!" said June.

"Graham, who died in 1997, was full of stories about his 38 year career with Rhondda, like the one of how conductors turned a blind eye to passengers bringing pigs and lambs on to the buses. He started at Porth in 1950, became a driver and eventually a garage chargehand. For him it wasn't just a place of work, it was his life. He was always taking photos of the buses and kept a record of the fleet. One of his proudest moments was when he received a watch and certificate for 25 years service."

Graham House

Very few former Rhondda Transport buses exist today but the fact one does is in no small way down to Graham who became firm friends with Martin Doe, a youngster who was a bus enthusiast and a frequent visitor to Porth depot.

"Martin wanted to buy his own bus in the late 1970s and a double decker that was about to be taken out of service was chosen," says June. But the company, by then National Welsh, was reluctant to sell the former Rhondda vehicle, an AEC Regent V, KNY 495D.

"It was unheard of for a boy to buy a bus but Graham encouraged him and helped all he could, eventually Martin became the owner, and still takes it to rallies today, helping to keep alive the memory of a company so fondly remembered by so many people."

Long lasting love affair with Regents

For nearly 50 years, the familiar roar of their engines could regularly be heard echoing around Rhondda. Earliest incarnations had open entrances at the back, while later versions had folding front entrance doors. What they all shared was the service they provided for the people of the valleys. They were the buses for which Rhondda Transport is best remembered — double deck AEC Regents.

There was no closer relationship in the transport industry than the one Rhondda Transport built up with the Associated Equipment Company. Its first buses in 1920, the primitive lorry buses, had the company's engines and the last were five Regents delivered in 1966 one of which remained at Porth depot until 1979.

Rhondda Transport bought 448 AEC buses and the majority of them, a total of 248 were Regents. Rhondda's sister companies in the British Electric Traction group, Cardiff-based Western Welsh and South Wales Transport at Swansea, bought Regents but they were split between low height (about 13ft 5ins) and normal height (about 14ft 6ins) vehicles. The two companies also dabbled with low height Bridgemasters and Renowns, but Rhondda never went down that road.

Despite the existence of low railway bridges in its operating area, the company only bought 14ft 6ins highbridge Regents and relied on its drivers' knowledge of the routes to avoid mishaps. Low bridge collisions were not unknown, but they were rare.

AEC introduced its Regent model in 1929, but Rhondda's first did not arrive until 1931 when the company was planning to replace its trams with motorbuses and update its old fashioned ADC, Bristol and Albion single deck vehicles whose history stretched back to the 1920s. It was a trial vehicle bodied by Brush and it arrived at the same time as a low-height Leyland TD1 and a Dennis Lance 2. The three were put through their paces on the

Radiators like this were seen everywhere in the Rhondda Valley when buses were king, testament to the close links between Rhondda Transport and AEC.

CHAPTER 8

Leaning slightly as it pulls away from Porth Square heading for Tonypandy, fleet No. 232, HTG700, was one of a batch of Weymann bodied AEC Regent IIIs delivered in 1948. This atmospheric scene will evoke nostalgic memories for 1950s Rhondda travellers.

tram routes and on the Ferndale to Cardiff service and it was the AEC Regent that won the day.

One person to whom AEC owed a debt of thanks for its subsequent custom from Rhondda Transport was Rhondda's works superintendent and later its chief engineer, Mr A Graham Slee, one of the company's longest serving managers. He was a strong admirer of the AEC engine and it is largely because of him that the company leaned so heavily towards AEC for its motorbus deliveries.

Rhondda's Regents fully justified his confidence. They tackled the valleys' notorious gradients with ease, storming effortlessly up the steepest of hills right to the end of their days. They were equally at home on the more rural routes between Talbot Green and Cardiff and on private hire duties when drivers could step on the pedal and let their charges go. They were suitable for any type of work, whether it was taking children to school or passengers to work or for private hire and trips to the seaside.

It was rare to see one of these buses broken down on the side of the road and even rarer to see one being towed back to Porth depot for repair. For 46 years they performed faithfully and reliably.

The first bulk delivery, consisting of 30 Weymann bodied Regents, arrived at Porth depot in two batches between 1933 and 1934 to replace the trams. They heralded a new era in transport provision in the South Wales valleys and received fleet numbers 101-130 with registration numbers TG6301-TG6330. At this time Rhondda developed another close relationship, this one with bus body builder Weymann of Addlestone, Surrey, and it continued to take vehicles from this company until 1959, the last Weymann Regents arriving in 1958.

The Weymann was an elegant bus with graceful curves and attractive lines. But Rhondda's first were not only superb to look at, they performed impressively as well. With powerful 8.8 litre diesel engines they significantly reduced journey times up and down the valleys compared to the slow trams they replaced. Just 30 double deckers with 52 seats succeeded 54 double deck trams with 48 seats and they afforded a level of comfort that previously the people of Rhondda could only have dreamt about. They had spacious, green and red patterned moquette upholstered seats, art deco interior light shades and, on the lower deck, attractive green coloured industrial patterning covering the ceilings and cove panels. The upper deck single skin ceilings were painted white and window surrounds on both decks were embellished with dark wood cappings, as were the bulkheads above waist level. These buses were followed by 11 similar vehicles in 1935, 131-141, registrations TG9550-TG9560, again with seats for 52, 28 upstairs and 24 on the lower deck.

They were the envy and admiration of all, but had a harsh life. During the war years, passengers packed these buses and the heavy loads carried over Rhondda's notorious road surfaces in all types of bad weather took their toll. Many had a noticeable nearside lean and some suffered cracked chassis members which required welding and extra leaves to the nearside road springs to correct stability.

At the end of the war they were in a sorry state, appearing run down and shabby. But new buses were in short supply and so they were heavily reconditioned and even rebuilt with new bodies in a bid to squeeze several more years' service out of them. The last of them wasn't withdrawn until 1955, by which time they had served Rhondda superbly for up to 22 years.

The Weymann Regents that arrived at Porth depot in 1937 were highly unusual for the time. For instead of boarding at the rear, passengers got on at the front and had the luxury of a sliding door to keep out the worst of the draughts. The first three of the 1937 delivery,147-149, BTX578-BTX580, seated 50 and had conventional entrances at the back, but the following 10, 150-159, CTG427-CTG436, had a completely different layout.

They had a forward staircase and passenger entrance with a sliding door and that was their problem. Buses at this time simply did not have the power to enable drivers to automatically close and open doors so the conductor had to do it manually. This meant that if he was on the upper deck collecting fares, he would have to dash downstairs to open the door for passengers to get on or off.

It was a tiresome chore, particularly when bus stops were close together, as was the case on Rhondda's local valley routes. So these vehicles, when new, were used on the Treorchy-Cardiff route which had fewer stops. They only seated 48 passengers but were equipped with comfortable, sofa type seats. They also had AEC's smaller 7.7 engine. After the war they were rebuilt to conventional rear entrance layout and some were rebodied by Burlingham at Blackpool, whose bodywork was not considered sufficiently robust. Others were sent to Longwell Green of Bristol to have the work carried out. Most were withdrawn from service between 1954 and 1956.

The Weymann bodied Regents that arrived in 1940 had a more modern and superior external image than their predecessors. Rhondda Transport also reverted to AEC's larger 8.8 litre engine for this batch which was numbered 163-172, ETG741-ETG750.

A solitary 1943 vintage Park Royal bodied Guy Arab I, second from left, languishes among a group of AEC Regent vehicles at Porth depot in the late 1940s.

Rear skirt panels on these buses were neatly embellished with a chrome rubbing strip which enhanced their appearance. Although the interior was similar to the previous rear entrance Regents, the batch had neater and more modern looking Sidhil & Hilton seats for 54 passengers which allowed more gangway space for people who had to stand and made it easier for conductors to collect fares.

Rhondda's traditional levels of comfort were retained and for the first time seats had 'wave top' chrome frames and hand grips. There was definitely a hint of refinement inside these vehicles with green patterned ceiling and cove panels on the lower deck.

On their arrival they were quickly put to work on the Treorchy-Cardiff and Ferndale-Cardiff routes where they performed impressively. Cascaded on to the valley routes in 1948, they were eventually withdrawn between 1956 and 1958.

Rhondda Transport's final batch of Regents ordered before the Second World War was delivered in 1941 and came as a complete shock to passengers. There were only three of them, 173-175, ETX581-ETX583, and they arrived at Porth depot in all-over camouflage grey with masked-off headlamps.

They were the first of Rhondda's buses that were built to the war time austerity design laid down by the

THE
R HONDDA
TRANSPORT COMPANY LIMITED

TIME TABLE

JUNE 1965
UNTIL FURTHER NOTICE

1/-

A typical late 1930s scene at Pandy Square which was as close as Tonypandy got to having its own bus station.

Ministry of War Transport. Commonly referred to as utility buses they were bodied by Park Royal and had the smaller 7.7 litre AEC engine. Compared to the graceful Weymann design they were considered by many to be angular and unattractive with a bare and bland interior.

Gone were the comfortable sofa type seats of previous batches. Instead these vehicles had wooden slatted seats on both decks and were dimly lit by exposed light bulbs. They had wood framed bodies mainly of unseasoned timber which leaked when it rained.

It was not unknown for passengers to let one of these buses pass by for the long journey to Cardiff in the hope of getting one of the more comfortable Regents from the earlier batches on the next turn. Dozing passengers were known to slide off the hard wooden seats into the aisle as the bus swayed around on bends. The utility design also had only two opening windows on each deck and a long journey on a warm summer's day in a bus full of cigarette smokers probably wouldn't have been a pleasant experience.

Worse was to come for Rhondda passengers however, because the next deliveries were of the utility Guy and

93

This 1953 AEC Regent III had a near full load of passengers for its mid-1950s journey to Cardiff.

Daimler double deckers. AEC stopped building buses during the Second World War and concentrated on army vehicles such as its famous Matador tractor unit.

Rhondda Transport sorely missed its favoured supplier and at the end of hostilities could not return to AEC and its Regents quickly enough.

Surprises as the Regents return

The first five of Rhondda's long-awaited post-war Regents arrived in 1946. They heralded a new generation of modern post-war buses and brought with them several surprises.

They were once again bodied by Weymann with 56 seats and looked very like London Transport's famous RT class of buses even down to the easy to clean rear

wheel hubs which gave them a smart appearance. Unfortunately, this did not last long as Rhondda found it prevented rear brake drum heat escaping on hilly routes during warm weather, something which could cause inner rear tyres to overheat and puncture.

These buses had top sliding window ventilators and the latest Deans lighter weight moquette upholstered seat frames. But their most significant features were the neat and low slung front radiator and reshaped front mudguards. Internally, light shades that resembled jelly moulds, and 24-volt batteries gave much improved lighting while a double skin ceiling was provided on the upper deck which prevented condensation and annoying water drips falling onto passengers.

They received fleet numbers 216-220 with registration numbers FTX190-FTX191 and GNY370-GNY372 and, equipped with AEC's 9.6 litre engine, were powerful vehicles. They performed impressively and gave passengers on the Treorchy-Cardiff flagship route a comfortable ride with smooth gear changes aided by

Hills were the bane of a bus driver's life in Rhondda as this one, coaxing a 1952 AEC Regent III up Saron Hill, Williamstown on a Tonypandy to Cardiff service during the mid-1950s would no doubt have testified.

One of the 10 Regents with front entrance design that were highly unusual in South Wales, seen in 1937.

the air-operated pre-selector gearbox. This made them popular with drivers. All were withdrawn in 1958 and sold to dealers.

Between 1947 and 1949, 40 Regents were delivered and they formed the backbone of Rhondda Transport's post-war fleet modernisation. They were all Regent IIIs and were known as the provincial equivalent of London Transport's RT bus with which they shared many similarities.

All were equipped with AEC's 9.6 litre engine and the Wilson type pre-selector gearbox which did not help engine braking on gradients. This meant heavier brake lining wear and inferior fuel consumption making them anything but the best vehicles for Rhondda's hilly routes.

There were three batches and the first 10, given fleet numbers 221-230 and registration numbers GNY767-GNY776, arrived in 1947. These were followed by 231-238, 240-243, HTG699-HTG706/708-711 in 1948 and 244-260, HTG712-HTG722 and JTG946-JTG951 a year later along with 239, HTG707.

All had traditional and attractive AEC front radiators and for the time modern looking, 'folded' front mudguards. Again they were supplied with Weymann 56 seat bodies with metal frames and were very robust. None was ever sent away for major body building and any work that was necessary was tackled at Porth depot. They came with front and rear destination indicators.

These buses were withdrawn between 1958 and 1962 and sold to dealers. They were replaced by new, more fuel efficient vehicles, a feature becoming increasingly important for Rhondda Transport at this time as the higher

Bus trip to evade police

There were some real characters among Rhondda's passengers down the years — one even turned Bill Thomas's bus into a getaway vehicle to evade pursuing police.

Bill recalled that it was just one of the more unusual events in 35 years with the company from 1962 to 1997 during which he worked as both driver and conductor.

"I was a conductor for 15 years then, in the 1970s after the Western Welsh takeover, more routes became one man operated so I learned to drive.

"I worked all the routes and the different shift patterns sometimes meant starting at Maerdy early in the morning to bring staff in for work and sometimes finishing well after midnight to take them home again.

"The depot never closed. There were always people working there making sure the buses were ready for their duties. Comradeship was superb and I loved every minute of my time with Rhondda Transport.

"Passengers were great too, and there were some real characters. One I remember was called Bristol Beat. I don't know why she got the name, perhaps it was because she was originally from Bristol!

"One day she got on my bus at Pontypridd and seemed in a big hurry to leave. 'Come on, let's go,' she said. It was departure time anyway, but I hadn't gone very far when suddenly I was overtaken by a police car with a flashing blue light signalling me to pull over.

"They were chasing Bristol Beat who had been stealing chocolate from one of the Ponty stores and was using my bus as a convenient getaway vehicle!"

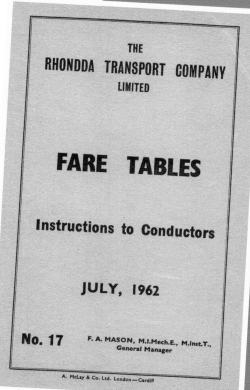

THE
RHONDDA TRANSPORT COMPANY
LIMITED

FARE TABLES

Instructions to Conductors

JULY, 1962

No. 17   F. A. MASON, M.I.Mech.E., M.Inst.T.,
          General Manager

A. McLay & Co. Ltd. London—Cardiff

Two conductors in conversation with an inspector at Taff Street, Pontypridd, in front of a 1947 Regent III during the mid-1950s.

Upstairs . . .

A top deck and lower saloon view of Weymann bodied, highbridge AEC Regent III 277, MNY 538, a vehicle delivered new to Rhondda in 1953.

. . . downstairs

cost of fuel and with it the much hated Government-levied fuel tax were generating financial worries.

The 14 Regents that arrived in 1952 looked squatter and more rounded than previous batches. This was because they were the first 8ft wide vehicles in the fleet which gave them a surprisingly different appearance to the earlier 7ft 6ins wide buses.

Even so, they were almost identical to the previous 45 Regents. Once again they had Weymann 56 seat bodies and were powered by AEC's 9.6 litre engine. But this time they were fitted with 'crash' gearboxes which made life harder for drivers, although they welcomed the change from slam type to sliding cab doors which could be left open providing much better ventilation in hot weather.

Passengers also welcomed the wider seats which had a new, red patterned moquette that gave a fresh image to the previous green and red which Rhondda had used since the 1930s.

They received fleet numbers 261-274, LNY342-LNY355, and weighed 7 tons 18 cwts compared to the 7 tons 10 cwts of their predecessors. Even so, they used 10 per cent less fuel and continued in service until 1965 when most were sold to dealers for scrap.

By 1953 Rhondda Transport was urging its bus suppliers to come up with more fuel efficient vehicles and the batch of seven Regents that arrived at Porth depot that year were the first serious attempt to reduce the unladen weight of vehicles.

As usual bodied by Weymann with 56 seats, these Regents still had a 9.6 litre engine and looked similar to previous batches but in detail were quite different. Numbered 275-281, MNY536-MNY542, they were designated as having the 'Aurora' type body which was a smarter, more modern looking bus with cleaner lines made possible by flush-fitting rubber mounted windows while the upper deck rear emergency exit window, traditionally in two glazed sections, now had a more modern one piece opening window.

Inside, the buses had lightweight, easily cleaned window cappings on both decks but passengers may well have noticed that the engine, coupled with the crash gearbox, gave a rougher ride. They were also noisy vehicles and their laden weight turned out at 7 tons 15 cwts, only a little under the weight of the previous batch. All were sold for scrap in 1965.

The first 1954 batch of Regents had a radical new design with the aim of making them as fuel efficient as possible. Gone were the graceful curves and attractive lines of Weymann's earlier buses, these looked more like Rhondda's war time utility vehicles.

Once again they were Regent IIIs with 9.6 litre engines, and 56 seat metal bodies but they were more angular than previous batches and the upper deck windows were noticeably shallower than those on the lower deck as part of a weight-saving exercise. It made them look odd and unbalanced.

The interiors of these newly-named Orion buses were extremely basic and lacked any frills or attempts at passenger comfort. They rattled and vibrated and provided a cheap image for a company that prided itself on the look of its fleet. But they weighed just 6 tons 12 cwts unladen and were more fuel efficient than previous batches, which was the main objective.

They were numbered 282-287, NTG135-NTG140, and were the first Rhondda buses to have front only triple track, route number and destination indicators. All were sold for further service in 1965.

They were followed in the same year by more Weymann Regent IIIs with identical Orion bodies, but these had the updated AEC 7.7 litre engine which was more fuel efficient. This batch, 288-297, PNY390-PNY399, had an unladen weight of 6 tons 10 cwts and were fitted with a synchromesh gearbox which gave a much smoother ride. They were sold to dealers in 1966.

Rhondda's 1956 Regents looked much like the two batches delivered two years earlier in 1954. But these were very different for they were the first Regent Vs to enter service with the company.

Other fleets by now had started placing Regents with rear platform doors and new look concealed radiator fronts into service but not Rhondda. It was much more traditionalist in its approach and the first Regent Vs arrived with open, rear platform entrances and old style exposed radiator fronts.

But while they might have looked old fashioned, they represented a major advance in bus design. AEC had put much development work into reducing the weight of its vehicles in a bid to make them more fuel efficient and the 27 new arrivals were a totally lightweight product with an improved suspension and a new 7.685 litre wet liner engine classified as the AV 470. They were numbered 298-9/400-424, STG869-STG876/TTX984-TTX998/UNY4-UNY7, and were just what Rhondda needed: a powerful engine that was fuel efficient, had good hill climbing capability and gave out lower noise emission levels. The last of the batch, 424, was a regular performer for several years on the Merthyr-Cardiff route when its average fuel consumption was 12 mpg, a 30 per cent improvement on previous models.

Negotiating the toilet block at Porth Square was all part of daily life for many of Rhondda's drivers as this late 1960s scene shows.

The unladen weight of these Weymann Orion bodies was just 6 tons 7 cwts, one of the lowest ever achieved for a modern double decker. But to attain it the vehicles were devoid of refinements although the suspension was improved to overcome the rough ride experienced with the previous batches.

These buses gave exemplary service and externally looked impressive with new sealed beam headlamps and neat exposed radiator. They were the first Rhondda double deckers to have nearside driving mirrors and four were specified with experimental, offside and nearside flashing trafficators. They were to be the last double deckers with elegant moquette upholstered seats. All future Rhondda double deck buses arrived with dark red pleated leather upholstery.

Drivers liked their spirited performance, easy to handle synchromesh gearbox and light steering. There was no problem keeping to time on the busiest of routes, although passengers and conductors found them cold in winter as they were without heating and platform doors.

Some left the fleet as early as 1967 due to cutbacks which saw Rhondda Transport needing fewer buses. But others were still being used on the backbone Pontypridd and Maerdy services as late as 1970 when they were 14 years old. School kids loved them and referred to them as the old bangers.

All were withdrawn by 1972, the last three, 422-424, transferred to Western Welsh when the company took over Rhondda in 1971. Sadly, not one of these vehicles has survived for posterity.

Long wait was well worthwhile

On a dark, wet winter's evening in January 1958, Rhondda Transport staff called at the bottom garage in Porth depot on their way home to see a bus that had been eagerly awaited for many months.

They were met by a beaming general manager, Mr Ivor Gray, and engineering employees who were busily examining this new vehicle. It had travelled all the way from Weymann's bus plant in Addlestone, Surrey, that day and was covered in road grime. For Rhondda Transport it represented nothing less than a transport revolution. Like previous batches, this double deck bus was also a Regent V, but it was radically different to everything that had gone before.

For the first time in the Rhondda fleet, this double decker had a front entrance and staircase with driver controlled, air operated folding doors which enabled the conductor to concentrate on collecting fares. It was also much safer, for no longer could passengers jump on or off the bus through an open exit/entrance at the

Terraced streets were typical Rhondda territory.

Rhondda Transport's final consignment of new AEC Regent Vs was delivered in 1966, but they were not the last of the type of this popular passenger carrier to arrive at the company's Porth depot. After the company was taken over by Western Welsh at the beginning of 1971, the depot received a Park Royal, 59 seat Regent V that had been new to Western Welsh as long ago as 1956. It came as a shock to passengers as it was a type of Regent Rhondda Transport had never bought.

It was a lowbridge vehicle with bench-like seats upstairs and a sunken gangway that intruded into the lower deck, which meant passengers all too often banged their heads getting up from their seats. The vehicle: 658, LKG658, was fitted with a 9.6 litre, AV590 engine and roared even more loudly than Rhondda's native 1958 and 1961 Regents. It had a rear entrance with platform doors, something the company had never stipulated for its own rear entrance Regents.

This new vehicle was given a fresh coat of paint and received the Rhondda fleet name. It was intended for works and schools services but perhaps Western Welsh wanted to show off that resplendent repaint further afield for it occasionally strayed onto the prestigious Treorchy to Cardiff service. Later it was used as a driver training vehicle before being withdrawn in 1971.

The following year, 10 more Western Welsh Regents arrived at Porth depot. These were 65 seat Northern Counties bodied examples, 703-712,

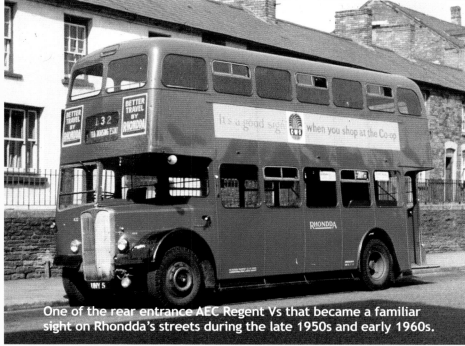

One of the rear entrance AEC Regent Vs that became a familiar sight on Rhondda's streets during the late 1950s and early 1960s.

Regent that roared louder than the rest

703CUH-712CUH and were very similar to Rhondda Transport's own batches of the type which were delivered between 1963 and 1966. They replaced 70 seat Rhondda Regents and were used on the Rhondda-Pontypridd and Tonypandy/Partridge Road-Maerdy services.

These had been allocated to Western Welsh's Cardiff and Barry depots where they were popular with drivers who described them as being easier to drive than the family car. They were not unknown in Rhondda as they had been used on the Maerdy-Cardiff route which was jointly operated by Rhondda Transport and Western Welsh's Cardiff depot.

They differed from Rhondda's in having two-tier destination displays and opening front upper deck and lower deck windows, an addition frowned upon by Rhondda which complained it let in the rain. Its examples had Northern Counties attractively curved upper deck windows and six-sided, single destination indicators, just another example of the different approach taken by the two companies, despite both belonging to the British Electric Traction group.

An AEC Regent in Pandy Square, 1962.

A depot line-up of AEC Regent Vs.

rear. This bus, and the 19 identical ones that soon followed, came with AEC's new look front with concealed radiators, which was a most attractive design. But there was even more innovation: previous batches had been 27ft 6ins in length. These new buses were 30ft and this meant they could seat 70 passengers, the highest figure ever provided for on a Rhondda bus. They were also the first in the company to be given matching fleet and registration numbers, 425-444, VTX425-VTX444, which made life easier for engineers and administrative staff, not to mention bus enthusiasts! There were heaters on both decks, although they never worked particularly well, tending to blow out cold air in winter when they were most needed and warm air in

summer. The buses had Weymann Orion bodies and like the previous batches the interiors were austere. They had exposed anti-theft light bulbs and two full length handrails fitted to the lower deck ceiling for standing passengers. Both the front and rear upper deck domes were fibreglass with a reinforced section on the front nearside to protect the body from overhead tree branches.

These buses weighed 7 tons 18 cwts and so Rhondda specified AEC's larger AV590, 9.6 litre wet liner engine coupled to a four forward speed synchromesh gearbox. This proved more than adequate for the steepest of hills, even when the buses were burdened with a full complement of passengers.

But not everyone was pleased to see their arrival. Rhondda Transport's formidable union, The General and Municipal Workers, promptly banned them from the Rhondda Fach and on the local routes in the Rhondda Fawr claiming they were too long to negotiate tight corners. So they were put on Treorchy/Ystrad-Talbot Green-Cardiff and the Pontypridd-Cardiff services, where they remained for most of their lives. Then the drivers, led by the union boss, Tom Morton, who also drove on the Treorchy-Cardiff service, complained of heavy steering, which was a problem getting round some tight corners in Gelli and Williamstown. This was in the days before power-assisted steering and Rhondda Transport's youthful engineer, David Cherry, at 29 one of the youngest chief engineers in the British Electric Traction group, found himself spending a lot of time consulting with AEC service engineers to find a solution to the problem. Eventually it was

decided that altering the front wheel set up sufficiently reduced the effort needed for steering to satisfy Mr Morton and the other drivers.

These buses, after 25 years the last Rhondda double deckers to be bodied by Weymann, survived until after Western Welsh took over Rhondda Transport in 1971. Most were withdrawn that year, although 444 lasted until early 1972.

The first six of the batch were transferred to Western Welsh's Cardiff and Barry depots after the takeover and 425 was often used on the Ferndale to Cardiff service, the route from which it had been banned in Rhondda's days!

Rhondda Transport bought 20 more Regent Vs in 1961 and they were, in the main, similar to the 1958 delivery. Leyland had tried to tempt the company into buying its revolutionary rear-engine Atlantean in 1960 and a demonstrator was used on the Treorchy-Cardiff route for which it was well suited.

Rhondda would have none of it however, and stuck to the tried and tested Regent V. The 20 that came in 1961 arrived in two batches, 445-453, 445GTX-453GTX, and 454-464, 454KTG-464KTG. They also had the powerful AEC AV590 9.6 litre engine which made them noisy machines although unlike the VTX batch which boomed, these simply roared along.

Bodywork was by MCW but still to lightweight Orion body specification. They were also unusual in having their lower deck emergency exit door placed at the back. The more usual position was on the off side rear and this arrangement meant they had three lower deck windows at the back instead of the usual two.

Like their earlier sisters, they were banned by the union from the Rhondda Fach and local routes in the Rhondda Fawr but were hugely successful on the Treorchy/Ystrad-Cardiff routes whose rural nature after Tonyrefail made for some fast running. They also found their way onto the summer service to Porthcawl and their 70 seats made them useful on private hire trips to Aberavon Beach or Barry Island.

The appearance of these buses with their shallow upper deck windows, not helped by Rhondda's all-over maroon livery, has often been criticised, but to any passenger of the time they offered a magical ride as the bus raced past fields and hedges on its way through the Vale of Glamorgan to Cardiff.

They were withdrawn in 1972 and most of the GTX examples found their way to China Motor Bus in Hong Kong where their MCW bodies were transferred to Guy

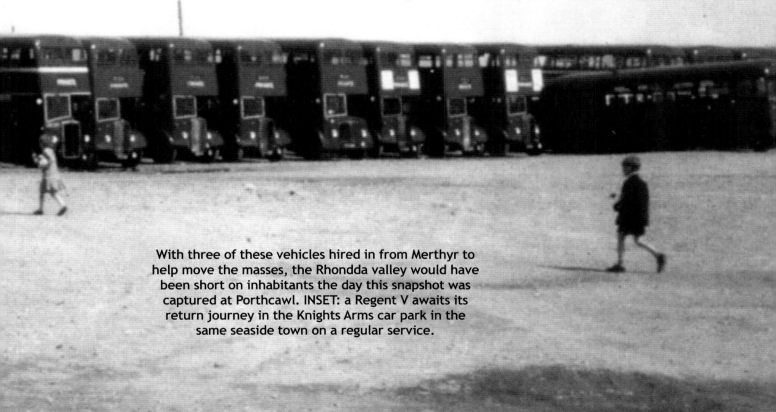

With three of these vehicles hired in from Merthyr to help move the masses, the Rhondda valley would have been short on inhabitants the day this snapshot was captured at Porthcawl. INSET: a Regent V awaits its return journey in the Knights Arms car park in the same seaside town on a regular service.

A line-up of Rhondda and former Western Welsh Regents at Porth in National Bus Company days.

Arab chassis that had originally been fitted with single deck bodies. The AEC chassis were scrapped. The KTG buses found themselves being used for works and schools services around the UK — 456, for example, was still working as a school bus in Oxford in 1981. One of the KTG batch survives to this day. It is 457 which was restored and kept in its original fleet livery at Rhondda Heritage Park as a proud reminder of Rhondda's Regents. It is now stored at Barry Bus Museum.

The four 'ugly sisters' arrived at Porth depot in 1962. From the front these buses looked very similar to the previous year's batch but a walk around to the side soon made the differences obvious.

Given fleet numbers 465-468, 465MTX-468MTX, these also had MCW bodies with a five bay structure, that is they had seven upper deck windows and five on the lower deck.

But these vehicles reverted to the 27ft 6ins length with 65 seats, 37 upstairs and 28 on the lower deck, which meant the windows were of shorter length. This gave them a decidedly odd appearance and the crews soon nicknamed them the ugly sisters.

These buses also had the economical, but less powerful 7.685 litre engine, and this gave out a more 'tinny' sound than the roar of the previous Regents, rather like a very large, wound-up clockwork toy. When new, one of them was used on the Merthyr to Cardiff route while the others served on the Ferndale to Cardiff run from which their larger sisters were still banned.

They were withdrawn and sold in 1972 and at the time of writing the remains of 468 can be found in a field in Leicestershire. It is hoped to eventually restore the vehicle as another reminder of Rhondda's Regents.

Rhondda's final Regents arrived in three batches between the end of 1963 and November 1966. There were 27 altogether, all identical vehicles, although the last five had a revamped, even more attractive interior. For the first time Rhondda turned to the Northern Counties company of Wigan to body its Regents and the result was some smart looking buses. The first caused quite a stir when it arrived at Porth depot in December 1963.

The advent of National Bus Company days brought with it a poppy red livery with a white. band right around the vehicle.

These two Regent Vs, seen at locations in Pontypridd show the difference that cream window rubbers made to the appearance of the vehicle. The bus to the left was bodied by Northern Counties while that below is an earlier MCW example.

"We are thinking of the passengers' comfort," said a spokesman for the company and for most the new arrivals were certainly a huge improvement over the previous MCW Orions.

Internally, they were specified in a paint free finish with much use of lightweight materials, providing passengers with a modern and pleasing travelling experience. The effect was completed by interior fluorescent lighting. Outside, their four-bay structure, with six upper deck windows on either side and four each side downstairs, was enhanced by cream window rubbers, a 1960s fad that Rhondda Transport adopted enthusiastically. They also had six sided destination displays, similarly mounted with cream rubber seals.

Rhondda's chief engineer, David Cherry, said various innovations on the vehicles would also reduce maintenance problems and improve engine efficiency.

The first of these new buses arrived in December/January 1963-4 and were given fleet numbers 469-478, 469UNY-478UNY. The second batch came in August 1965, 479-490, ETX479C-ETX490C, while the third went into service in November 1966, 491-495, KNY491D-KNY495D. They seated 65 passengers, 37 on the

upper deck and 28 downstairs, and as they were 27ft in length were immediately put on the local and still busy valley routes where they remained for most of their working lives. The last was withdrawn in 1979 by which time Regents had proudly served Rhondda Transport for 46 years. It was 495, which survives to this day in private preservation and can be seen at most of the annual South Wales bus rallies.

General manager Ivor Gray makes a long service presentation to Don James of the wages section. Mr Cock, the accountant, is behind the general manager while Megan Jones, Ivor Gray's secretary is seated front right. The others present were directors.

Liveries brought a rainbow of colours

Rhondda Transport may best be remembered for its large fleet of maroon liveried double deck AEC Regents, but at various times the company's buses appeared in primrose, blue and cream, green and even grey!

The colour of the vehicles was always an issue that warranted the most serious consideration. From the earliest days Rhondda councillors took it upon themselves to decide which livery the trams should use. Rhondda Tramways, as the company was known until 1934, leased the tracks from the council which had the right to hire the trams free of charge for official events. The council decided where the stops should be and what advertisements the vehicles should carry. They also discussed the livery and at one stage green was suggested. This idea didn't seem to gather much favour with local councillor, Dr WE Thomas, declaring in June 1908: "We don't want any green in the Rhondda!"

In the end a maroon and primrose colour was chosen, an unlikely combination perhaps, but one that worked surprisingly well as Stagecoach in South Wales demonstrated when it painted one of its Northern Counties single deck Volvo buses in the traditional tramways colours to mark Rhondda Transport's centenary in 2006.

The tramcars were painted in the usual tramway style with shaded numerals at the back and front, gold lining-out and a garter scroll on the side panels. The six, short-lived trolleybuses of 1914 were painted similarly but had Rhondda Tramways as a fleet name on their side panels.

A different livery was chosen for the first motorbuses in 1920. They were all single deck vehicles until 1931, were painted dark red below the windows with cream above and had black mudguards. A large Rhondda fleet name appeared on either side with the middle letters underlined and this style was maintained right through

When Rhondda adopted a green and cream livery for its coaches in 1967 it rarely looked better suited to a vehicle than on its Leyland Leopards such as this one.

The Rhondda Transport Company's depot yard at Porth was a sea of red for nearly all of the company's existence. When this picture was taken in the mid-1960s many of the vehicles the BET colour adorned were AEC Regent Vs.

to 1964, although over the years it gradually became smaller. By 1927 the livery had changed, with a dark band around the waist which appears in photographs of the time to be black, although there is a debate about whether it was actually a darker red or even brown. By now the roof was also red, but the window surrounds stayed cream. Another variation appeared in 1931 with dark red as the base colour, a darker waist band of either darker red, black or brown, dark window surrounds and a cream roof. Mudguards were again painted black.

By the beginning of the 1930s Rhondda Tramways was receiving large batches of modern single and double deck AEC Regals and AEC Regents. With them came a new standard livery. It was all-over red with black mudguards, a dark waist band on the single deckers and three dark bands on the double deck vehicles. The large Rhondda fleet name appeared on both sides of all buses together with the rear which was also given large tramway style fleet numbers.

There were lots of surprises as the 1930s ended with the 1937 Dennis Lancet saloons used as coaches being given an intricate RTC Luxury Coaches logo, probably in an effort to set them apart from everyday vehicles. Then, in 1939, Rhondda received a trio of coach bodied

AEC Regals which were delivered in a blue livery with cream streamline flashes, although they were later repainted into standard red. They also had an RTC logo, a rather strange looking monogram with the letters interlocking which, perhaps wisely, was dropped in the 1950s in favour of the standard fleet name.

Camouflage was the order of the day during the years of the Second World War and Rhondda repainted the Regents used on its Cardiff services with grey roofs. The utility buses that followed were painted all-over grey on the orders of the Ministry of War Transport.

Thankfully, as the war came to an end, buses once more appeared in a livery that became known as 'Rhondda red' with black mudguards, red wheels and silver-painted radiator grills. The image was relieved with black edging bands and this continued until a batch of AEC Regents arrived in 1958 with a new-look, rounded radiator grill. These did not have the lining-out and the fleet name gradually became smaller.

Stylish ways

From its earliest beginnings Rhondda Transport was always proud to display its name on the side of vehicles in its bus fleet. Some of the incarnations are featured below.

By 1964 buses were being painted all-over red with red mudguards and a new style Rhondda fleet name, still with the middle letters underlined but with sloping characters, and this remained the style to the end.

Coach liveries were more complicated as Rhondda painted the vehicles to suit their individual styles, but basically they appeared as cream with red stripes and carried a circular logo on the front and sides which was painted red with a small Rhondda fleet name in the centre.

In 1961 the company received its first dual purpose vehicles. These were ordinary single deck buses, but with coach seats, that could be used on ordinary services or for private hire. They were painted red below the windows and cream above, in usual British Electric Traction style although Rhondda carried out experiments later to make the buses appear more like coaches by increasing the amount of cream. They were unsuccessful as the company found the lighter colour made the buses look shabby when unwashed. So the 1964 batch of dual purpose vehicles reverted to red under the windows and cream on top.

Then in early 1967 there was huge excitement among the local children. 'Have you seen the new green Rhondda bus?' was the cry. This could not be right — Rhondda's buses were red, not green, and all the kids dashed down to the main road to investigate this phenomenon. True enough there it was, one of the

1964 dual purpose Willowbrooks in a new, bright green and ivory livery working the Porth to Porthcawl service which always seemed to be graced with dual purpose vehicles. It was painted in a 'sandwich' style, with a green roof and lower body and ivory between and the green extended to the front in a V-shape.

From 1966 Rhondda and Western Welsh were jointly managed and the previous year WW had introduced a blue and ivory livery for its fleet of coaches and dual purpose vehicles. It had proved a success and it was decided to do the same for Rhondda's, albeit much smaller, private hire fleet.

In a decision that would no doubt have horrified Dr Thomas, all those years previously, green and ivory was chosen and what a splendid choice that was. The livery greatly enhanced the look of the vehicles used for coaching and private hire operations and always looked a cut above the rest.

This Weymann bodied AEC Regal was unique in that along with two sister vehicles it was liveried in blue and cream when it arrived in 1939.

Smart looking vehicles were a general trait for Rhondda Transport. Until 1959, when a new paint shop was built at Porth depot, it had a bus painting garage at Treorchy and two vehicles could usually be found there. Bus bodies were prepared for repaint at Porth which saw to the replacement of dented panels or reshaping and filling of roof domes damaged by overhanging tree branches that were a problem on Rhondda's rural routes around Cowbridge, Llantrisant and St Athan. Repaints would normally coincide with the Certificate of Fitness inspections carried out by the Traffic Commissioners.

Rhondda's pride in the fleet meant that it wanted as few people as possible to see its buses in a patched-up panel state so vehicles were usually driven up to

One of the rear entrance AEC Regent Vs delivered to Rhondda in 1956 about to enter service in fully lined out red livery.

Treorchy after dark on Friday nights and brought back to Porth depot the following weekend resplendent in a new coat of paint and ready for the stringent inspection.

Originally buses were painted in an undercoat, several top coats and finally varnished but in the 1950s it was decided that an undercoat and one top coat of good quality ICI Rhondda red paint was sufficient. After the Second World War buses were usually repainted once midway through their average 12-year working life with the company. Rhondda Transport's livery has often been described as sombre, an all-over maroon not enhanced by any cream stripes similar to the ones that its sister BET companies, South

With drivers behind the wheel these AEC Regents, complete with two tone livery and pre-registration trade plates were about to set off for Rhondda Transport in 1933.

Wales Transport and Western Welsh, carried in the 1940s and 1950s. But the Rhondda fleet always looked immaculate and when vehicles were being painted poppy red in the National Bus Company days of the 1970s and looked decidedly care worn, it was a particularly sad time.

By then Rhondda Transport was a dormant company, its buses fast becoming memories. For some it will be a positive that it missed the era of all-over advertisement liveries and contravision that followed.

Exhausted end to trip

Michael Huckridge was brought up in Gilfach Goch and has fond memories of adventures experienced while on some of Rhondda Transport's tours.

"The company always ran day tours from Porth depot and if you wanted to catch one you were allowed free travel on the local bus to pick up the tour," he said.

"All you had to do was to show your tour ticket to the driver when you got on the service bus. When I was a child I remember going on one tour to Hereford. On the way back the exhaust broke on the coach filling the back of the vehicle with smoke. By the time we arrived back at the depot most of the passengers looked like miners!

"The annual social club outing was always a big event, but it was a bit of a problem from Gilfach Goch because of low bridges. So the double deckers had to go about five miles in the wrong direction to Williamstown and then double back in the direction they had come on the opposite side of the valley.

"On one occasion there was nearly an accident when the driver of one of Rhondda's buses on an excursion to Aberavon Beach, tried to follow a low height double decker under a bridge. But the Rhondda bus was normal height, about a foot higher, and would not have fitted underneath. Luckily, another driver stopped him just in time.

"The Rhondda bus drivers were brilliant. I always wanted to know about their buses when I was a kid and they were always happy to chat to me. But it was that kind of company.

"I remember when I was only about 10 being shown around the engineering works at Porth depot, the staff so obviously just loved their jobs."

Part of the uniform once worn by Rhondda drivers and the badge on the caps crews wore.

When passengers turned their backs

The date of June 1, 1966, is one of the most significant in the history of Rhondda Transport. For on that day the company's management came under the control of its sister company, Western Welsh, and Rhondda lost both its general manager and chief engineer.

Company chairman, JH Richardson, son of the long-serving Rhondda general manager TG Richardson, was at pains to point out that it was not a takeover or a merger and that Rhondda would retain its individual identity. It meant that Western Welsh's general manager, Ivor Gray, now assumed the same title for Rhondda Transport whose own general manager was downgraded to simply manager.

The company's well-respected chief engineer, David Cherry, took up the same post at Western Welsh as well as retaining his responsibilities at Rhondda.

Mr Richardson explained the move had been made 'because of the difficult times in which the bus industry now finds itself.' He was of course referring to the increase in private car ownership, rising costs and heavy taxation. All this made it necessary to establish closer relationships between the two companies in the interests of efficiency.

"That closer relationship has now been established at management level and will be developed at work and, I hope, socially too. Although I trust the friendly spirit of rivalry will be kept up at games and sport," said Mr Richardson.

There was a further shock for Rhondda's employees for plans were also revealed to promote closer co-ordination between the company and British Rail whose Western Region general manager, Mr RC Hilton, became a member of the Rhondda board of directors.

However these changes were portrayed, they represented a huge loss of prestige for a company that started running trams in 1908 and had done such

Leyland Atlanteans came late to Rhondda Transport despite much persuasion from the manufacturers. This Northern Counties bodied example arrived in 1968.

CHAPTER 10

An interesting line up of Leylands in the depot yard captured during the mid-1960s. From the left they are a Tiger Cub delivered in 1954, a Weymann bodied Leyland Fanfare coach of 1959 vintage and a 1964 Willowbrook bodied, 41 seat dual purpose Tiger Cub.

sterling service during the war years. But Rhondda Transport had always been susceptible to economic circumstances affecting the wider community and just as it had reaped the rewards of the good times of rising passenger numbers in the 1940s it was now having to cope with the effect of a major decline. In 1955 the company had carried 37,674,000 passengers a year, but by 1966 this had been slashed to just 22,925,000.

Rhondda Transport was forced to increase fares, which had the effect of turning people away from travelling on its buses which in turn led to less revenue. The company also suffered from special problems of its own, not least the difficult geographical terrain over which it operated. The amount of fuel it used, the cost of brake linings and wear and tear on vehicles were all higher than for companies operating on a flatter terrain. Like other operators it was suffering from rising car ownership but another problem was Rhondda's declining population which fell from 100,000 in 1963 to 97,000 in the three years up to 1966.

It had hoped for more passengers in 1964 when the Rhondda Fach railway closed, but in reality the train loadings had dropped to such low levels that there was little benefit and the new custom could be met with one additional vehicle for peak time working. New housing estates were being built in the Vale of

Glamorgan and in the Rhondda itself, but these had not helped and, as the company's new manager, Bill Cooper, pointed out rather cynically, these came with garage spaces which he believed encouraged the continued growth of private car ownership.

Collieries were continuing to close in the 1960s and Mr Cooper commented that this had brought about "a very considerable drop in passenger loadings, especially on the workmen's vehicles which have always been provided at early hours of the morning for the transport of these people, and considerable loss of revenue has resulted."

By April 1967 the situation was becoming parlous and Mr Cooper made a strongly worded plea to the bus crews in that month's edition of Staff News.

"It should now be made known to all members of staff that the financial position of the company is a matter for most serious concern," he wrote, adding that "there is a limit to what can be achieved by curtailment of services and we know from experience that higher fares do not necessarily provide the answer. It is in all our interests that every effort should be made to encourage traffic and to ensure also that we do not suffer any loss of revenue. A favourable result must be reflected in the extent to which we must impose further economies. Please think it over."

There was another fares increase that summer, but the extra revenue Rhondda Transport had hoped for wasn't forthcoming as its buses continued to carry fewer passengers. Money was tight in the valley, where unemployment at the time was around eight per cent. There were added financial problems for the company including a wage award, higher fuel prices and increases in National Insurance contributions. But Mr Cooper was optimistic. "It will be apparent to everyone that we must now set ourselves to collect all the revenue to which we are rightly entitled," he wrote in Staff News in September 1967. "If passengers continue on the present level and we ensure that correct fares are charged, the position should improve, as I hope it will," he continued.

He remained optimistic about passenger growth over the next 12 months as new homes were being built on the Penrhys Mountain housing estate and new factories came on stream, including Fram Filters at Ynysmaerdy and later the Royal Mint. Then in the summer of 1968 Rhondda Transport faced a major problem with

absenteeism. "We are still confronted with a very high sickness list and coverage of our essential stage carriage services is frequently in jeopardy, but I should like to record my appreciation of the efforts made by most of our staff in helping to maintain our services," said Mr Cooper.

But events were happening on the national stage that were beyond Rhondda Transport's control. Since 1931 the company had been owned by British Electric Traction, the country's largest privately owned bus group. On November 22, 1967, it announced it was selling out to the state for £35 million and for the first time in its 60-year life Rhondda became a nationalised bus company.

The National Bus Company was created on January 1, 1969, out of the Transport Act of 1968 and Rhondda became a subsidiary of the world's biggest single bus operator with 21,000 vehicles and 81,000 staff.

Like its sister companies that had also been part of BET, South Wales Transport, Western Welsh, Thomas Bros of Port Talbot and N&C Luxury Coaches, Rhondda began 1969 facing the great unknown, the prospect of operating as a state-owned concern.

It was a time of great uncertainty, but Rhondda Transport comforted itself in the fact that the management alterations three years previously had not resulted in major change in its operations. Perhaps largely thanks to Ivor Gray, who had been Rhondda's general manager in the late 1950s, and David Cherry, the Western Welsh influence had been minimal. Both these men had huge respect for Rhondda Transport and the company continued to do things its own way. Although new buses in the fleet resembled those arriving at Western Welsh, Rhondda was allowed its idiosyncracies, down to destination indicators and types of seats.

But the changes under the National Bus Company were destined to be more profound. In the summer of 1968 JH Richardson left Rhondda Transport and his place was taken by Bernard Griffiths who wrote in that September's Staff News:

"Many important changes are taking place in our industry which will affect us all in one way or another and it is difficult to forecast with any degree of accuracy what the future holds for us. I am quite certain, however, that if we can maintain that high tradition of loyalty and service for which the Rhondda Transport Company is rightly known, then all should be well."

What he was not expecting, and probably at this time no-one else knew either, was that less than three years

A group of staff stand proudly alongside one of three Windover bodied 32 seat AEC Regal III coaches delivered new to the company in 1948.

A 1971 Leyland Atlantean crosses a busy junction outside the former Evan Roberts store in Cardiff city centre as it carries passengers on the last leg of its journey.

later the bus industry in South Wales would go through its greatest upheaval of the 20th Century. In November 1970 it was announced that SWT would take over N&C, Thomas Bros and United Welsh, another Swansea-based bus firm already in the state sector. But there was an even greater shock for Rhondda Transport: it was to be taken over by Western Welsh.

The staff were stunned. Earlier that summer, the directors had visited the National Bus Company subsidiaries in South Wales and there had been no hint of such a radical change although it is inconceivable that it was not at least in the minds of the board.

A special booklet was produced to mark the two-day visit on Tuesday and Wednesday, June 9 and 10. The directors arrived at Porth depot at 5.15pm on the Tuesday and were gone by 5.30pm, dashing off to the Angel Hotel in Cardiff for dinner. There were few at Rhondda Transport who did not regard

a 15-minute visit to a company that ran 164 vehicles and had a staff of 798 as a complete insult.

But industrial relations were not good at Porth depot that year. The crews were pursuing a pay claim and when Rhondda Transport implemented a fares increase awarded by the Traffic Commissioners on October 11, the staff refused to charge the higher fares. The company sent out warnings and each member of staff received a personal letter, but the industrial action continued and seven employees were disciplined. As a result the crews went on immediate strike. Buses were stopped in the middle of their journeys and every vehicle returned to Porth depot. The complete shut-down continued for two weeks losing the company £39,000 which contributed to an overall loss for the year, of £93,400. The mileage lost during the strike was also significant, standing at 188,000.

The dispute caused major problems. Children had to walk to school and people had to find alternative ways of getting to their place of work. Takings went down in the shops and hospital appointments were missed. Mr Cooper estimated that it led to a further drop in passengers of between 1.5 and two per cent.

So as Rhondda Transport entered its final few months of life, relations were strained and they were not helped by the Western Welsh takeover and the difficulties that were bound to

An Atlantean at work. This Alexander bodied vehicle seen in Sardis Road, Pontypridd, was one of the last buses ordered by Rhondda Transport.

Carol figured

Checking the waybills and mileage cards of drivers and conductors became a daily task for Carol Gibbons when she joined Rhondda Transport on January 1, 1969.

"It was a difficult job because the driver's figures had to tally with the amount of diesel used by the bus," said Carol, who worked in the mileage and revenue office and whose surname then was Thomas.

"It was made more complicated because of crew changes on the vehicle and sometimes buses had to go off route because of accidents or roadworks. My work colleague, Jessa Wasley, would calculate the amount of diesel used which had to fit the driver's mileage cards.

"But conductors' waybills were the bigger headache because the ticket machine would have to tally with the cash collected in fares. If it fell short, the conductor had to make up the difference from his wages, although he didn't get the money if he had an excess amount in his cash bag. The ticket machines were repaired by an employee nicknamed Billy Watch, he got the name because he also repaired watches. We didn't have computers. We kept records in big ledgers and everything had to tally.

"The figures would be inspected by the company who kept a close check on revenue. If a bus route took significantly less one week than it had the previous week, the service would be monitored and sometimes plain clothed inspectors, called 'private eyes' would travel on the bus. If the conductor was found to be acting dishonestly by pocketing fares for himself, he could expect to be dismissed.

"The company had uniformed inspectors working all the routes and the crews devised their own warning system. If a driver gave the thumbs up to the driver of a passing bus, it meant there was no inspector along the route. If he gave the thumbs down it meant an inspector was about and when he was spotted the driver would hit the brakes three times to warn the conductor.

"I started work for Rhondda Transport when I was 18, it was my first job and my pay was £6 18s 6d a week. We had a great team. Iorrie Smith was in charge of the office, he was a lovely man, and my boss was follow. Staff were upset about the loss of identity and National Bus Company was an unknown entity. On January 1, 1971, Rhondda Transport became a dormant company and 65 years of proud history came to an end. The legal lettering on the buses changed from Rhondda Transport Company Ltd, Aberrhondda Road, Porth, to Western Welsh Omnibus Company Ltd, 253 Cowbridge Road West, Cardiff. It was a sad and uncertain time for both staff and passengers. They would probably have been even more worried had they known what the next few years were about to bring.

Highest cost but lowest profits

As passenger figures continued to fall during the 1960s, Rhondda Transport was forced to make almost annual visits to the South Wales Traffic Commissioners seeking permission to increase fares.

The so-called 'fares inquiries' started in 1952 and the period up to 1967 became known as 'the 15-year fares war' because at each hearing the applications were vociferously opposed by local

authorities. The company said it needed to increase fares because of rising fuel bills and the Government's hated tax on fuel. Rhondda's hilly terrain meant its vehicles used more fuel and they suffered greater wear and tear than buses operated by other companies. The 1952 inquiry heard that Rhondda Transport had the highest running costs but the lowest profits of six major bus companies in South Wales. Even so, its profits for the year were £85,288, a rise of £18,538 on 1951 and the local authorities could not understand why raising fares was necessary. They believed shareholder dividends were too high. Increased fares did not always succeed in raising revenue. Passengers became reluctant to pay the higher prices and travelled less. In November 1952 Rhondda was given permission to raise fares and when it came before the Traffic Commissioners asking for yet more higher ticket prices the following August it was revealed that since the previous increase passengers

it all out

Gladys Hawk whose husband Reg worked in the depot garage. An incident I remember well occurred in 1969 when cracks were discovered in the Maerdy reservoir wall. It was feared it would collapse and the water would cascade down the Rhondda Fach. Some of our buses were parked up at Maerdy ready to begin an emergency evacuation should it be necessary and their place was taken at Porth depot by police and rescue vehicles.

"At this time, we had a red button alarm in the office to be pressed if we were ever robbed, there was a lot of cash on the premises at the time, and one of the new members of staff was warned not to press it unless there was an emergency, but one day he did, accidentally. I have never seen so many police swarm all over the office so quickly, they only had a few yards to come and any would-be robbers simply would never have been able to make their getaway.

Depot colleagues, from left: Carol Thomas, Merle, Susan Evans and Hannah Jones in front of a newly delivered coach.

"We also had a lost property department and it's amazing what people would leave behind on a bus, as well as the usual wallets and handbags there were bird cages, false teeth and odd shoes. Drivers would bring them to the department and they were kept in a cupboard for three months. If no-one had claimed them by then the staff could take their pick, although I don't think there were any takers for the false teeth.

"On one occasion I needed an umbrella so I chose a lovely black one. I later lost it, that's right, I left it on a bus!"

Any excuse for a photograph! A group of drivers poses in front of a Leyland Leopard while on a private hire assignment.

between Nantgarw and Cardiff had fallen by 17 per cent which the company said would lose it £2,000 over a full year.

Inquiry chairman HJ Thom commented: "The stage has now been reached where increases in fares are likely to defeat their own objective and not produce the expected revenue. We may have to face the undesirable alternative of cutting down or terminating unremunerative services." This statement was an early warning of what would increasingly happen as passenger numbers plummeted during the late 1950s and early 1960s.

The process started as early as March 1959 when instead of granting a fares rise on the Porth-Pontypridd route the commissioners authorised fewer Sunday buses. By the mid-1960s the frequency on a number of routes was cut, including the prestigious Treorchy-Cardiff service which now saw three instead of four buses an hour Monday to Friday. There were however still four buses an hour on Saturdays.

Another method of reducing operating costs was the introduction of driver-only buses, known in the 1960s and 1970s as one man operation. From 1964 Rhondda Transport tried to introduce this type of operation on its lesser used routes, but by 1967 had only one route converted entirely to driver-only operation. This was the lightly used 23-minute rural service between Talbot Green and Cowbridge, which ran 15 times a day on weekdays and nine times daily on Sundays.

One person operation, as it is called in this more equality driven era, was introduced on some other routes at quiet times and on a few schools and works services, but even by the end of 1970 Rhondda Transport had only 39 vehicles out of a fleet of 164 that were capable of being used on driver-only routes, including 16 of its newest vehicles, the double deck Leyland Atlanteans of 1968/9. These were being used on the Cardiff services which the company did not think were suitable for conversion to driver-only operation. There was also opposition to the move from the union, which understandably did not want to see jobs lost, and even the complaining councils were uneasy because Rhondda already had some of the highest unemployment levels in the country and they did not want to add to them.

Another headache for Rhondda Transport was the number of buses that could not be converted to one person operation. Nearly half the fleet, 80 vehicles in all, were AEC Regent Vs, front-engined buses where the driver sat in isolation in his cab.

Experiments were carried out elsewhere with the aim of altering the lay-out of these vehicles to make them suitable for driver-only operation, notably at Rhondda's sister company, South Wales Transport of Swansea, but they were unsuccessful.

Converting services to one person operation was a painfully slow process for Rhondda in the last couple of

years of its existence. Months before the Western Welsh takeover it made the Treorchy/Porth-Porthcawl routes driver-only operated and the Merthyr-Cardiff service was similarly converted with just one peak hour working being retained for crew operation. Yet by February 1971 there were only 23 full-time one-person operated buses running out of Porth depot.

At the time of the Western Welsh takeover, Rhondda still had 286 conductors on its books out of a traffic staff total of 618, a significant factor given that the company estimated that between 65 and 70 per cent of its costs were down to the number of staff employed.

Such figures would not be acceptable to the newly-created National Bus Company, of which Rhondda Transport became a subsidiary in 1969. More driver-only buses were introduced at Porth depot as the 1970s progressed, but it was a slow process. It wasn't until 1979 that the last Regent V was withdrawn when the backbone Blaenrhondda/Blaencwm-Pontypridd route was finally converted to one person operation.

Biggest upheaval in bus industry

Rhondda Transport's heyday was disappearing into the history books by the time it was taken over by Western Welsh in the South Wales bus industry's biggest ever upheaval at the start of January 1971.

Even so it was a sizeable operation and immensely important in an area like Rhondda which suffered some of the highest unemployment figures in the country.

At the time of the takeover, the company employed 798 staff and in 1969 its buses operated 5,466,385 miles and carried 20,615,360 passengers, although this was half the number that had been carried less than 20 years previously.

At the end of 1970 Rhondda Transport owned 158 vehicles, all of them kept at its only depot at Porth. A total of 90 were double deckers, 74 of which were AEC Regent Vs, the rest rear-engine Leyland Atlanteans. There were 53 single deckers and 12 saloons described as dual purpose — bus bodies fitted with coach seats for use on private hire and excursion duties. Of these, 62 were Leyland Tiger Cubs and three were Leyland Leopard vehicles, the first of their type in the fleet. The newest vehicles, only introduced in July and August that year, were three Plaxton Panorama Elite coaches that had replaced the Bedford VAL coaches of 1964. All

the buses were painted traditional Rhondda maroon livery with sloping letter fleet names. The dual purpose vehicles and coaches appeared in the green and ivory livery that the company had introduced in early 1967 and had similar Rhondda fleet names.

The company operated 33 routes, the local ones in the Rhondda Valleys were prefixed with the letter R, and other services panned out to Pontypridd, Merthyr Tydfil, Cardiff, Talbot Green, Bridgend, Maesteg and Porthcawl. There were a number of works, schools, hospitals services and express routes to Barry Island, Tenby and Aberavon Beach.

As well as its depot at Porth, which was the largest in Wales and probably the biggest in what had been the British Electric Traction group, Rhondda Transport owned the freehold of Talbot Green bus station and rented an office in Hannah Street, Porth, where it based its Rhondda Travel Agency.

The company's office was in Aberrhondda Road, Porth. It was split into five sections. There was a general office

Porth depot entrance, decorated for the Coronation of King George VI in 1937. A pair of 1936 AEC Regals with Weymann bodies wait inside the yard, and behind is the stable block of Charles Jenkins' timber yard.

where, under the supervision of cashier WL Smith, there were 29 clerks.

The traffic department, under Mr Horace Purcell had six clerks; the cash office had two clerks and three cash checkers; the ticket office, under HT Jenkins, had four clerks and a Setright ticket machine maintenance operator; and finally a typing department under the direction of manager's secretary, Mrs Megan Jones, with three typing clerks. Rhondda had 77 engineering staff under work study engineer BJ Roberts and work study assistant DI Williams. It was split into a fitting shop

with 44 employees, an electrical shop with nine staff, a paint shop with five, and a body shop with 17. In charge of the all-important stores was H Jones whose staff were two storemen and a stores boy. There were 20 people on the day and late shift maintenance staff, foreman E Croker and 11 shunters, who parked up the buses in the depot, six cleaners and two other grades. The night maintenance and cleaning staff under foreman RA Roberts consisted of two chargehands, six shunters, 10 cleaners and eight other grades. The vast majority of Rhondda Transport's employees were traffic staff and in 1970 they consisted of senior

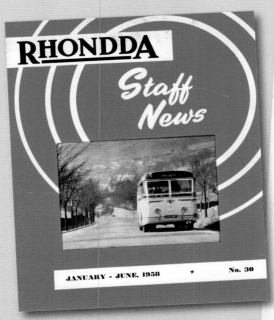

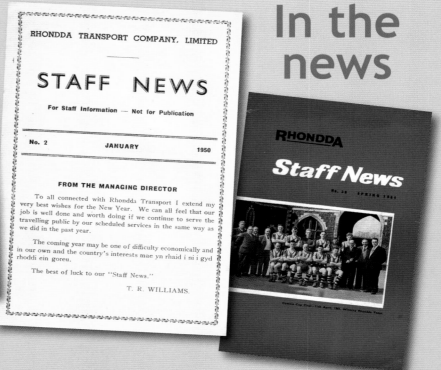

In the news

Some of the office staff, including the eight engaged in handling the wages, during the mid-1960s.

depot inspector WS Griffiths, 22 inspectors, three regulators, 300 drivers, 286 conductors and six car drivers, making in total 617.

The company had five directors: chairman was Bernard Griffiths and members were DW Glassborrow, ER Williams, JTE Robinson and Ivor Gray, who was also general manager of Western Welsh. Rhondda's secretary/accountant was CM Williams, the manager was Bill Cooper, whose name appeared on the legal lettering of the buses as WF Cooper, engineering superintendent was R Nicholls and assistant accountant was WC Jones.

A selection of Rhondda Transport's Staff News publications.

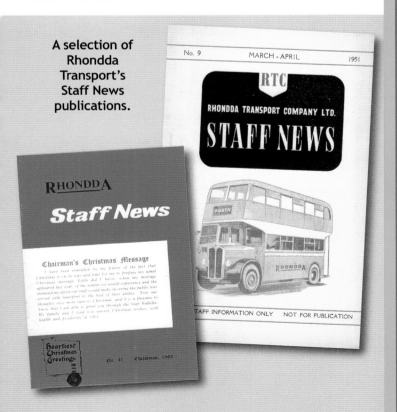

Mischief on school runs

School runs could often present problems for Rhondda Transport's crews with mischievous children finding ways of livening up journeys to school with any number of tricks, as Ken Jones of Ferndale remembered.

"Every day I travelled to and from Porth County Grammar School, a distance of about five miles. School buses were also used by the public and our bus was supposed to carry Maerdy as its destination. We always had a double decker and upstairs it was possible to change the destination," said Ken.

"We could change it to anything we fancied without the driver or conductor knowing, and would-be passengers would be thoroughly confused by a bus arriving at their stop with something like Merthyr or Treherbert on the destination blind."

Rhondda Transport's largest school run served the three grammar schools at Porth. There was Porth County School for Boys, Porth County School for Girls, both of which took pupils from all over the Rhondda Fach and Fawr, and Porth Grammar Technical School. Pupils were picked up outside the schools in Cemetery Road, Porth, and hundreds of youngsters would pile out at the end of the day for the homeward trek.

Sometimes crews would be overwhelmed as dozens of pupils dashed to catch their bus. One day a driver on a single deck vehicle faced with an on-coming horde of youngsters forgot to apply the brake. The bus rolled back downhill, straight into a Leyland Atlantean that was unusually being used on a school run that day. Luckily, no-one was injured but the Atlantean had to return to Porth depot with a shattered windscreen.

Rhondda Transport's school services were important sources of income for the company in the 1950s and 1960s and the company could send out any vehicle to run them. It was great fun wondering whether one of the newest buses or even a coach might turn up!

As the 1970s progressed, after the takeover by Western Welsh and during National Bus Company days, Porth depot became less involved in school work and by 1975 didn't tender for school runs which were taken over by private operators.

Times when it all went wrong

Late in the afternoon of March 1 — St David's Day —1969, a single deck Rhondda Transport bus crawled its way up the three-quarter mile, 1 in 6 hill from Ystrad to the top of Penrhys Mountain. The vehicle stopped to let six people off at the newly-built housing estate before starting the steep descent towards Tylorstown. What happened next were probably the most terrifying moments in the lives of the 24 passengers still on board.

The bus suddenly veered out of control and as its passengers screamed in terror, gathered speed, slammed three times against the cemetery wall on the left hand side, smashed through the crash barrier opposite, left the road and hurtled down the steep grassy slope.

It was probably the most dramatic accident in the history of the Rhondda Transport Company and the miracle was that no passengers were killed. The sole casualty of this tragic incident was the driver, Reg Morby of Porth, who sadly died after suffering a heart attack at the wheel. When the bus was winched back up the mountainside the following day it was a mangled wreck. Even so, fleet number 388, 388WTG, a 1964 Leyland Tiger Cub, was sent for rebodying, to its builder, Willowbrook, and returned to service in 1970.

All the passengers were taken to hospital, but only eight were detained. They included the conductor, William Bevan, who lived near the scene of the accident in Vivian Street, Tylorstown. A friend and colleague of 52-year-old Reg Morby, William was the secretary of the Rhondda Transport Ex-Servicemen's Social Association of which Reg was a founder member. A well-respected and well-liked driver, Reg had worked for Rhondda Transport for 37 years and company managers and staff packed Glyntaff Crematorium in Pontypridd for his funeral service.

His regular passengers fondly remembered him as someone who was always placid and smiling.

This 1964 Leyland Tiger Cub was a mangled wreck after it careered down the mountainside at Penrhys.

CHAPTER 11

Serious accidents involving Rhondda Transport buses, such as this one, were exceedingly rare and the company did all it could to promote safety among its crews. An awards ceremony was held each January for drivers and conductors who had attained accident free periods and it was always attended by top company managers, police representatives and Rhondda's mayor.

The mayor was at the two-day awards ceremony held in 1958 even though, he said, he had been awoken at 5 am one morning by a loud bang. Going downstairs, he found a single deck bus in his living room. "Still, I bear no malice to the driver, for my house has been nicely repaired!" he quipped.

Company managers took up space in Rhondda Transport's Staff News to promote safer driving and these occasionally contained some strong language. In 1950 the number of accidents was the highest in the company's history which general manager TG Davies described as alarming. There had been 546 accidents in which three people were killed and 269 injured. A total of 346 buses were damaged and the number of days they were out of service amounted to 552.

"Three serious accidents occurred owing to drivers attempting to drive under low bridges at Abercynon, Pontypridd and Cardiff," stormed Mr Davies, who said

Accidents with buses, particularly double deckers, often required plenty of muscle when recovery was called for. This Wynns heavy duty recovery vehicle was sent to the rescue after a Leyland Atlantean came to grief at Berw Road, Pontypridd while on its way to Nantgarw Colliery.

the company had hit a very bad patch. He continued: "The cost to this company for repairing damage to our own vehicles in June, July and August amounted to well over £3,000."

It all sounds very worrying, as indeed it no doubt was, but it has to be seen in the context of the number of bus journeys made and passengers carried. In 1950, Rhondda Transport's buses were covering well in excess of seven million miles a year and were carrying more than 40 million passengers.

Even so, it is clear some accidents could, and should, have been avoided. In 1949 for example, there were 100 accidents in which bus drivers were at fault: there were 22 collisions with street lamps or sun blinds of shops, 45 with other vehicles on the road, and 33 collisions with walls and other property.

However, given Rhondda's narrow roads and its steep gradients, it is probably remarkable that there were not more accidents, particularly in the late 1950s and

This may look as though there had been an accident on the Porth to Porthcawl route, but 32 seat ADC 415A vehicle, fleet No. 44, TX2885, had apparently only pulled to the side of the road.

1960s when traffic figures started to rise. In 1956, when there were three fatal accidents involving Rhondda Transport's buses, 231 of the company's drivers had no accidents on their records, which was a commendable 67.4 per cent.

Most of the time the company could be proud of its accident record and that was down to the ability of its drivers who all too often had to hit their brakes to avoid collisions with wandering sheep and dogs or careless children running across the road. The Staff News often carried letters from passengers praising drivers for their ability in avoiding collisions, including one from a Mr James Jones of Pentre in July 1950.

"Today I was a passenger on the 4.40pm bus from Porth Square," wrote Mr Jones. "As the bus was proceeding along from Llwynypia station a child darted out into the middle of the road right into the path of the on-coming bus. An accident seemed inevitable, but with great presence of mind, and a superb piece of driving, the driver averted what seemed a sure fatality." That driver was Arthur Williams who,

only a year before, had been forced to swerve to avoid two toddlers who ran across the road in front of his bus at Bridgend.

When praise was due, Rhondda Transport managers gave it, but they were not slow to lecture their drivers and conductors when they thought it necessary.

There were 282 accidents involving the company's buses in 1958 and 178 vehicles were damaged and off the road for 570 days during the year.

"Be a better driver!" urged chief engineer Mr David Cherry, who said the cost of carelessness to the company was considerable. "No-one causes an accident deliberately, but the good driver takes care to avoid mistakes and the better driver takes care to prevent accidents caused by the other driver's mistakes," said Mr Cherry.

The engine had been removed from this double deck vehicle after it sustained serious front end damage.

In 1960 as many as 40 to 50 vehicles entered the depot works as a direct result of accident damage. It varied from broken windows and panel scratches to major accidents that needed large scale structural, electrical and chassis repairs. During the year, each Rhondda bus was damaged an average of three times. Mr Cherry appealed to drivers to help keep the fleet in a first class condition.

"Damage is also caused by works and depot staff on both night and day shifts and, while I appreciate that the depot is somewhat congested at times, most of the damage is caused by reversing into stanchions, walls or stationary vehicles, which can be avoided with a little more care," he said.

Staff News in 1967 contained an article acknowledging that Rhondda Transport had 'many good drivers, as the general public and many conductors are aware, but unfortunately there are also a few not so careful drivers.'

It continued: "This company has a good accident record and it is a challenge to all drivers to maintain this or even better it, despite the hazards which confront them on the roads today."

Among the other most serious accidents involving Rhondda Transport buses was one where a woman was crushed to death and a young mother and her baby had a miracle escape when a double deck Rhondda bus crashed out of control in Cardiff's central bus station. It happened at lunchtime on December 15, 1965, when the 11.03am Ferndale to Cardiff service was making its way to the bus stand. Suddenly it skidded out of control, mounted the pavement and careered into the doorway of the Sun Life Assurance offices. The accident victim was walking along the pavement when the bus pinned her to the wall. The mother was wheeling her four month old baby in his pram and the collision showered the pram with bricks, glass and masonry, but the child slept through it all. The concrete canopy of the office block sliced through the top deck of the bus but fortunately there were no upper deck passengers at the time. Two lower deck passengers were taken to hospital suffering from the effects of shock. The driver,

Mr Haydn Thomas of Cymmer, Porth, was taken to hospital with an injured shoulder and shock while his conductor, Mr Neville King, of Treherbert, was unhurt. The bus, 445, 445GTX, a 1961 MCW Regent V, was eventually repaired and returned to service.

On another occasion, on March 12, 1968, a 75-year-old man was trapped and another was seriously injured when a double deck Rhondda Transport bus crashed into the front of a shop in Brook Street, Williamstown.

The 18-month-old vehicle, at the time the company's newest double decker, was on the Gilfach Goch to Penygraig service when it was involved in a collision with a stationary car and a lorry before swerving across the pavement and hitting both men into the shop front, which was wrecked. Shop assistant, Ramona Edmunds of Penygraig, described the incident as terrifying.

"I was serving a customer when I heard a loud sound of metal being scraped outside," she said. "The next moment we saw the bus careering towards us and coming through the window. All of us just dropped

A rear end shunt caused extensive damage to AEC Regent III 263, LNY344.

A selection of the vehicles that rallied to the rescue when Rhondda buses broke down or suffered an accident.

Careering off the Penrhys Mountain road resulted in severe damage to 388WTG, a 1964 Tiger Cub with Willowbrook bodywork. It was later rebuilt.

everything and fled into the passage at the back of the shop."

Three passengers on the bus were taken to hospital suffering from shock while the driver, Mr William Edwards of Llwynypia, was uninjured. The bus involved was 495, KNY495D, one of the 1966 batch of Northern Counties-bodied AEC Regent Vs. It was repaired and returned to service. It survives to this day owned by bus preservationist Martin Doe.

Dozens of school children remarkably avoided serious injury when the brakes on an elderly double deck Rhondda bus failed one morning in 1952. The vehicle had descended Court Street, the steep hill leading to Pandy Square, when it suffered brake fade, caused when brake drums overheat because of constant use on severe and long downhill gradients. The bus, packed with children on their way to school, failed to stop at Pandy Square and careered across the main road at De Winton Street and on towards St Andrew's Church where it finally came to a halt on the flat near the church gates. In his report on the accident, the driver stated that he was "thankful for stopping at the gates of heaven." It was certainly a miracle that the bus didn't collide with any other vehicles or overturn as the outcome would undoubtedly have been far more serious, particularly if the accident had happened during the heavier traffic conditions of the 1960s. No blame was attached to the driver who was following instructions by travelling down Court Street in second gear, which limited his speed. The bus involved was 106, TG6306, an AEC Regent of 1933 vintage which was long overdue for replacement.

Another serious incident occurred late on a Saturday night in 1957 when a double deck bus on a service from Cardiff overturned after colliding with a car coming in the opposite direction. The vehicle was on the last departure from the city to the Rhondda when it was hit by the car on a bend near the village of Groesfaen on the A4119. The car driver had crossed the white line on the bend. None of the passengers or the bus driver and conductor were seriously hurt. The vehicle involved was 1956 Regent V, 408, TTX986. It was repaired and returned to service several weeks after the accident.

One bus with a particular unfortunate accident record was one of Rhondda's Guy Arab wartime utility buses delivered in 1943 with a 56 seat, Park Royal body. It was 182, FNY391, and on January 17, 1946, it skidded on ice and toppled 20ft down an embankment at Grover's Corner in Glyncoch, Pontypridd.

Hundreds of people went to see it as it lay on its side, still in its grey camouflage livery. It was sent off to Beadle in Rochester to be fitted with a new body and returned with new green leather seats which made it stand out against its fellow batch members which had retained their austere wartime interiors.

Unfortunately it was involved in another serious accident in 1951 and was sent away for repair, this time to Longwell Green of Bristol. The bus was eventually withdrawn and scrapped in 1957.

This unlucky vehicle which came to grief in 1951 suffered two serious accidents in its 14 year life. After this mishap the repair work was carried out by Longwell Green of Bristol.

Double route

Rhondda Transport had a big influence on many families in the valleys it served, but for one in particular the company even provided a route to matrimony — not once, but twice!

At 86 years of age, Avril Richards of Merthyr recalled how she had met her husband Bill Westcott while travelling as a passenger each day from Tonyrefail, where she lived, to work in Cardiff.

"At the time Bill was a conductor, a role he took on when he became old enough after starting with the company as a tea boy at 14. After service during the Second World War he came back as a driver. He had attained his 32 year service badge before he sadly died aged just 50.

"I'll never forget the first time I brought Bill home to meet my family. We lived on the Gilfach road near the old trolleybus depot.

"My elder sister, a nurse at Parc Hospital, Bridgend, would catch the Porthcawl bus to get to work and when I took Bill home the first thing she said to him was 'I know you, you're that quiet boy on the buses.' I was amazed!

"Although 10 years older than me he was a little on the shy side and it was a long time before he had plucked up the courage to ask me out.

"Amazingly it was Rhondda Transport that had been responsible for bringing Bill's parents together too. His father Thomas Westcott — known as Long Tom, because of his height — was a tram driver during the First World War while his mother Hannah had worked for the company as a conductress. After they were married Tom and Hannah lived at 10 Cemetery Road, near Porth depot which must have been convenient for them.

"I have lots of memories of travelling on Rhondda buses. Back in those days it was was the only way of getting about for most people. One of my clearest memories relates to my childhood. We were always made to wear hats and gloves then. In those days the buses were often filthy as the colliers travelled in them and you had to be careful where you sat.

Some careless driving was perhaps the reason that this 1948 AEC Regent resulted in a rather awkward situation. It appears to have slid sideways on the greasy Porth depot yard and ended up hanging precariously over the river.

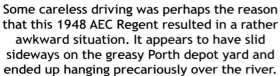

to marriage

I remember my gloves always got dirty. They would be covered in coal dust. After we were married I remember Bill would often drive coaches on many chapel outings to seaside destinations such as Barry and Porthcawl.

"Later I worked in Cardiff so travelled regularly on Rhondda buses between Tonyrefail and Cardiff. Buses were very social in those days. You always met and spoke to different people."

A link with Rhondda Transport and the family was retained for many years after the company ceased operation. Avril's son Richard Westcott obtained the original construction date plate from the depot at Porth and fixed it to the gates of his haulage business at Pyle.

Romance blossomed on the bus to Cardiff.

Single deck pair proved their worth

Rhondda Transport had an amazing miscellany of single deck bus types in its infancy. However, there is no doubt that as it settled into its role as a major bus operator it developed a fondness for two in particular which between them made up a significant part of the fleet for many years.

The first of these was the AEC Regal, one of the most successful single deck buses of the 1930s and 1940s, many of which continued to deliver sterling service until the advent of the 1960s. The second was the Leyland Tiger Cub, which brought significant advances in passenger transport on its early 1950s arrival.

Together they were prime people movers in the Rhondda Valleys for decades and during their lives the various batches that the company ordered carried millions of passengers.

Rhondda Transport took to the AEC Regal with enthusiasm. It was ideal for routes where double deckers couldn't be used, including those with low railway bridges or others with steep gradients which gave the company lots of problems.

Early Regals were all front engined, half cab buses, with rear entrances. This meant the driver sat in isolation in his cab alongside the engine, while conductors collected the fares and looked after passengers getting on and off the vehicle. There were three versions between 1929 and 1950. These were the Regal, Regal II and Regal III, and Rhondda had examples of each.

The company had built up a close relationship with AEC in the 1920s and when the Regal was introduced in 1929 Rhondda Transport was among its first customers. The first batch arrived in 1930. They were rear entrance 30 seaters which were numbered 66-71. One of them, 68, was destroyed in a fire the following year, but the others remained in service right through the Second World War until 1947. This was an exceptionally long

Passengers board a 1961 dual purpose Metro Cammell Weymann Tiger Cub at Cardiff bus station for the Limited Stop express service to Maesteg.

life span for such a vehicle at this time. These early Regals were followed by a further 10 in 1931, 81-90, the first of which was exhibited at the prestigious Commercial Motor Show that year.

This vehicle was a Brush built model, but the others were bodied by Weymann, Rhondda's favoured body builder. They were also 30 seaters, although most were later altered to 32 seats, and were followed by a solitary example, 91, in 1932. They were eventually withdrawn between 1946 and 1948.

Four more Weymann-bodied Regals arrived in 1934, this time with 34 seats, but an order for another 10 similar buses was cancelled and it was not until 1936 that the next Regals turned up at Porth depot although these were of the updated Regal II type. They came with Weymann 34 seat bodies but were later rebodied by Longwell Green or Park Royal. Two second-hand Regals, 143 and 144, with bodies by Metcalfe, were also bought in the same year.

A further 17 Regals arrived in 1937, 21-37, and 33 was also exhibited at that year's Commercial Motor Show. They had Weymann 34 seat bodies and in 1948 were fitted with more powerful AEC 9.6 litre engines. Most were rebuilt by local company Starkey in 1947 and they were eventually withdrawn between 1949 and 1952.

As Britain headed towards war in 1939, Rhondda bought 14 more Regals with Weymann 34 seat bodies, 40-53, followed by the first of the company's Regal coaches which were delivered in a blue livery with cream, streamline flashes and with large roof-mounted luggage racks. Numbered 160-162, they had 31 coach seats and lasted until 1952, by which time they had been repainted in a more usual red livery.

The war years put a hold on new Regals, but Rhondda received nine on loan from Western Welsh. As oil was in short supply, WW operated some which pulled two wheeled, coal fired trailers which produced gas as an alternative fuel. They were hitched to the back of the buses which could run for about 80 miles before the trailer had to be restocked with anthracite.

The first post-war Regals arrived in 1946 in the shape of four Burlingham, 34 seat examples and six built by Weymann, 58-63, with 35 seats along with a solitary Longwell Green example, 92, with 34 seats. The Burlingham examples, 54-57, are notable for being the first and only Rhondda bus type Regals to be fitted with front entrances. They were withdrawn in 1958.

New buses remained in short supply, mainly due to constraints on the availability and use of materials in the immediate post-war years and only four Regals were delivered in 1947, fleet numbers 93-96, this time with Longwell Green, 34 seat bodies and entrances at the rear once again. Deliveries were much healthier in 1948 with the arrival of 14 Regals, now of the updated Regal III type. Of these, 11 were 34 seat, rear entrance Longwell Green models, Nos. 64-65, 97, and 301-308, but three were magnificent Windover coaches, 98-100, with manually operated front doors. They had 32 coach seats and gave 10 years exemplary service on Rhondda's private hires and tours.

Six more Longwell Green Regal IIIs with 34 seats and rear entrances arrived in 1949 which were the last of the type to be bought new by the company. They were joined in 1952 by 13 second-hand Regals from Rhondda's sister company in the British Electric Traction group, Devon General. Fleet numbers 1-10 had Harrington bodies, dating back to 1938, while 12-14 had 1940 Weymann bodywork.

Regals continued to be familiar vehicles on Rhondda's routes — including the notoriously steep Trebanog Hill, Clydach Vale and Penrhys Mountain services — well into the 1950s. They survived into the early 1960s, 310-314 being withdrawn in 1961. They were the last AEC single deck vehicles ever bought by Rhondda Transport. All had proved sound performers and the company was well pleased with them. But their day was over and in 1950 an altogether more modern type of vehicle arrived — built by AEC's main competitor, Leyland.

Leyland's Royal Tiger roared for the first time in 1950 but it was 1952 before Rhondda Transport really began to take an interest in the vehicle. This single decker was a significant advance on the AEC Regals that the company had bought for the previous 20 years.

More than anything this was because it had an underfloor engine which meant the space taken up by the forward placed engine on the Regals could be used to create more seats.

Rhondda's Regals had only 35 seats, but the new Royal Tigers had 44 and that was an important consideration at the start of the 1950s when passenger figures rocketed.

Having an underfloor engine also meant drivers no longer needed to be in a cab isolated from passengers. They could now sit in the main frame of the vehicle and keep an eye on people boarding and leaving the bus. AEC, the company with which Rhondda had built up such a close partnership over the previous 30 years, did develop an underfloor engine single decker, the

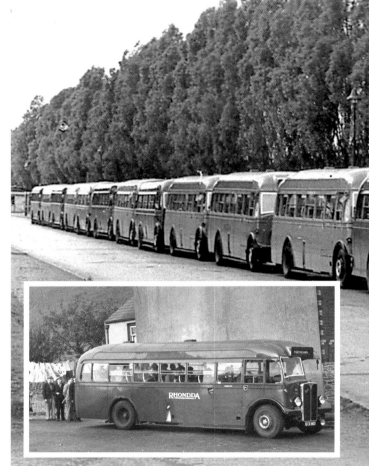

Regal IV. But surprisingly, while its sister company, Western Welsh, bought some, Rhondda turned away from AEC for its single deck deliveries and for the rest of its existence it only bought Leyland engined single deckers.

Rhondda's first Royal Tigers were 12, PSU1/13 examples bodied by Weymann. They arrived in 1952 and had seats for 44 passengers, were 8ft wide and fitted with vacuum brakes. They had an emergency door at the rear, which meant three windows at the back, a combination that was to become ubiquitous with the company's single deck buses as the 1950s progressed. Numbered 315-326, LNY356-LNY367, they were soon put to use on the lengthy Pontypridd to Pontyclun and Pontypridd to Porthcawl runs.

Drivers found them hard going as they weighed just under eight tons unladen, which was a real heavyweight for a single decker. Rhondda's batch of 1956 AEC Regent V double deck buses, also bodied by Weymann, were only 6 tons 7 cwt and they seated 61 passengers. The Royal Tigers proved to be thirsty machines at a time when Rhondda, like other bus companies, was concerned about fuel consumption when oil prices were rising and at the same time the Government was increasing its fuel tax.

The Weymann single deckers were quickly followed by three Royal Tiger coaches, 327-329, LTG267-LTG269. These were PSU1/15 examples, also with vacuum brakes, which were used on Rhondda's private hires and coach tours all over the country. They were robust

Four of these AEC Regals were destined for Rhondda Transport in 1947. INSET: One of three similar vehicles which followed a year later.

looking machines with Leyland's own bodywork and had 41 coach seats with a centre door that was manually operated. Rhondda also found these expensive vehicles to operate so was delighted when Leyland came up with the much lighter, and less thirsty, passenger carrier, the Leyland Tiger Cub.

Even so, the Weymann Royal Tigers lasted until 1963-4 while the coaches were withdrawn in 1960. But Rhondda was not yet done with the Royal Tiger. Amazingly, as late as 1967, it took another three into the fleet.

They were acquired from Southdown Motor Coaches. These were three Leyland PSU1/16 coaches which were already 14 years old. Two had bodywork by Harrington, the other by Duple. They were 41 seaters and were given fleet numbers 330-332. Elderly they might have been, but they looked resplendent in

This was the only Brush bodied AEC Regal, in the Rhondda fleet. No. 81 was bought by the company in 1931.

With bodywork by Burlingham this front entrance AEC Regal entered service in 1946.

Despite running down the long descent from Clydach Vale to Tonypandy, the destination blind on Royal Tiger 325, LNY366 still says Clydach Vale. The vehicle joined the fleet in 1952.

On private hire this centre entrance 41 seater Leyland Tiger Cub coach was bodied by Strachan.

Rhondda's attractive green and cream livery. They were meant to work the company's private hires and tours but often found themselves on works and schools services where they were disliked by conductors because they had a manually operated centre exit and only one button for the bell. They lasted just nine months and for Rhondda Transport at least, the Royal Tiger roared no more.

The salvation of Rhondda Transport, as with many other bus companies, came in the shape of the Leyland Tiger Cub. For local bus work or for private hire and express duties, Rhondda Transport found the Tiger Cub ideal.

It was a lightweight underfloor-engined chassis introduced by Leyland in 1952 at a time when fleets like Rhondda were suffering rising fuel bills and battling against the Government fuel tax which continued to rise throughout the 1950s.

The Royal Tigers weighed 7 tons 9 cwt when unladen, but the Tiger Cubs were just 5 tons 12 cwt and that made them much more fuel efficient. Rhondda, like other BET companies, saw the Royal Tiger as overweight, over specified and over priced. BET was an important customer and Leyland took note of its concerns, coming up with a bus powered by one of its own 0350H 91bhp 5.76-litre diesel engines with a newly designed lightweight, high, straight frame and a vertical radiator set behind the front axle. This was the Leyland Tiger Cub and Rhondda Transport welcomed the newcomer with open arms.

The biggest bus company in South Wales, Rhondda's BET sister, Western Welsh, bought a total of 349 Leyland Tiger Cubs during the 1950s and 1960s, but the much smaller Porth-based operator still utilised the services of a respectable 84 of these reliable passenger carrying workhorses. While WW dabbled with the Leyland Tiger Cub's great rival, the AEC Reliance, Rhondda remained steadfastly loyal to the Tiger Cub, taking only one other type of single deck vehicle into its fleet between 1953 and 1968, a mere three Bedford VAL coaches.

The first four Tiger Cubs, all bodied by Weymann, arrived at Porth depot in 1953. They looked very similar to the Leyland Royal Tigers that had been taken into stock the previous year, but despite that they were a very different kind of bus.

Fleet numbered 330-333, NTG141-NTG144, they were of the PSUC1/1 designation and like the Royal Tigers seated 44 passengers. They were followed the next year by 19 similar buses, 334-352, PNY 371-PNY 389 and in 1955 by 353-356, SNY231-SNY234, the only buses delivered that year. These were designated PSUC1/1T, which meant they were fitted with two-speed axles, but all three batches were bodied by Weymann, which was Rhondda's favoured supplier at the time. These vehicles soon became familiar sights on local routes in the valleys and on the longer Porth/Treorchy-Porthcawl and Pontypridd-Pontyclun/Porthcawl services. Rhondda was pleased with their performance on all its single deck routes, including the tough hilly climbs, and they were well liked by both passengers and crews.

These buses, with their famous Tiger Cub engine 'purr' and the ubiquitous Weymann triple window configuration at the rear — the centre one comprising the emergency exit — would continue with Rhondda Transport for the remainder of its existence. The first four, which were the first buses in the fleet to have route number blinds, stayed with the company until 1966 when they were sold to dealers. One, 332, later returned to its old seaside haunts when it was sold to Porthcawl Omnibus Company. Some of the PNY batch went in 1968 but seven of them, 334, 340, 343, 349, 350, 351 and 352, as well as the SNY vehicles, continued until after Rhondda was taken over by Western Welsh in 1971. They had completed a remarkable service career of 18 years. In 1956 a very different kind of Tiger Cub arrived on the Rhondda scene. These were 41 seat coaches with a centre entrance, and were given fleet numbers 357-359, UNY8-UNY10.

These vehicles were bodied by Strachans, a coach building firm based in Acton, London, and were designated PSUC1/2 which meant they had a dropped frame extension

Times were changing when these 1959 Leyland Tiger Cubs were snapped at Porth depot, as the 'pay as you enter' signs indicate. INSET: one of the 1954 intake of Weymann bodied sister vehicles.

First class comradeship

Graham Richardson worked for Rhondda Transport for 39 years from 1965 to 2004 and recalled many of the changes those years brought with them.

"I started as a conductor, that's how you had to do it, you couldn't become a driver first. Comradeship in the old company was first class, it couldn't be bettered," he said.

"When I first joined the company was still running double deckers with open entrances at the rear. There were no heaters in them and they were freezing in winter. Drivers used to have potatoes which they would rub on the windscreens to prevent the glass freezing up.

"I later became a driver and I worked for five companies which ran Porth depot: after Rhondda Transport there was Western Welsh, National Welsh, both when it was part of the National Bus Company and later when it was privatised, Rhondda Buses Ltd and Stagecoach in South Wales."

The 15 Weymann Hermes bus bodied Leyland Tiger Cubs delivered in 1959 were quite late examples of this model. They were also the last Weymann bodied vehicles to be delivered ending an association between Rhondda Transport and the Addlestone firm which dated back to 1931. Fleet No. 367 is seen in Porth operating a short extension of the service from Tonyrefail.

The ubiquitous Tiger Cub badge.

at the rear for a luggage boot and a higher-ratio rear axle to give them greater speed. Strachans was a well-respected builder of buses and coaches, but these were perhaps not its finest achievement. They were distinctly box-shaped with small side windows and looked more like prison buses than front line coaches although the company had been delighted at the lightweight vehicle's fuel saving, tyre economy and low maintenance bills.

At the beginning of 1959, some of the finest coaches ever built arrived at Porth depot. Rhondda had

In green and cream livery, this Harrington bodied 41 seat Leyland Royal Tiger coach was one of three aquired from Southdown Motor Services in 1967.

An impressive line-up of
1954-55 Leyland Tiger Cubs
at Porth depot in 1971.
Sadly they had all recently
been withdrawn

returned to Weymann for its 41 seat, front entrance coach, the Fanfare, one of the most graceful designs of the 1950s. These, 360-362, XTG360-XTG362, Rhondda's first single deckers with matching fleet and registration numbers, were designated PSUC1/2T, which meant they had all the attributes of the previous batch plus a two-speed axle. They were sent on private hire work all over the country where they ranked with the best. "These coaches should encourage the public not only to go by bus, but to go by Rhondda," the company proclaimed in its newsletter.

Rhondda received 15 more Weymann buses in early 1959, very similar to the 1953 to 1955 batches, but with the updated Hermes styling, complete with its even more elegant curves. Again seating 44 passengers with the three rear windows, this batch, 363-377, XTG363-XTG377, were also PSUC1/1 and were often used as deputy vehicles for private hires.

These vehicles tackled with ease any duty for which they were allocated and continued in service well into National Bus

Company days by which time they had been dispersed to other depots. Some even received NBC poppy red livery and most were not withdrawn until 1975 with the last two, 371 and 377, being taken out of service in 1976, after a remarkable, hard working lifetime of more than 17 years.

No new vehicles were delivered to Rhondda in 1960 and the next to arrive were three Tiger Cubs early in 1961. They were the first dual purpose vehicles in the fleet, 378-380, 378GNY-380GNY. Bodied by MCW, they seated 41 passengers and were designated PSUC1/2T, which made them similar to the Fanfares. When they were not deputising on private hire or express duties they could be found on the Treorchy/Porth to Porthcawl

One of five Park Royal bodied
45 seat, front entrance Leyland
Tiger Cubs delivered in 1961,
385KTG waits at Cardiff central
bus station to embark on a
return journey to Merthyr
in the early 1960s.

One of the Leyland Leopards ordered by Rhondda in 1970, but delivered to Western Welsh the following year.

The 1964 intake saw 12 single deckers acquired, including six Willowbrook bodied 45 seater Leyland Tiger Cubs. This one is seen at the bottom of Cymmer Hill in Porth.

A Leyland Tiger Cub makes a tight turn, so common in Rhondda Transport territory, as it heads for Blaenllechau.

One of three Tiger Cubs bought in 1961. They were the first dual purpose vehicles in the fleet and, bodied by MCW, they seated 41 passengers.

services, which were allocated dual purpose vehicles after 1961, or, from 1964, the new, fast Maesteg to Cardiff route which Rhondda ran jointly with Western Welsh. They were sturdy looking machines and their appearance was greatly enhanced when they were repainted in green and ivory livery in 1967. They were downgraded to bus work after the Western Welsh takeover in 1971 and were painted all-over red. Two were withdrawn in 1973 but one, 380, survived to 1976.

The three were followed by five Park Royal examples, 381-385, 381KTG-385KTG, which were PSUC1/1Ts. They had an offside rear emergency exit — which meant they could seat 45 — and a curved window at the rear. They were built to standard British Electric Traction design which perhaps wasn't the most attractive.

What these buses lacked in looks, they more than made up in creature comfort. They were the last single deckers to be fitted with moquette seats — double deckers had lost theirs with the arrival of the 1958 batch of Regents — and as a result they could deputise on private hire duties.

Their engines purred and travelling on them was a real pleasure, particularly on their usual haunt, the 92-minute long Pontypridd to Porthcawl route which Rhondda ran jointly with Western Welsh's Bridgend depot. They were eventually withdrawn in 1976.

In 1962 the power unit for Leyland Tiger Cubs became the 125 bhp 6.75 litre 0400H and in May 1964 Rhondda received its first examples to this specification, six 45 seat buses and three 41 seat dual purpose vehicles designated PSUC1/11T. The buses were numbered

Umbrella loss led to new job

Losing an umbrella proved a lucky experience for Brenda Hughes, a regular traveller on Rhondda Transport's buses — the incident ended up with her working for the company!

"It really was a lucky break," said Brenda whose name was Hopgood before she married. "It resulted in me working in the company's wages office for nearly 10 years from 1961 until 1969.

"I lived in Aberhondda Road, only a few yards from the company's offices, but worked as a civil servant in Llanishen in Cardiff and that meant three changes of bus to get there. One day I left my umbrella on the bus and went to Rhondda's lost property department to see if anyone had handed it in, which they had. While I was there I got chatting and said it was a shame I didn't work there because it was so

near my house. The office manager, Cled Jones, asked me if I would like an immediate interview, I said yes, and they took me on there and then! It wasn't the easiest of jobs. There was a team of eight who were all a great bunch and we had to work out the wages for more than 800 staff who would come to the office every Thursday for their pay packets. There were no direct payments into bank accounts in those days, everyone got cash in a brown envelope, the wages clerks were certainly the most popular people on Thursdays!

"The company was meticulous about accuracy, if you were just 6d out, you had to find it. Cled was a great boss, but he was very strict and made sure we did our jobs properly. I have had lots of jobs, but working for Rhondda Transport was certainly my favourite."

386-391, 386WTG-391WTG, the dual purpose vehicles 392-394, 392WTG-394WTG, and had Willowbrook bodies to a BET design referred to as 'the new look' which gave better front and rear views for drivers and passengers. The buses were often found on the Pontypridd to Porthcawl service but, as usual, people using the Treorchy/Porth to Porthcawl route had the comfort of the dual purpose vehicles unless they were needed for private hire. These served the company well until they were taken out of service in 1976-7.

Just four Tiger Cubs arrived in 1966, 300-303, HTG300D-HTG303D, followed in June 1968 by Rhondda Transport's last batch, 12 buses, 304-315, RTG304F-RTG315F, and three dual purpose vehicles, 316-318, RTG316F-RTG318F. All were PSUC1/12T, bodied by Marshall and, like the other vehicles of their type, gave long and exemplary service over some of the toughest terrain in the country.

Most of these vehicles were withdrawn by the end of 1980 by which time they were scattered at various depots in what was now the National Welsh fleet. One of them, RTG309F, was hired to Jones of Aberbeeg between November 1977 and June 1978 and was repainted in that company's blue livery.

The very last Rhondda Tiger Cub was 311, RTG311F, which by now had been renumbered 2868. It lasted until early 1981 when it was sold for further service in the Republic of Ireland. Unfortunately, as far as is known, not one of Rhondda's Tiger Cubs has survived for posterity. Only photographs of these splendid passenger carrying vehicles remain as a reminder of the arduous, day in, day out service that they rendered over a period of 28 years to Rhondda Transport.

A front and rear view of the Atlantean demonstrator provided by Leyland in its attempt to woo Rhondda away from its Regent V love affair in 1960. The vehicle is seen in Cardiff bus station. The company wasn't to be turned however, and it was some years before they entered the fleet.

Arrival of the Atlanteans

The day of the Atlantean dawned very late for Rhondda Transport. Leyland had started work on this revolutionary rear-engine double decker in the early 1950s with the prototype being exhibited at the 1956 Commercial Motor Show.

The first production example appeared at the same show two years later, but it was to be 10 years before one arrived at Porth. Leyland tried to woo Rhondda by sending its demonstration Atlantean to the company in 1960 where it was trialled on the Treorchy to Cardiff service. Later years proved this to be an ideal route for the vehicle. However, if Leyland had hoped to get the same favourable result from Rhondda Transport as it had from its sister company, Western Welsh, which ordered large numbers, it was sorely disappointed.

While WW bought 66 Weymann bodied 70 seat Atlanteans between 1960 and 1962, Rhondda was not for turning. It remained loyal to the tried and tested Regent V, ordering another 20, 30 ft examples which were delivered in 1961. Rhondda might have had a point as there were many early teething troubles with WW's Atlanteans, although its engineers got to work and by 1966 these were largely resolved with the vehicles having full lives with the company, some lasting until as late as 1977.

Rhondda continued ordering Regent Vs but at the end of August 1968 there was great excitement at Porth depot's bottom garage. The company's first Atlanteans, all PDR1/1s, had arrived and were lined up, ready to enter service. There were six, numbered 496-501, RTX496G-RTX501G, all looking resplendent in their glistening new paint. Rhondda had been well-pleased with their Northern Counties bodied Regents that were bought between 1963 to 1966 and stuck with the Wigan

Gone was the much loved Rhondda fleet name, instead the words Western Welsh adorned the front of this 1968 Northern Counties bodied Leyland Atlantean.

body builder for its first Atlanteans. As usual they were 14ft 6ins, normal height vehicles with cream rubber window surrounds and six sided destination indicator.

They were immediately put to work on the Treorchy to Cardiff and Maerdy/Ferndale-Pontypridd-Cardiff services where they were well received by passengers who described them as smooth running and comfortable. Like the Regents, they had tastefully decorated interiors using sky blue as a base colour with bright fluorescent lighting, contrasting with the austere Regent Vs that they were to replace. With 42 seats upstairs and 31 on the lower deck, these 30ft vehicles accommodated 73 seated passengers, three more than the Regents.

In July 1969 they were followed by another 10 identical vehicles, 502-511, VTG502G-VTG511G, and all were fitted out for one-person operation with periscopes installed so the

Tonypandy was the destination of this solitary 1969 Atlantean, about to leave the depot.

driver could see what was happening upstairs. This had been the reason for Rhondda finally turning to the Atlantean. As passenger numbers started to decline rapidly towards the end of the 1960s there was a need for more driver-only buses and the Regents couldn't be converted. AEC was also not offering a double decker that could be used for pay-as-you-enter operations so Leyland finally received the orders it had hoped for eight years previously.

Even so, Rhondda's Atlanteans were initially crew operated as was another batch it ordered in 1970. These arrived after the Western Welsh takeover in 1971 but were to the complete Rhondda specification, including its livery. There were nine, 512-520, BTG512J-BTG520J, which replaced the last nine rear entrance Regent Vs of 1956, and were also PDR1A/1s with 73 seats. But these were bodied by the Scottish bus builder Alexander and although their interiors were rather more spartan than the Northern Counties examples, arguably they

This Leyland Atlantean with Alexander bodywork was one of the last batch of double deckers, BTG512J-BTG520J, ordered by Rhondda Transport in 1970, but delivered in early 1971 after the company was taken over by Western Welsh.

had more handsome exteriors. All 25 Atlanteans were used on Rhondda's Cardiff services until the company began introducing more driver-only operations on its schools and works services in the early 1970s.

Because of their one-person operation capability, the Atlanteans began to be used on these less prestigious services and were replaced on what were the flagship routes by Rhondda's Regents which could not be converted to single manning.

Western Welsh also started transferring in its own vehicles, including some of its early Weymann Atlanteans, to run the Treorchy-Cardiff route which remained crew-operated until 1976 when it became pay-as-you-enter using Leyland Nationals.

As the 1970s progressed, Rhondda's Atlanteans could turn up anywhere, even with a driver and conductor on the backbone Blaenrhondda/Blaencwm-Pontypridd service which did not become one person operated until 1979.

Most of these vehicles were withdrawn between 1981 and 1984, the last, BTG520J, going in the late winter of that year. Not only was this the last Rhondda Atlantean, it was also the last double deck bus ordered by the Rhondda Transport Company. In a way it was a sad farewell to what had unmistakably been an unforgettable era.

The first of Rhondda's Leyland Atlanteans, 496, at Cardiff's central bus station, when still quite new. Rhondda came late to the Atlantean having remained loyal to the AEC Regent long after many other BET companies had succumbed to the rear engined double decker.

Bedfords brought a touch of luxury

Delivered in 1964 this was one of only three 47 seat Duple bodied Bedford VAL luxury coaches purchased by Rhondda. All three proved popular with passengers for their comfort and airiness.

Three coaches which arrived at Porth depot in 1964 created a huge stir as they were completely different to anything that Rhondda Transport had previously bought. These were the company's first 36ft long vehicles and the most luxurious ever operated.

They were Bedford VAL coaches bodied by Duple and, as the company's engineer, David Cherry, told staff: "They are a complete departure from standard as far as this company is concerned."

For the first time in 11 years the company had turned away from its beloved Tiger Cub, although the Bedford VAL was powered by a Leyland 400 engine. It had a three-axle coach chassis with two front steering axles and a five speed transmission with synchromesh on all gears except first and reverse. The twin front wheels were fitted with power assisted steering.

Seating capacity was 52 but on the Rhondda coaches this was limited to 47. According to the company this was to provide passengers with the maximum comfort.

Mr Cherry said: "The interior trim has been designed to produce a finish that is both gay and colourful and pleasing to the eye, and the seats are of a luxury coach type for maximum comfort. These coaches will, I am sure, prove most popular both with the passengers and staff, and will encourage people to 'Go By Rhondda' during the coming season."

The vehicles, 395-397, 395WTG-397WTG certainly looked eye catching in their red and cream livery with scrolled fleet names and were even more attractive when they were repainted in the newly adopted green and cream coach colours in early 1967.

They were not solely used for coach duties. They occasionally found their way onto school services as well, much to the delight of the youngsters. The drivers were not so pleased. "They are hopeless on hills," complained one who was contemplating with dread driving his VAL up Clydach Vale, one of the steepest gradients on the Rhondda Transport network.

The three coaches were withdrawn in 1970 and by 1973 were operating for the Geoff Watts company of Stourbridge, Worcestershire, where they were employed as staff vehicles for workers at the Austin car production plant in Longbridge, Birmingham.

Plaxton coaches ended an era

The last vehicles ever delivered new to Rhondda Transport arrived in 1970, just a few months before the company was taken over by Western Welsh. They were three luxurious coaches that arrived fully decked out in the company's green and cream livery.

Given fleet numbers 322-324, YTX322H-YTX324H, the 49 seat Plaxton Panorama Elite coaches were Leyland Leopards, a type that Rhondda was very late receiving. Leyland had started producing the model in 1959 as a more powerful version of the Tiger Cub. Western Welsh took a fleet of 20 in 1962, but Rhondda stayed faithful to the Tiger Cub, apart from the Bedford VALs of 1964.

The company received its last Tiger Cubs In 1968 and these were followed in April that year by its first three Leyland Leopards, 319-321, RTG319F-RTG321F, which were dual purpose with 49 seat Willowbrook bodies.

Then in 1971, the last single deck buses ordered by Rhondda arrived. These were also Leyland Leopards but unlike the previous deliveries, which were 36ft long. This was the type's shorter variant with 45 seats and fitted out for bus work. They were given fleet numbers 325-334, BTX325J-BTX334J, and spent most of their lives on former Rhondda services before the last was

Another of Rhondda's smart 1970 Plaxton Panorama Elite coaches.

finally withdrawn from public service in 1984. The 1968 dual purpose vehicles eventually received National Bus Company poppy red and white livery and were transferred to other Western Welsh depots. Two of the 1970 coaches, 322 and 323, went the following year to Greenslades Tours of Exeter and ended up with National Travel South West, 322 ending its days in the early

One of the last three vehicles delivered to Rhondda which arrived in 1970 was this Plaxton Panorama Elite coach.

1990s on school bus duties with S & M/Linkfast Group in Essex. Meanwhile, 324 was renumbered 109 and transferred in 1973 to Jones of Aberbeeg. It ended up with National Welsh as UD170 and received poppy red and white livery for use on local express services before withdrawal as 1104 in the late winter of 1984.

One of the 1971 Leyland Leopards still exists. This is 2332 which ended up as a towing vehicle with the Stagecoach company, not being withdrawn until 1999. This vehicle has been preserved and is undergoing restoration work.

Fighting and friendship

Gwyn Burgoyne and Bob James both served Rhondda Transport for decades as drivers, times which brought with them a mix of memories, both good and bad.

Gwyn worked as a driver for 38 years and remembered times when crews had to fight for their rights.

"I was a union representative and it's true that we were regarded as formidable by the company. If you don't fight, you get nothing. So we were tough when the company wanted to introduce driver-only vehicles which meant fewer conductors. These were people's jobs and we wanted to keep as many as we could. Our union was the General and Municipal Workers, which was less usual for transport workers, but we thought they could look after us the best. The branch secretary for many years was Tom Morton who stoutly defended our rights. There's no doubt he had a lot of power in the company. There was much comradeship at Rhondda Transport."

Bob meanwhile was another who drove for many years and transported thousands in that time.

"There was immense comradeship at Rhondda Transport, it was run like a family firm, said Bob. "We played lots of sports. There were thriving rugby, football, cricket, darts, skittles and bowls teams. They would go all over the place to play. We had regular tournaments with other bus depots, some of our friendliest rivalries were with Western Welsh.

"Lots of events were organised for the staff's families. There were Christmas parties and summer outings for the children. We had our own social club which was well used.

"Staff also had annual trips. Most years we went to Caswell Bay in Gower — always on a Rhondda Transport bus, of course!"

Ivor Gray receives a framed certificate to mark 25 years of loyal service from RTC chairman WT James.

Largest depot was never big enough

Rhondda Transport's Porth site was the largest bus depot in Wales, but for much of the company's existence space was at a premium with parked buses taking up virtually every inch of available space.

Construction work on the depot began in 1906 and by 1908 two tram sheds had been built, one known as bottom shed, which was situated near the entrance in Tynewydd Square, and the other, top shed, further inside the site. There were also machine shops, offices and power station buildings.

When the trams were phased out in 1933-1934 to be replaced by motorbuses it meant completely reorganising the workshop facilities while alterations were carried out on bottom shed, removing the tram rails and transforming it into a single span structure without the hindrance of pillars.

Space problems began to become a major issue during the Second World War when demand for bus travel soared. On the cessation of hostilities in 1945, Rhondda's bus fleet had grown to more than 200 vehicles on a site originally designed for 50 trams. The workshops needed upgrading and modernising as newer, lightweight, all-metal bodied buses started to arrive requiring less body maintenance than previous vehicles which contained a significant amount of wood. Such development was impossible on the cramped site.

Depot expansion was essential and eventually eyes turned to a level plot that was being used as an unofficial football ground across the river from top shed, which by now had been renamed top garage. To reach it a bridge was needed and in 1950 construction of one was finally given the go-ahead. The contract was awarded to the Fairfield Shipbuilding and Engineering Company of Chepstow and in 1953 the bridge, capable of carrying 20 tons, was ready to enable a new central fitting shop, body shop and stores to be built on the new site. Rhondda Transport's general manager, Tom

Some of the equipment installed in the engineering section where vehicles put in an appearance for regular maintenance and sometimes, more serious repairs.

CHAPTER 13

An atmospheric late 1950s scene at Porth depot as three buses prepare to set off for their next duty. The view typifies the vehicles most favoured by Rhondda Transport — the AEC Regent and Leyland Royal Tiger. On the lamp post is the microphone by which returning drivers gave their roster details to the office staff.

Strange, told employees: "It is most appropriate that we are able to start these extensive projects, which will modernise and greatly assist our maintenance and operating conditions, during the Coronation year of our gracious Queen Elizabeth II."

By May 1955 the old workshops had been demolished and the new purpose-built, fully enclosed modern facility with several inspection pits was fully operational. With a vast expanse of glass roofing it was described as the brightest in the country. At the same time new bus fuelling equipment was installed and an automatic bus washing machine, strategically located to the north east side of the bottom shed, now called bottom garage. This meant buses could enter the depot, refuel, wash and park-up overnight as directed by the depot supervisor.

The transformation was completed by the demolition of Green Meadow House in Aberrhondda Road, which had been used by the general manager, and a new, two-storey office block built in its place. This opened in March 1956 and housed the general office, which was the largest department employing 30 people during the 1960s, the traffic department, cash office and typing department. From this date also the legal address on the buses had to be amended from Rheola Road, Porth,

to Aberrhondda Road. But the developments did not resolve all the depot's problems.

Space continued to be at a premium, top garage could only accommodate 54 vehicles and bottom garage had room for just 35 buses which meant more than half the fleet had to be parked in the open, which presented huge challenges.

Coal-burning braziers were essential in winter. These were not there to keep staff warm, but to prevent bus engines from freezing solid. Nights in the valleys can be bitterly cold and there was a real risk of vehicle radiators and water pumps seizing up. So engines were kept running during the night with the braziers dispersed among the buses to keep them warm and ensure they would be ready for service the following morning. Staff in the workshops also made up aluminium radiator blinds from recycled bus panels, painted in Rhondda red, which were fitted to the front radiators of buses during the winter months to prevent freezing.

The space shortage on the 25,808 sq yard depot site also meant buses had to be parked up closely together, something which inevitably resulted in some bangs and scrapes. This led to an appeal by chief engineer, Mr David Cherry, for staff to take special care when parking vehicles. Porth depot was a busy place, 24 hours a day, seven days a week, although everyone had from 7 am on Christmas morning to 7 am Boxing Day off with only a small security staff retained on site. Originally buses had operated on Christmas Day, but this was phased out in the early 1950s and limited Boxing Day services ended in the mid-1960s while most services did not begin until midday on Sundays.

The Porth depot entrance in the tramway days of the 1900s. There were two roads, or tracks, in each garage bay, making eight in all. Nine Road, as it was known, ran to the right hand side of the garage, alongside the River Rhondda Fach. It is still known as Nine Road.

But Rhondda Transport's buses could be on the road for up to 22 hours a day, with the late night buses not arriving back at the depot until 1.30 am and morning services starting up as early as 3.30 am. The night shift was kept busy refuelling and cleaning vehicles. There were four fuel tanks with capacities of 6,000, 8,000, 10,000 and 11,000 gallons of diesel situated next to the administrative offices in Aberrhondda Road and these were topped up by two deliveries a week.

Buses were originally repainted at the company's paint shop in Ynyswen, Treorchy, but in 1959 a new paint shop was opened alongside the fitting shop and stores at Porth depot.

There was further modernisation in 1967 when the old ticket offices at the Tynewydd Square depot entrance were demolished and replaced by a new, single storey facility. Rhondda Tramways originally had a depot in Tonyrefail to house the trolley buses used on the short-

Work in progress on Porth's new fitting shop in May 1954. LEFT: the web of steel framework. CENTRE: the interior nears completion, May, 1955. RIGHT: the new depot office block which opened in 1956.

lived Gilfach Goch route and later the replacement motorbuses, but it closed in 1931 and Porth became the company's only depot. It rarely used outstations, or overnight parking sites, and buses always travelled from the depot to take up their services, returning there each night. The company paid crews to reach start points with timings agreed with the trade union.

Bottom garage at Porth still survives although it is now used by WG Thomas, a private coach and tours company which ironically took over many of Rhondda Transport's old school runs. Top garage was demolished in 1982 when heavy snows made the roof unsafe. The area is now used as an open air parking space by Stagecoach in South Wales which operates Rhondda's bus routes.

The new central workshops and stores after construction was finally completed in May 1955.

A view of the top of the depot in the late 1950s. Stockpiles of coal at the Lady Lewis Colliery can be seen in the background.

The head office building remains after being taken over by the local authority, who later decided to sell it. Some of the tram lines can still be seen at top garage.

But there is more to a garage and depot than simply the buildings. The staff within play their own individual part in helping things run smoothly and it seems at Rhondda Transport they did just that.

A happy, close knit management team of devoted and loyal staff is how Lyndon Rees recalled Rhondda Transport's office staff in the late 1950s when he was a traffic trainee.

"The typing pool girls were usually a law unto themselves and were known as 'the untouchables'. They were totally patronised by their bosses, although they did a good job of organising the annual dinner and dance at Bindle's Ballroom in Barry," recalled Lyndon.

Secretaries can be formidable personalities, ruthless in the protection of their bosses, and that was certainly true at Rhondda Transport whose general manager's secretary for many years was Megan Jones. Lyndon remembered wryly that she looked and sounded like well known actress, Peggy Mount.

"Some said she was actually the general manager but, after a frosty start, I got on with her quite well, subject to regular offerings of nice chocolates! No-one got into the general manager's office, not even the senior managers, without Megan's approval," he said.

"A little confusingly, the chief engineer's secretary was also called Megan Jones, so we distinguished the two by calling her Small Megan. The traffic manager's secretary was the glamorous Olga Evans.

"There were two lovely girls in the front lobby office, Doreen James and Megan Morby. They handled enquiries and a host of private bus hire quotations under the guidance of Horace Purcell, who was in charge of private hires and tours. To indicate once again how Rhondda Transport was often a family concern, both girls had husbands working for the company.

"A source of much interesting statistical information was Tom Davies, who handled all the passenger traffic, fleet mileage and bus fuel consumption records."

From the shine, it looks as if 1958, Weymann bodied AEC Regent V, 435, VTX435 has already had a new coat of paint as it stands in the paint shop, during the 1960s.

By July 1955 the new and well-equipped fitting shop was fully in use.

A scene inside the old bodyshop in the early 1950s. A wooden framed bus is undergoing rebodying.

An impressive line-up in the depot of 1933-35 buses.

Working for Rhondda was

Rhondda Transport was very much a family affair for Bill Hanley. His father, Tom Hanley, was a tram driver and worked for the firm for 48 years while his brother Jim worked in the depot fitting shop for 27 years.

"I remember my father taking me to the depot when I was just six and I got to know it along with the people who worked there very well," said Bill. "There was a Rhondda Transport social club on the other side of the river which my father would go to, and the crews would use a canteen at the depot entrance in Tynewydd Square.

"But it wasn't until 1964 that I joined the company as an employee. I had been working as a fitter with the Co-operative, and the pay was terrible. So I

called in to see my brother Jim, who was night foreman at the depot, and got a job in maintenance and cleaning. Three years later I became deputy foreman and in 1971 was promoted to the role of garage foreman.

"That meant arranging the maintenance of the buses, refuelling the vehicles and allocating buses to the crews. It was all properly organised even though buses could be three-deep parked up in what we called the bull ring, a parking area between the two garages. Breakdowns could cause problems and difficulties arose in making sure there were always enough buses to go round," said Bill.

"My worst experience in the job came one night when I was on shunting duties, which involved

a family affair

One of the buses that Bill Hanley 'bumped'.

parking up buses. Space was always tight at the depot. It was a very wet night and I got into the cab of a double decker with wet hands. As I reversed the bus my hands slipped on the steering wheel, and it went straight into two other vehicles, which meant all three had to go out of service for repairs. Strangely, the bus I was driving was one of the 1958 Regent Vs, VTX439, and the two vehicles I hit were the next in sequence, 440 and 441.

"I continued to work at Porth depot until 1987, by which time Rhondda Transport had been taken over by Western Welsh. I have always regarded that bitterly as one of the biggest robberies that ever took place. We had a superb fitting shop which was taken away by Western Welsh. The depot was never the same after the takeover."

Parking space was always at a premium in Porth depot!

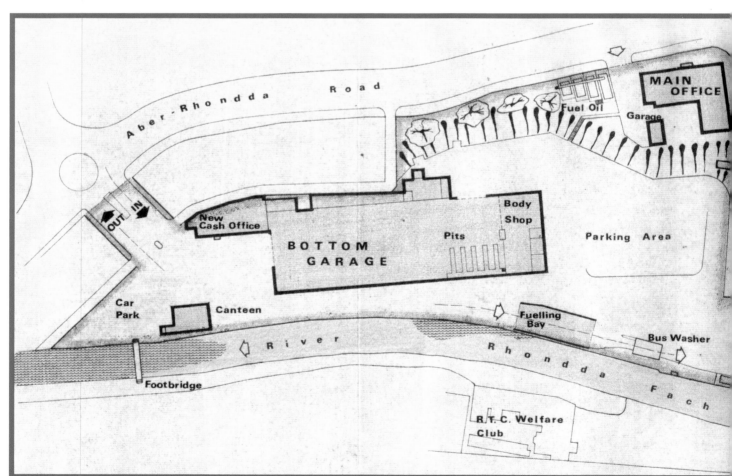

Through the wash in 1972. The Rhondda Transport Club can be seen in the background.

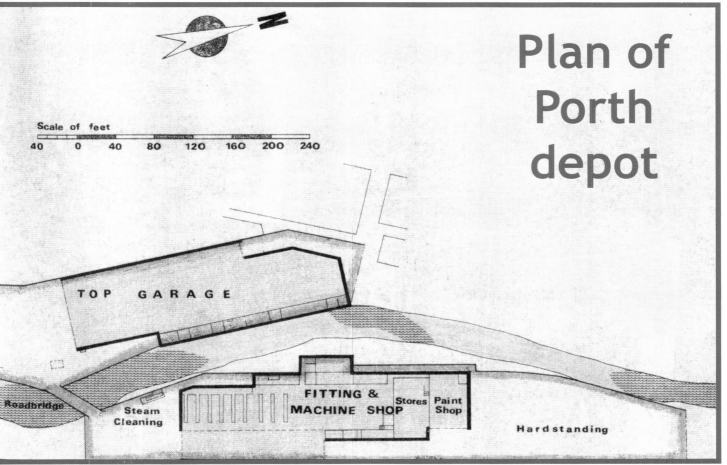

Plan of Porth depot

Scale of feet

40   0   40   80   120   160   200   240

TOP GARAGE

Roadbridge

Steam Cleaning

FITTING & MACHINE SHOP

Stores

Paint Shop

Hardstanding

All change as the name game begins

As the bells rang out to herald the start of the New Year in January 1971, they also sounded the death knell for the Rhondda Transport Company. The last bus to enter Porth depot the night before was owned by Rhondda, the first out of the garage that morning was a Western Welsh vehicle.

Rhondda Transport as a separate company was no more. Its depot with 158 vehicles and 802 staff had become the largest within the Western Welsh Omnibus Company. For the travelling public, there was little difference. Their buses were still red and continued to carry the Rhondda fleet name. But for the staff, the change was noticed immediately, as Carol Gibbons, at the time Carol Thomas, who worked in the general office, recalled: "On December 31 we answered the phone, Rhondda Transport Company. The next day we had to say, Western Welsh, Porth depot. It was the end of one era and the beginning of another."

The axe fell on a number of office staff who had given many years faithful service to the Rhondda company. Manager, Mr Bill Cooper, said the takeover would result in an overall saving of £10,000 in a full year, which today seems a remarkably small sum for such a large sacrifice. On the changeover Mr Cooper became Western Welsh's Rhondda area manager, but the following month was promoted to WW traffic manager and was succeeded at Porth by the company's assistant area manager at Haverfordwest, Derek Price.

So not only did the Rhondda staff have to adapt to the Western Welsh way of doing things, which was often very different, they had to get used to a new boss as well. But there were some benefits, recalled Carol. "Rhondda Transport classified office staff as clerical workers but with Western Welsh we became local government workers who were on higher pay rates. My wage with Rhondda was £6 18s 6d a week and with Western Welsh that doubled."

As in many places minibuses played a part in helping to slow declining passenger numbers as they reached the parts other vehicles couldn't.

CHAPTER 14

The steep gradient from Tylorstown to Penrhys presented a challenge for Rhondda buses whether they were going up or down. Here two vehicles pass one another. About half way up the climb is a 1971 Willowbrook bodied 45 seat Leyland Leopard. Going down is a 1972 Marshall bodied Leyland Leopard.

Even so, the takeover was not popular at Porth depot. It was seen as a huge loss of prestige for a company that pre-dated Western Welsh. Rhondda was established in 1906, WW had only been created in 1929 with the merger of South Wales Commercial Motors and the bus operations of the Great Western Railway. WW's general manager, Ivor Gray, who had been Rhondda's general manager from August 1957 to January 1962, understood the problems, although he maintained the takeover was entirely logical in the interests of economy and greater efficiency.

"But, however necessary the move, there must inevitably be some pangs of regret at the passing of RTC, whose proud history goes back to the early years of the century," said Mr Gray. "I can understand, and indeed, share, this feeling of nostalgia having managed Rhondda and worked amongst the staff. Fortunately, busmen are adaptable and so I am sure that our 'new mates' will soon get used to the idea of belonging to Western Welsh."

Many did not and as company chairman Mr JTE Robinson said in his speech at Western Welsh's long service awards in February: "Whatever the change, the Rhondda will still be the Rhondda." Rhondda's sports sections and societies continued as before. The former company's football team remained outside WW, both

sides playing in the South Wales Transport League, and there was intense satisfaction when, that September, the redoubtable Porth depot side beat Western Welsh 3-1! But Rhondda's house magazine, Staff News, which had done an excellent job in keeping the employees up to date with all that was going on in their company, was discontinued and now there was only a page or so of Porth depot news in WW's own Staff Bulletin.

It was not an easy takeover and a confrontation blew up early on when WW wanted to promote a Cardiff depot bus driver to the position of inspector at Porth. Rhondda Transport had an agreement with its trade union that only Porth employees could become bus inspectors at the depot and on this occasion the company backed down. But the Rhondda crews still had to get used to WW's inspectors from other depots boarding their vehicles to check fares.

Initially the travelling public would have noticed little change as it was intended to retain Rhondda's identity and although the legal address on the buses changed from Aberrhondda Road, Porth, to Cowbridge Road West, Cardiff, buses at Porth depot continued to carry Rhondda fleet names. Nine new Leyland Atlanteans bodied by Alexander and 10 Willowbrook-bodied single deck Leyland Leopard buses, to full Rhondda Transport specification, were put into service and were joined by 658, one of Western Welsh's 1956 batch of rear entrance Park Royal bodied AEC Regent Vs. This was a shock because it was a low height vehicle with bench-type seats upstairs. Rhondda Transport had only ever bought one similar vehicle and that was a Leyland TD 1, number 80, back in 1931. The Regent looked resplendent in full Rhondda livery, but was only intended to help out on works and schools services and driver instruction duties. But perhaps someone wanted to show off that livery more widely for it occasionally strayed onto the prestigious Treorchy-Cardiff service.

Meanwhile, the first six of Rhondda's 1958 batch of Weymann forward entrance Regent Vs were transferred to Western Welsh's Cardiff and Barry depots and one, 425, became a frequent performer on the Ferndale to Cardiff service, a route from which it had been banned when new because it was 30ft long. The first of the 1959 Weymann Hermes Leyland Tiger Cubs was transferred to Bridgend depot, 363, which, like other single deckers in the former Rhondda fleet, began carrying a 2 prefix to its fleet number to distinguish it from buses in WW's numbering scheme. The transferred vehicles all received Western Welsh fleet names. Changes were also introduced to Rhondda's route numbers.

The local R-prefixed services were now numbered in the 5XX series, while routes from 100 up were renumbered in the 3XX series. So the R20 Pontypridd service became 520 while the 120 Treorchy to Cardiff route became the 320.

Then there was another change at the top. Mr Gray, whose father Albert Gray had been Western Welsh's first general manager, announced his retirement. He left that April and was succeeded by Mr Keith Holmes, assistant general manager of Northern General. His arrival coincided with another change in policy. It was announced that the Rhondda fleet name would be phased out and all Porth-based vehicles would carry the Western Welsh identity. There was a furious reaction and protest letters appeared in the Rhondda Leader newspaper. A WW spokesman explained: "Different buses serve different areas at different times and we wouldn't want a Rhondda bus operating in West Wales."

It seemed a lame excuse, particularly as Western Welsh was busy divesting itself of its loss-making West Wales operations at the time.

In a bid to get people used to the change, the company announced that Rhondda vehicles would only receive the WW name on repaint, but that meant vehicles working alongside each other on the same routes had different identities, which appeared odd. One of the 1964 Regent Vs even appeared with Western Welsh on the sides and the Rhondda fleet name at the rear! Also at this time, the company did not seem able to make up its mind what colour to paint its coach-seated single deck buses. Initially one of Rhondda's vehicles, a Marshall-bodied Leyland Tiger Cub of 1968, 316, received the blue and ivory livery WW had introduced in 1965 but then the company decided to phase out the scheme in favour of red and cream into which it repainted a sister

By now Western Welsh had taken over and the Rhondda fleet name was being replaced.

National Welsh were the owners of this Leyland Atlantean when it was photographed at work in Barry, though it was new to Rhondda in 1968.

vehicle, 317. It meant Rhondda now had vehicles with two different identities while its dual purpose vehicles appeared in three different colour schemes, including its own green and cream. But worse was to follow.

Back in 1967, British Electric Traction, which was the parent company of Rhondda Transport and Western Welsh, had sold its bus interests to the state for £35 million which led to the creation of the National Bus Company on January 1, 1969. In 1972 the NBC announced that its bus subsidiaries, which included Western Welsh, would paint their vehicles either poppy red or leaf green. WW chose the red livery and soon former Rhondda buses were appearing in this new, bright shade which contrasted sharply with their former livery. But the company was continuing to hear protests about the loss of identity and in early 1975 it agreed to bring back the Rhondda fleet name for vehicles operating from Porth depot. By now they included former Western Welsh vehicles such as the Northern Counties bodied Regent Vs, similar to Rhondda's examples, that had been transferred in 1972, three 1963 Weymann Leyland PD2s and eight of the attractive Northern Counties AEC Renowns of 1965-1966.

These changes to liveries and identities were doing little to help the bus industry's fundamental problems in the 1970s which were declining passenger numbers and rising costs. Porth depot was not immune and

Western Welsh axed the Porth/Treorchy-Porthcawl service, which in the 1950s had needed up to 16 double deckers to take the crowds home from the seaside, and the Merthyr to Cardiff route which Rhondda Tramways had fought so hard to run in the late 1920s. Frequencies were also cut on other routes. The Treorchy to Cardiff service, which in the 1950s had run every 15 minutes and was boosted at busy times with three or four buses, now ran only twice hourly.

Driver-only operated buses helped, but these continued to be only slowly introduced at Porth depot. The Maerdy-Tonypandy/Llwynypia service was not converted until 1975, the Treorchy to Cardiff route a year later. The former tramways route from Blaenrhondda/Blaencwm-Pontypridd continued to be crew operated for most of the 1970s, the last former Rhondda Transport AEC Regent V, KNY495D, running for the final time on the service in 1979.

By now Western Welsh itself was no more. Back in 1972, Mr Keith Holmes had also become general manager of the long-established, Chepstow based Red & White bus company which operated on routes in the South Wales valleys and was a subsidiary of the National Bus Company. From then Western Welsh and R&W vehicles had a common fleet numbering system based on the year they were delivered. So Rhondda Regent V 489 became H1165, which meant it was the

One of the smaller vehicles that became a common sight on Rhondda roads in the days of National Welsh, long after the demise of Rhondda Transport .

11th vehicle delivered in 1965. The H indicated it was a normal height double deck vehicle while L was used for low height buses. It just added to the problems for Rhondda's engineers and administrative staff. Meanwhile, R&W remained a separate company owning its own land, buildings and vehicles but gradually it became more closely involved with WW and on Thursday, April 27, 1978, the companies merged.

A competition had been organised to choose a new name and out of 674 entries, National Welsh Omnibus Services Ltd was chosen. This time there was no gradual changeover and from midnight on April 26 staff at Porth depot worked flat out to replace the Rhondda fleet name on all vehicles, with National Welsh on the nearside and the Welsh equivalent, Cymru Cenedlaethol, on the offside. It seemed like a good idea at the time, after all National Welsh was part of the National Bus Company and operated in Wales, albeit only in the south eastern corner. But they were hardly 'catchy' names and ignored the fact that a significant part of NW territory was outside Wales. Also not taken into account was the loyalty built up over many years to Rhondda Transport, Western Welsh and Red & White, but that attitude was soon to change.

As passenger numbers continued to fall during the end of the 1970s, it was clear decisive action was needed. National Welsh carried out a market analysis project, an in-depth study of customer demands and public attitudes towards its bus services. The aim was to maximise passenger loadings and minimise the number of buses needed. Porth depot came under close scrutiny and from May 1981 new services were introduced, although the core routes remained. All depots gained local identities to encourage loyalty and at Porth this emerged as New Rhondda.

But National Welsh continued to lose money. Passenger figures dropped from 42.6 million a year in 1981 to 36.3 million in 1984 while in the same period it lost £800,000 even after receiving more than £8 million in

revenue support from local authorities to keep loss-making services running. There were further cutbacks and Porth depot's vehicle allocation fell from 77 to 66 vehicles in January 1984. In Rhondda Transport's heyday, 30 years earlier there were more than 200.

Among the buses withdrawn were BTG520J, a 1971 Leyland Atlantean, and BTX334J, a Willowbrook-bodied Leyland Leopard, both ordered by the old Rhondda company and the last former Porth based vehicles in public service. The last ex-Rhondda Leyland Tiger Cub to go was RTG311F, which had been renumbered U2868. It was withdrawn in early 1981 and saw further service in the Republic of Ireland.

It was not all doom and gloom at Porth, however. There were innovations. A fast Maerdy to Cardiff service was introduced in 1981, the X8, using coaches in a blue, red and white livery that did the journey in 70 minutes instead of the 90 minutes taken by the 332 all-stops route. It was followed by a limited stop X9 service which completed the Tonypandy to Cardiff journey in 52 minutes compared to 78 minutes on the old route which by now had been renumbered the 522. A new midibus service was introduced in the Rhondda Fach called Skyliner, with vehicles painted in a bright blue livery, that connected villages previously without a bus. There were special day out tickets to travel in the Rhondda Fach and Rhondda Fawr for just £1.35.

But generally it was a tale of decline. The Treorchy to Cardiff route which needed so much duplication in the 1950s was cut back to run from Tonypandy only and there was just one bus an hour. The backbone route from Blaencwm/Blaenrhondda-Pontypridd was pruned to just two buses an hour. The service had needed up to one bus every five minutes back in Rhondda Transport's day. The standard of vehicles had dropped as well. Porth depot used ageing vehicles from both the Red & White and Western Welsh fleets and the buses looked scruffy, their poppy red livery fading into a washed out pink. Rhondda Transport had always taken pride in the appearance of its buses. That was now lost forever.

By now however, the National Bus Company's days were numbered. A Conservative government was in power which decided that privately-owned buses would turn around standards and decreed that NBC should sell off its subsidiaries. National Welsh was sold to its management in May 1987, the 31st NBC company to be disposed of in this way. It had a fleet of 462 buses and 1,483 employees and soon began introducing minibuses in a bright yellow livery across its operating territory. The Blaenrhondda/Blaencwm-Pontypridd service was converted and where once Rhondda Transport's Regents reigned, now there were 21 seat Iveco minibuses.

It was an attempt to stave off the severe competition that National Welsh now faced, not only from the municipal companies but also from private operators like Clayton Jones of Pontypridd. Taff Ely buses in Pontypridd, Merthyr Tydfil and Inter-Valley Link based in Caerphilly succumbed to the onslaught and disappeared but while National Welsh survived it was mortally wounded. It had made a small profit in its first year as a private company but by 1990 it was heavily in debt. In a bid to keep the wolf from the door, the company sold its eastern area depots in February 1991 to Western Travel of Gloucester, another former NBC company that had been sold to its managers, and they created a new Red & White company in south east Wales.

Porth depot remained with National Welsh which began painting its vehicles in a maroon and cream livery. There was huge excitement when, after a gap of 14 years, the depot's allocation appeared with Rhondda fleet names once more. The company started to operate profitably, but it was saddled with huge debt problems and on January 3, 1992, administrative receivers moved in. Swansea-based South Wales Transport and Red & White were both interested in taking over the Rhondda operations but the following day it was announced a consortium from the Midlands was taking over. A phoenix was rising from the ashes, a new Rhondda bus company was about to be born.

One of 27 Weymann bodied AEC Regent Vs which arrived at Rhondda in 1956.

Sheep in the driver's cab

Driving Rhondda Transport's double deckers took a lot of skill and some ingenuity, recalled Lyndon Evans, who worked at Porth depot for 45 years.

He began his career as a conductor, moved on to driver and spent his last 25 years working on National Express and its continental tours, but always from Porth.

"Modern coaches were much easier to drive than those double deckers," he said. "There was no such thing as power assisted steering at the time and that could make things really tricky, particularly if there was a full passenger load on board. I remember coming through Trehafod with 70 people on the bus and had to stand up in the cab to exert enough muscle to pull the bus around the bends," said Lyndon.

If driving double deckers was no picnic, it was made up for by the terrific camaraderie and sense of fun at Porth depot. "It was absolutely fantastic," said Lyndon. "We had lots of nicknames for the crews too.

"There was Dai Back Seat, so called because he refused to get up from the back seat of the bus. Passengers had to pay him as they boarded the vehicle, the entrance was always at the back at the time. Then there was Inspector Fluffy, real name Clarence Francis, who got his name from the time when, as a conductor, he was guiding a driver as he reversed a bus, but the vehicle was still involved in a collision. The case went to court and when asked what had happened Clarence said 'I was blowing my whistle but I fluffed it'. Another was known as Alan Hospital because he was injured in every game he played in for the depot's football team."

Some of the crews were also notorious for their practical jokes, such as the time a driver went to his allocated bus at the depot.

"To his great surprise a sheep jumped out from the cab as he opened the door," said Lyndon.

New company with old buses

Four days after National Welsh went into receivership, the company's Porth and Aberdare depots, plus the vehicles, were bought for around £2 million by a consortium from the Midlands headed by bus entrepreneur, Julian Peddle.

The new company was named Rhondda Buses Ltd (RBL) and was an independent company. But that was not the full story. While Mr Peddle was the major shareholder, owning 60 per cent, three of the major transport groups, Stagecoach, First and Arriva, also had shares through their bus subsidiaries. This not only put the new company in an unique position, it also gave it formidable strength against would-be competitors as well as the buying power of these major groups.

Aberdare depot was quickly sold off and the company turned to the task of deciding which routes to run from Porth. A timetable similar to the one that had been operated by National Welsh began with a significant addition. Rhondda Buses took over the 36-mile Aberdare to Porthcawl service, started by the old Red & White company in 1928, and which National Welsh had also run from Aberdare depot. It retained its well-known route number, 172. On February 12 RBL took over National Welsh's Caerphilly depot which it closed four days later with the loss of 80 jobs before re-opening it a week later as Caerphilly Busways, with just 20 staff and operating amicably with Cardiff Bus which had started services in the town.

Many of the vehicles bought from National Welsh were quickly disposed of and RBL kept 80 buses and minibuses for its Rhondda depot and 25 at Caerphilly, although there were still too many for its needs and more were sold. But the inheritance was a motley collection of ageing buses and it was clear to the new company that modernisation was a priority.

The first new vehicles began to arrive in the summer of 1992 and the company quickly found the Dennis Dart ideal for its purposes. It eventually built up a fleet of 33 for the valley routes and there were new Mercedes Benz minibuses as well while the flagships for the company were two Optare Prismas which were bought in December 1995 and used mainly on the X8 and X9 Rhondda express services. There was also judicious buying of second-hand vehicles, which included Leyland Lynxes for the Tonypandy-Cardiff service. For a while RBL kept a small double deck fleet, mainly for the Maerdy-Cardiff service which by now had been renumbered 132. But in March 1997 it withdrew its last example, 717 (GTX741W), a Bristol VRT which had been bought by National Welsh in 1980. Double deckers had arrived at Porth depot for the first time in 1931 when it was owned by Rhondda Tramways; 66 years later, there were none and that is how it has remained.

The new company decided to retain the livery used by National Welsh at its Porth depot. This was maroon and cream with a scrolled Rhondda fleet name and it was extended to the minibus fleet as well, so ending NW's Bustler identity. But this was found to fade over time and in February 1996 a new standard livery of red, cream and maroon was adopted which worked surprisingly well. The fleet's appearance was pristine, although Rhondda Buses began using contravision with enthusiasm, usually at the rear of its vehicles. There were also buses displaying garish, all-over advertising liveries at this time, but the historic Rhondda name was kept alive which helped create passenger loyalty.

RBL chose to grow by acquisition, not competition, and for the six years it ran

Two Leyland Nationals at Tonypandy, May 18, 1991.

A Leyland Lynx arrives at Pandy Square on the fast route to Cardiff in the Rhondda Buses era of the mid-1990s.

services there was none of the cut-throat behaviour that had played a major role in the demise of National Welsh. In May 1993 it took over Cyril Evans of Senghenydd and on April 1, 1995, it bought Parfitts of Rhymney Bridge which was competing with Red & White in Merthyr Tydfil. Rhondda Buses passed on the commercial operations run by Parfitts in the town to R&W, which by this time was owned by Stagecoach, but retained the council-run services and routes in the upper Rhymney Valley and Tredegar. This meant that its operating area was significantly larger than the old Rhondda Transport Company. More than 60 years after Rhondda Tramways had been refused a licence, Rhondda buses were finally reaching Newport!

But the company was hemmed in on both sides by two major bus groups. To the west was First while Stagecoach was the main operator to the east, and there was much speculation about which of them might make a takeover bid. This ended on December 23, 1997, when Rhondda Buses was sold to Stagecoach. There were 100 vehicles in the fleet, 61 at Porth depot, 22 at Caerphilly Busways and 17 at Parfitts. Now everyone looked to see what the new owners would do with the company.

Stagecoach began revamping Rhondda Buses immediately. The Rhymney Valley and Caerphilly operations were integrated into its South Wales subsidiary which traded as Red & White and was based at Cwmbran. Buses from Porth depot began to run as Stagecoach Rhondda. Repaints into Stagecoach's brash corporate livery followed quickly. The base colour was white with three stripes in orange, red and blue wrapped around the vehicle and could not have been more different from Rhondda's more staid colours or from the all-over maroon of the old company. But at least vehicles continued to carry the Rhondda fleet name although now it was

This MCW Metrorider is bridging a gap in time outside what was once Rhondda Transport's busy canteen.

secondary to Stagecoach. The first buses to be repainted were the two flagship Optare Prismas which emerged with their new stripes in January 1998 and the rest of the fleet was soon similarly adorned.

Stagecoach also turned its attention to Porth depot's routes and early on switched the operation of the Aberdare to Porthcawl service back to Aberdare depot, which by now it also owned. This cut out the dead running needed for Porth based vehicles to start and end the service at Aberdare. Schedules for other services were tightened and action taken to ensure maximum efficiency. But the company was prepared to trial services. It introduced a fast Tonypandy to Cardiff service which used the new Tonyrefail by-pass, for example. Often however, these trial services were withdrawn quickly if passenger figures didn't match expectations, as happened with this service.

The company paid particular attention to fleet renewal. It had inherited vehicles from Rhondda Buses of which more than 70 per cent were less than five years old and to these Stagecoach added more Dennis Darts, although by now they were of the low-floor variety. There were also transfers into the depot from other company subsidiaries, including a number of comfortable Northern Counties bodied Volvo B10M-55s received from Stagecoach Manchester for premier routes.

Towards the end of 2001 the group announced a new livery to take it into the new century. Out went the stripes and in came swirls in blue, orange and white, similar to the scheme that is still used today. It was followed by a revamp of identities and what had been Stagecoach Red & White and Stagecoach Rhondda now became Stagecoach in South Wales. Sadly the Rhondda fleet name began to disappear, although as in 1971, only as vehicles required a repaint.

Seen at Pontypridd bus station, this 1997 Wright bodied Dennis Dart was one of the first low floor vehicles delivered to Rhondda Buses.

The Volvo B10M-55, which the Stagecoach company repainted in the primrose and maroon of Rhondda Tramways to celebrate Rhondda's centenary

Stagecoach pulled out all the stops in 2006 to make Rhondda's centenary a special occasion which culminated in a three-day event over the May Day Bank Holiday at Rhondda Heritage Park.

A Northern Counties-bodied Volvo B10M-55, fleet number 20885 (P885MNE), was repainted into the primrose and maroon colours that had been used by Rhondda Tramways with a special exhibition telling the company's story laid out inside.

Repainting the last vehicle at Porth still in the stripes livery with Stagecoach Rhondda fleet names was delayed until after the centenary event. This was low-floor Dennis Dart 33622 (S622TDW), new in 1998. It was the last vehicle ever to carry the historic Rhondda fleet name.

Pride of place at the event went to two Rhondda Transport AEC Regent Vs that Stagecoach repainted for the occasion. One was 457KTG, new in 1961 as 457 and now owned by the heritage park. It appeared as it would have looked as new, with old-style upright fleet names and black mudguards and grill. The other, owned by Martin Doe, was the last Regent V delivered new to the old company, KNY495D, fleet number 495, which received the later livery of fleet name with sloping characters, red mudguards and black grill.

A special commemorative colour booklet, Tramcars & Clippies, was also produced for the occasion which gave a potted history of Rhondda over the previous 100 years from its formation in April 1906. It was certainly as big a celebration as the one organised to mark the company's Golden

An Alexander bodied Dennis Dart standing at Porth depot in Stagecoach Rhondda livery in March 2002.

Jubilee in 1956, but by now operations at Porth depot were very different.

Back in 1956, Rhondda Transport operated 207 buses, 130 of them double deckers, mainly AEC Regent IIIs with a smaller number of the new AEC Regent V. All had open entrances at the rear. The rest of the fleet consisted of front-engine, single deck AEC Regals, also with rear entrances, and some later under-floor engine Royal Tigers and Tiger Cubs. In 2006 there were just 62 buses at Porth depot and they were all single deckers: 30 low-floor Dennis Darts, seven step entrance Dennis Darts, eight Volvo B10M single deckers, 15 Mercedes 709D/711D/811D minibuses and two Optare Primas, the only ones in the Stagecoach South Wales fleet.

Fifty years earlier Rhondda Transport had employed around 1,000 people at Porth depot. By 2006 this had fallen to just 160. The old company's buses were running more than seven million miles a year and in 1955 carried nearly 38,250,000 passengers. In 2006 Porth depot was carrying 90,000 passengers a week, around 4,680,000 a year.

In 1956 every inch of space of Porth depot was utilised and space was so limited that buses had to be parked just inches apart. By 2006 Stagecoach only needed what had been the top garage in Rhondda Transport's days and bottom garage was being used by WG Thomas, a private operator who had taken over many of the old company's school services.

Once Rhondda Transport's buses ran most of the valleys school services and took miners to 18 collieries working three shifts a day. The last pit in the Rhondda, Mardy Colliery, closed in 1990 and this loss of valuable colliery contracts had a huge effect on the profitability of Porth depot during National Welsh days. Back in 1948, Rhondda Transport was carrying 50,000 workmen every day, and more than half the company's fleet was used solely for works services. This traffic declined markedly in the 1960s and had largely disappeared by 2006.

Falling passenger figures and declining profitability is something all bus companies have had to face since the mid-1950s and the huge drop experienced at Porth depot is not unusual. So it is a credit to Stagecoach that it has managed to increase the level of service on many of its Rhondda routes in the last 10 years.

But there have been regrettable cutbacks. In 2014 the company blamed Welsh Government finance cuts for its decision to withdraw the 89 year old, 244 Pontypridd to Bridgend service that Rhondda Tramways introduced in 1925, as well as the fast Maerdy to Cardiff service introduced by National Welsh in 1981 as the X8 which Stagecoach later renumbered the X32.

Generally, however, Rhondda's legacy has been well looked after by Stagecoach. At the time of writing it operated 77 vehicles at its Porth depot including 26 of the latest low floor Dennis Enviro 200 single deckers which were new in 2012 or later. They are used on the former tram service from Blaenrhondda/Blaencwm-Pontypridd which runs every 10 minutes, a similar frequency to that operated in the 1950s.

The Tonypandy to Cardiff service runs three times an hour once more, although the demolition of a low bridge at Tonyrefail means it takes a slightly different route to the one used by Rhondda Transport. Optare Versas are used on this service and they couldn't be any more different to the AEC Regents and Atlanteans that were popular in Rhondda Transport's days. Four minibuses an hour using low floor Optare Solos have been introduced on the Porth to Tonyrefail service which was extended to Gilfach Goch at one end and to Pontypridd at the other.

As Stagecoach said in its Rhondda centenary booklet, the area differs tremendously from the community served by Rhondda Tramways. But while there are fewer passengers and fewer buses, the people of the valleys still rely heavily on this mode of transport.

Today the area covered by Porth depot is served by ultra modern low-floor vehicles which contrast hugely with the double deck Regents and single deck Tiger Cubs that made up much of the Rhondda Transport fleet.

The roar of the Regents and the purr of the Tiger Cubs no longer echo in the valleys. They may not have had the comforts of today's buses but many of the older people in the valleys remember them with great fondness. They also vividly recall Rhondda Transport's friendly drivers and conductors who were always prepared to do their passengers a friendly turn, even if it was not always strictly in the company's rule book!

163

Ensuring that the legend lives on

One of two surviving AEC Regent Vs at Rhondda Heritage Park after being restored. The 1961 MCW bodied Regent V is currently at Barry Bus Museum.

Posterity has not been kind to Rhondda Transport. Of 634 buses the company bought between 1920 and 1970, just eight remain and the future of all but two of them is uncertain. Two others, the only known surviving single deckers, now look very different to when they ran from Porth depot.

Today the two best known former Rhondda buses are both Regent Vs, one from the 1961 batch, MCW bodied 457KTG, and the last of its type delivered to the company, Northern Counties-bodied KNY495D of 1966.

It is 495 which is seen most regularly at bus rallies and events around South Wales and the fact that in 2016 it will celebrate its 50th year is down to the determination of solicitor and Rhondda boy, Martin Doe, and former Porth depot chargehand, Graham House.

Withdrawn by what had become National Welsh in 1979, 495 looked to be heading for the scrapyard but enthusiast Martin, who always wanted to own his own bus, and the equally enthusiastic Graham were determined to save it for posterity. The company was reluctant to sell it to Martin, then a 24-year-old trainee solicitor with nowhere to store the vehicle, but with support from Graham, National Welsh was eventually persuaded to part with it.

"I didn't have anywhere to store it so it stayed at Porth for the next three years," said Martin. "Graham always managed to deflect Porth depot managers who kept asking when the bus was going to be moved."

Eventually the day could be put off no longer and 495, looking rather shabby in its National Bus Company poppy red livery, was found a new home at the Welsh Industrial and Maritime Museum in Cardiff, but not before it was repainted in traditional Rhondda Transport fleet colours, the livery it has proudly worn ever since.

The museum closed in 1999 and Martin found a new home for it in Newport Transport's depot in the town's

Corporation Road, where it was garaged for a number of years while work was carried out on it. The vehicle received another repaint courtesy of Stagecoach for Rhondda Transport's centenary in 2006 and continues to look resplendent inside and out. Yet its survival is an accident of fate, for it was not the vehicle Martin originally wanted to buy.

"I wanted 478UNY, a similar bus from an earlier batch," he said. "But unfortunately it was involved in a shunt accident while on a private hire contract and it was quickly scrapped."

The fact that 495 continues to grace bus rallies and events is in no small way down to the Cardiff Transport Preservation Group, based at the former Western Welsh depot at Barry. Volunteers have carried out extensive repairs to keep it roadworthy. The group has also been busy with 457, owned for around 20 years by the Rhondda Heritage Park at Porth. Unfortunately, it had been stored in the open and subject to all weathers and needed a substantial amount of work to keep it fully operational.

The 1961 bus was withdrawn by Rhondda in 1972 and eventually found its way to a driving school in Sheffield from where it was rescued by Andrew Gibbs who passed it on to the heritage park which used it at various promotional events. It needed extensive renovation including repairs to a badly dented roof and body panels.

Today the future of both these buses looks good but that cannot be said of another three ex-Rhondda Regent Vs. As each year passes, it seems less likely that they will be returned to roadworthy condition and proudly carry their original Rhondda fleetname once more. They include 468MTX, one of the 1962 batch of MCW-bodied Regent Vs, nicknamed 'the ugly sisters' at Porth. It is currently languishing in a Leicestershire field where it has been deteriorating for 20 years.

Withdrawn by Rhondda Transport in 1972, it was eventually bought by a showman named Joe Weston, who liked to be known as Grumpy Joe, and nicknamed The River Jump Bus. Joe's stunts included firing people from cannons across the River Avon and 468 was used as sleeping accommodation and an office. When Joe died the bus was sold to a farmer living near Leicester.

Leicestershire bus enthusiast Andrew Tucker, who himself owns a restored AEC Renown, said: "We need to

One of two preserved Regent Vs at Rhondda Heritage Park. The other vehicles on this page have not been so fortunate, currently deteriorating in various locations. These vehicles are, clockwise from top left: 468MTX, VTX444, VTX442 exterior and interior, TG6311.

KNY495D was purchased by Martin Doe in 1980 and has now been in preservation three times as long as it was in service. It is seen here at Rhondda Heritage Park at Trehafod, having been restored to its original livery.

inspect it to see what kind of condition it's in. After that, we need to find someone who is prepared to restore it. Unfortunately, it is likely to be a very expensive project."

The remaining two Regent Vs are in even worse predicaments. They are both from the 1958 Weymann-bodied batch, Rhondda Transport's first 30ft long double deckers: VTX442, bought by Denyer Brothers of Stondon Massey near Brentwood in Essex who ran buses and coaches and is believed to be still there, and VTX444, which was bought as a source of spares by Denyer Brothers, but is believed to have been sold to an enthusiast and rescued from their scrapyard.

Mystery of a 1933 survivor

Little is known about the condition of an even older survivor, a Weymann bodied AEC Regent that was one of a batch which arrived at Rhondda Transport in 1933.

Delivered to the company as a 52 seater, one of 30 double deckers that replaced the trams, TG6311, fleet number 111, was sold in 1946 to Welsh Metal Industries of Caerphilly as a demonstrator and fitted with a replacement 56 seat body. It ended up with Yeoman's of Canon Pyon who used it on local services around Hereford. Withdrawn in 1951, it became a caravan and still exists surrounded by trees in the Herefordshire village of Pembridge.

An 'unusual' success story

When he was 20, he was a Rhondda Transport bus conductor, but by his early thirties he had a garage full of Rolls Royces and was a multi-millionaire.

That is the rags to riches story of Gordon Mills, the most famous conductor ever employed at Porth depot. Gordon found fame as a songwriter and managed pop stars Tom Jones, Engelbert Humperdinck and Gilbert O'Sullivan. He bought a mansion in Surrey, but was brought up in a terraced house in Trealaw.

Gordon did his National Service and on his return in the late 1950s took a job as a conductor with Rhondda Transport, but music was always in his blood and he became friendly with two colleagues, Rhondda drivers Ray Rees and Mal Kisby. Outside work the three played together, Mal on the guitar while Ray and Gordon both played harmonica.

He quit Porth depot to seek fame and fortune with his own group and started to write songs. His first hit came in 1963 with I'll Never Get Over You which reached number four in the charts for Johnny Kidd and The Pirates. Gordon also co-wrote Tom Jones's first hit, It's Not Unusual.

From collecting fares for a few pounds a week he became a songwriter worth millions of pounds, but his life was tragically short. He died in 1986 from stomach cancer at the age of just 51.

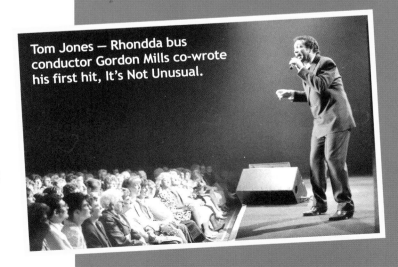

Tom Jones — Rhondda bus conductor Gordon Mills co-wrote his first hit, It's Not Unusual.

Thanks to the efforts of Martin Doe, who bought the vehicle, Graham House and restorers Taff Wagons, Rhondda Transport Regent V 495, KNY495D, was handed over to the Welsh Industrial & Maritime Museum at Cardiff on July 16, 1985 in the hope of keeping the legend alive. When the museum closed, the vehicle ownership reverted to Martin Doe. The bus is now at the former Western Welsh depot at Barry which is run as a working bus museum by the Cardiff Transport Preservation Group along with another similar former Rhondda Regent. The picture above was taken when 495 was handed over to the WIMM.

We looked after one another

Derek Williams of Ynyshir says he will never forget the community spirit that existed during his time with Rhondda Transport. He joined in 1959, worked his way up the ranks and finally retired as depot supervisor in February 1999.

"I started with the company as a conductor. That was the way you had to do it in those days. The company had about 180 vehicles then and my first wage packet contained £3.89 which is what they paid you for three weeks training.

"After that, when you became a conductor, it went up to between £8 and £9 a week. There were three main rosters, known as the Pandy, Maerdy and

Cardiff rosters, and they comprised 112 different shifts which each driver and conductor worked their way down. The minimum time you stayed in each job was strictly laid down by the union, so I spent six-and-a-half years as a conductor, seven years as a driver, before becoming an inspector and then a depot inspector. I finished up as depot supervisor and retired after 40 years.

"That meant I worked for Rhondda Transport, for Western Welsh when it took over the company in 1971, for National Welsh, which was created when Western Welsh and Red &White merged in 1978, for the new Rhondda Buses company, which took over Porth depot when National Welsh went out of

One of the two single deck survivors is not quite as old but when last heard of, it was still in running order, albeit a long way from its original haunts. It was GNY764, fleet number 64, a 34 seat Longwell Green-bodied Regal III, which was withdrawn in the summer of 1958 and sold to Thomas Bros of Port Talbot, a Rhondda Transport sister company. It was later shipped to Malta and operated by a small family transport concern running around seven buses.

But by the time it began its Malta duties, it had become a very different vehicle. Its original rear entrance body was replaced by a 40 seat Debono forward entrance body dating from 1963 and looked superb in its yellow Maltese livery. It received a new Cummins engine and the registration was changed, initially to DBY312, then EBY484.

The second single decker survivor is a much newer vehicle, BTX332J, a Willowbrook 45 seat Leyland Leopard which was ordered by Rhondda Transport but actually delivered after the Western Welsh takeover in 1971.

Even so, it was to Rhondda's specification and livery and numbered in the company's series, although it became 2332. It remained at Porth depot all its life and was withdrawn in the winter of 1984 after the company had become National Welsh.

But its service in South Wales was not over. It was shortened and converted into a towing bus for Cwmbran depot, which became part of the new Red & White company in 1991, and lasted into Stagecoach days, not being withdrawn until 1999. It was bought from Stagecoach in 1999 by the Friends of Rhondda Heritage Park and stored at various sites until its ownership passed to Martin Doe. The vehicle is currently stored at Lydney awaiting long term restoration with hopes that it can eventually be restored to its former Rhondda livery.

There is another bus with strong Porth depot connections surviving today, although it did not arrive until long after the demise of Rhondda Transport. It is a double deck, ECW-bodied Leyland Olympian, MUH289X, which arrived at Porth in 1982 as a National Welsh vehicle and remained there until it was withdrawn by the new Rhondda Buses company in July 1995. For most of its life at Porth depot it was generally used on the 332 Maerdy to Cardiff service. The Cardiff Transport Preservation Group bought it in June 2011 and have done a magnificent job restoring it to its original poppy red livery.

Sadly, those eight vehicles are believed to be the sole remnants of Rhondda Transport. Not one of the rear entrance Regent III and Regent V buses, which were once such familiar sights around the valleys, have made it. The splendidly kept coaches that took thousands of local families on much needed breaks to the seaside and further afield, are all gone.

Today buses at Porth depot are all extremely comfortable, low-floor, modern vehicles operated by Stagecoach in South Wales. But there are still many older people in the Rhondda who remember the old days with affection, and rather wistfully, too.

like a family

business in 1992, and finally for Stagecoach which bought out Rhondda Buses just before Christmas in 1997. But for me there's no doubt that the original Rhondda Transport was the best to work for. It was like a family-run company, we all looked after each other; they were a great bunch. We had our own social club across the river from the depot and there were lots of memorable events, particularly the Christmas parties and summer outings. I worked for the company for 40 years and I don't remember a day that I didn't like. It was a wonderful career."

Derek Williams in front of one of the last surviving Rhondda Regent Vs in 2014.

Half a century of fleet building

In the earliest days of operation of their legendary public transport provider the people of the Rhondda valleys were conveyed to their places of work, rest and play by trams and for the briefest of periods, by trolleybuses.

However for the greatest time in the existence of the Rhondda Transport Company it discharged the important task of moving the valley's people far and wide through the use of a continually growing fleet of motorbuses.

These ranged from the most basic incarnation of such vehicles where for passengers the ride was rough and the protection minimal, compared to the vehicles that came as the years rolled on, to some of the 20th Century's most modern buses and coaches.

The Rhondda Transport Company operated motorbuses for a total of 51 years, stretching from 1920 to 1970. The passing of those years saw it purchase a total of 634 buses of which 593 were new vehicles and 41 that had been pre-owned.

Vehicles were bought in all but six of those years. Different times brought with them different types and quantities of buses but 1921, 1938, 1950, 1951, 1957 and 1960 saw nothing new emerging from the doors of the sprawling Porth depot.

The company also had 28 buses on loan, all during the Second World War: 17 from the London Passenger Transport Board, 9 from Western Welsh and 2 from South Wales Transport. The total number of vehicles operated was therefore 662, of which roughly equal numbers were single deckers and double deckers, the first of the latter appearing in 1931.

The supplier most favoured by Rhondda was AEC and a breakdown of the vehicles operated is: AEC 448, Leyland 111, Daimler 29, Bristol 23, Guy 17, Dennis 16, Albion 9, ADC 4, Bedford 3, Thornycroft 1, Tilling-Stevens 1. The following is the complete fleet list which it is hoped will help as a guide to the distribution of these vehicles down the proud Rhondda years.

Part of the collection of Rhondda Transport Company former bus registration plates on display at Barry Bus Museum.

CHAPTER 16

A typically tight parked line-up of early double decker buses on a rainy day in Porth depot. Closest to the camera is one of 10 Guy Arab IIs with Park Royal bodywork delivered in 1943 during the Second World War and still operating many years later.

1920

1	L 6482	AEC YC Lorry-bus 26
2	L 6479	AEC YC Lorry-bus 26
3	L 6480	AEC YC Lorry-bus 26
4	L 6484	AEC YC Lorry-bus 26
5	L 6481	AEC YC Lorry-bus 26
6	L 6483	AEC YC Lorry-bus 26
7	L 6492	AEC YC Lorry-bus 26
8	L 6493	AEC YC Lorry-bus 26
9	L 6494	AEC YC Lorry-bus 26

1921

No acquisitions

1922

10	NY 996	Daimler Y Strachan/Brown B32
11	NY 995	Daimler Y Strachan/Brown B32
12	NY 997	Daimler Y Strachan/Brown B32
13	T 7750	AEC YC B--R
16	T 8232	AEC YC Lorry-bus

1923

14	NY 3450	Bristol 4 ton BBW B32F
15	L 5050	AEC YC Charabanc 30
17	Not known	AEC YC

1924

18	NY 6731	Bristol 4 ton W Lewis B32F
19	NY 6327	AEC YC Charabanc 35
20	NY 6371	Tilling-Stevens TS3A B30RP
21	NY 6510	Bristol 4 ton W Lewis B32F
22	BX 1208	AEC YC B--F
23	BX 1206	AEC YC B--F

1925

24	NY 7468	Bristol 4-ton W Lewis B32F
25	NY 7533	Bristol 4-ton W Lewis B32F
26	NY 8086	Bristol 4-ton W Lewis B32F
29	NY 8869	Bristol 4-ton BBW B32F
30	NY 8871	Bristol 4-ton BBW B32F
31	NY 8870	Bristol 4-ton BBW B32F
32	NY 9280	AEC 413 B30
33	NY 9282	AEC 413 B30
34	NY 9284	AEC 413 B30
35	NY 9347	AEC 413 B30
36	NY 9349	AEC 413 B30
37	NY 9351	AEC 413 B30
38	NY 9502	AEC 413 B30
39	NY 9498	AEC 413 B30
40	NY 9500	AEC 413 B30
41	L 9385	AEC 413 B32
27	NY 1503	AEC YC 32 seat
28	NY 484	Daimler Y 28 seat

1926

| 42 | TX 1755 | AEC 413 United B30 |

1927

43	TX 2887	ADC 415A Hall Lewis B32D
44	TX 2885	ADC 415A Hall Lewis B32D
45	TX 3039	ADC 415A Hall Lewis B32D
46	TX 3037	ADC 415A Hall Lewis B32D
47	TX 4436	Bristol B BBW B32R
48	TX 4432	Bristol B BBW B32R
49	TX 4434	Bristol B BBW B32R
50	Not known	Thornycroft

1928

51	TX 6379	Bristol B BBW B32D
52	TX 6381	Bristol B BBW B32D
53	TX 6383	Bristol B BBW B32D
54	TX 6385	Bristol B BBW B32D
55	TX 6387	Bristol B BBW B32D

1929

| 56 | TX 8642 | Albion PMB28 Brush B32 |
| 57 | TX 8640 | Albion PMB28 Brush B32 |

1930

58	TX 8715	Albion PMB28 Brush B32
59	TX 8713	Albion PMB28 Brush B32
60	TX 8928	Leyland LT1 B32
61	TX 9227	Albion PMA28 B32
62	TX 9223	Albion PMA28 B32
63	TX 9225	Albion PMA28 B32
64	TX 9858	Albion PMA28 B32
65	TX 9860	Albion PMA28 B32
66	TG 743	AEC Regal Park Royal B30D
67	TG 745	AEC Regal Park Royal B30D
68	TG 747	AEC Regal Park Royal B30D
69	TG 749	AEC Regal Park Royal B30D
70	TG 751	AEC Regal Park Royal B30D
71	TG 755	AEC Regal Park Royal B30D

1931

72	TG 1780	Bristol D BBW B32F
73	TG 1782	Bristol D BBW B32F
74	TG 1784	Bristol D BBW B32F
75	TG 1846	Bristol D BBW B32F
76	TG 1845	Bristol D BBW B32F
77	TG 1844	Bristol D BBW B32F
78	TG 2119	Dennis Lance II MCW H28/20R
79	TG 2121	AEC Regent Brush H52R
80	TG 2120	Leyland TD1 Leyland L27/24R
81	TG 2401	AEC Regal Brush B32D
82-90	TG 2466-74	AEC Regal Weymann B30R

1932

91	TG 2475	AEC Regal Weymann B30R
92-95	TG 4041-44	Dennis Lancet Weymann B30R
Unknown	TG 2788	Dennis Lancet Weymann B30R

One of Rhondda's smart, Marshall bodied, dual purpose Leyland Tiger Cubs of 1968, seen in National Bus Company colours in later life.

This Willowbrook bodied Dennis Lancet 2 was one of two ordered by Rhondda in 1937.

1933

101-12	TG 6301-12	AEC Regent Weymann H28/24R

1934

1-6	TG 6790-95	Dennis Lancet Weymann B31R
7-10	TG 7931-34	AEC Regal Weymann B34R
113-30	TG 6313-30	AEC Regent Weymann H28/24R

1935

131-41	TG 9550-60	AEC Regent Weymann H28/24R

1936

11	ATG 515	AEC Regal II Weymann B34R
12	ATX 414	AEC Regal II Weymann B34R
13	ATX 629	Dennis Lancet Dennis B34R
14-20	ATG 516-22	AEC Regal II Weymann B34R
142	TG 2903	AEC Reliance Hall Lewis B32R
143	TG 3869	AEC Regal Metcalfe B30F
144	ANY 28	AEC Regal Metcalfe B32F

1937

21-32	BTX 280-291	AEC Regal Weymann B34R
33-37	CTG 422-426	AEC Regal Weymann B34R
145-6	BTX 292-293	Dennis Lancet 2 W/brook C35F
147-9	BTX 578-580	AEC Regent Weymann H26/24R
150-9	CTG 427-436	AEC Regent Weymann H24/24F

1938

No acquisitions

1939

38-9	DTG 701-2	Daimler COG5 Weymann B34R
40-4	DTG 703-7	AEC Regal Weymann B34R
45-53	DTX 906-14	AEC Regal Weymann B34R
160-2	DTG 708-10	AEC Regal Weymann C31F

1940

163-72	ETG 741-50	AEC Regent Weymann H28/26R

1941

173-5	ETX 581-3	AEC Regent Park Royal H30/26R

Vehicles on loan from London Passenger Transport Board

ST 899	GJ 2075	AEC Regent Tilling H27/25RO
ST 903	GJ 2079	AEC Regent Tilling H27/25RO
ST 915	GJ 2091	AEC Regent Tilling H27/25RO

1942

176-8	ETX 832-4	Guy Arab I 6LW Weymn H30/26R

Vehicles on loan from London Passenger Transport Board

ST149	GF 446	AEC Regent LGOC H28/20RO
ST365	GK 3027	AEC Regent LGOC H28/20RO
ST872	GJ 2048	AEC Regent Tilling H27/25RO
ST1011	GK 6287	AEC Regent Tilling H27/25RO

Vehicles on loan from Western Welsh

538	TG 1821	AEC Regal Metcalfe B34
549	UH 9924	AEC Regal Metcalfe B32
550	UH 9985	AEC Regal Metcalfe B32
564	UH 8632	AEC Regal Hall Lewis B30
565	UH 9628	AEC Regal NCME B28
566	UH 9629	AEC Regal NCME B31
567-8	UH 9630-1	AEC Regal NCME B28
569	UH 9632	AEC Regal NCME B31

1943

179-80	FNY 60-1	Guy Arab I 6LW Pk Ryl H30/26R
181-6	FNY 390-5	Guy Arab II 6LW Pk Ryl H30/26R
187-92	FNY 530-5	Guy Arab II 6LW Pk Ryl H30/26R

Vehicles on Loan from London Passenger Transport Board

ST873	GJ 2049	AEC Regent Tilling H27/25RO
ST874	GJ 2050	AEC Regent Tilling H27/25RO
ST899	GJ 2075	AEC Regent Tilling H27/25RO
ST910	GJ 2086	AEC Regent Tilling H27/25RO
ST933	GK 1009	AEC Regent Tilling H27/25RO
ST940	GK 1016	AEC Regent Tilling H27/25RO
ST1029	VX 7487	AEC Regent Dodson H54RO

Vehicles on loan from South Wales Transport Company

312	WN 5812	AEC Renown Brush B40F
322	WN 6222	Dennis Lancet Weymann B32R

1944

193-4	HTA 881-2	Daimler CWG5 Duple H30/26R
195-9	FNY 809-13	Daimler CWA6 Duple H30/26R

Vehicles on loan from London Passenger Transport Board

ST844	GJ 2020	AEC Regent Tilling H27/25RO
ST964	GK 6240	AEC Regent Tilling H27/25RO
ST977	GK 6253	AEC Regent Tilling H27/25RO

1945

200	FNY 814	Daimler CWA6 Duple H30/26R
201-7	FTG 114-20	Daimler CWA6 Pk Ryl H30/26R
208-14	FTG 202-8	Daimler CWA6 Brush H30/26R

1946

54-5	FTX 188-9	AEC Regal Burlingham B34F
56-7	FTX 364-5	AEC Regal Burlingham B34F
58-63	GNY 66-71	AEC Regal Weymann B35R
92	GNY 72	AEC Regal Longwell Green B34R
215	FTG 256	Daimler CWD6 Duple H30/26R
216-7	FTX 190-1	AEC Regent III Weymn H30/26R
218-20	GNY 370-2	AEC Regent III Weymn H30/26R

1947

93-6	GNY 73-6	AEC Regal Longwell Green B34R
221-30	GNY 767-76	AEC Regent III Weymn H30/26R

1948

64-5	GNY 764-5	AEC Regal III Longwell Grn B34R
97	GNY 766	AEC Regal III Longwell Grn B34R
98-100	GNY 761-3	AEC Regal III Windover C32F
231-8	HTG 699-706	AEC Regent III Weymn H30/26R
240-3	HTG 708-11	AEC Regent III Weymn H30/26R
301-8	GTX 863-70	AEC Regal III Longwell Grn B34R

1949

239	HTG 707	AEC Regent III Weymn H30/26R
244-54	HTG 712-22	AEC Regent III Weymn H30/26R
255-60	JTG 946-51	AEC Regent III Weymn H30/26R
309-14	HTX 580-5	AEC Regal III Longwell Grn B34R

1950

No acquisitions

1951

No acquisitions

1952

261-74	LNY 342-55	AEC Regent III Weymn H30/26R
315-26	LNY 356-67	Leyland PSU1/13 Weymn B44F
327-9	LTG 267-9	Leyland PSU1/15 Leyland C41C

Acquired from Devon General

1	ETT 996	AEC Regal Harrington B33F
2	DOD 456	AEC Regal Harrington B35F
3	DUO 324	AEC Regal Harrington B35F
4	ETT 993	AEC Regal Harrington B33F
5	DDV 428	AEC Regal Harrington B35F
6	DDV 433	AEC Regal Harrington B35F
7	DDV 434	AEC Regal Harrington B35F
8	DDV 437	AEC Regal Harrington B35F
9	DDV 448	AEC Regal Harrington B35F
10	DDV 449	AEC Regal Harrington B35F
12	DOD 462	AEC Regal Weymann B35F
13	DOD 468	AEC Regal Weymann B35F
14	DOD 476	AEC Regal Weymann B35F

This line up of vehicles was going nowhere after heavy snow blocked their progress in 1982 when Porth depot was owned by the National Bus Company.

1953

| 275-81 | MNY 536-42 | AEC Regent III Weymn H30/26R |
| 330-3 | NTG 141-4 | Leyland PSUC1/1 Weymn B44F |

1954

282-7	NTG 135-40	AEC Regent III Weymn H30/26R
288-97	PNY 390-9	AEC Regent III Weymn H32/28R
334-52	PNY 371-89	Leyland PSUC1/1T Weymn B44F

1955

| 353-6 | SNY 231-4 | Leyland PSUC1/1T Weymn B44F |

1956

298-9	STG 869-70	AEC Regent V Weymn H33/28R
357-9	UNY 8-10	Leyland PSUC1/2 Strachan C41C
400-5	STG 871-6	AEC Regent V Weymn H33/28R
406-20	TTX 984-98	AEC Regent V Weymn H33/28R
421-4	UNY 4-7	AEC Regent V Weymn H33/28R

1957

No acquisitions

1958

| 425-44 | VTX 425-44 | AEC Regent V Weymn H37/33F |

1959

| 360-2 | XTG 360-2 | Leyland PSUC1/2T Weymn C41F |
| 363-77 | XTG 363-77 | Leyland PSUC1/1 Weymn B44F |

1960

No acquisitions

1961

378-80	378-80 GNY	Leyland PSUC1/2T MCW DP41F
381-5	381-5 KTG	Leyland PSUC1/1T Pk Ryl B45F
445-53	445-53 GTX	AEC Regent V MCW H39/31F
454-64	454-64 KTG	AEC Regent V MCW H39/31F

1962

| 465-8 | 465-8 MTX | AEC Regent V MCW H37/28F |

1963

| 469-78 | 469-78 UNY | AEC Regent V NCME H37/28F |

1964

386-91	386-91 WTG	Leyland PSUC1/11RT Wbrk B45F
392-4	392-4 WTG	Leyland PSUC1/11RT Wbrk DP41F
395-7	395-7 WTG	Bedford VAL14 Duple C47F

1965

| 479-90 | ETX 479-90C | AEC Regent V NCME H37/28F |

1966

| 300-3 | HTG 300-3D | Leyland PSUC1/12T Mrshll B45F |
| 491-5 | KNY 491-5D | AEC Regent V NCME H37/28F |

1967

Acquired from Southdown Motor Services

| 330-1 | MUF 430-1 | Leyland PSU1/16 Har/ton C41C |
| 332 | NUF 71 | Leyland PSU1/16 Duple C41C |

1968

304-15	RTG 304-15F	Leyland PSUC1/12T Mrshll B45F
316-8	RTG 316-8F	Leyland PSUC1/12T Mrshll DP41F
319-21	RTG 319-21F	Leyland PSU3/4R Wbrk DP49F
496-501	RTX 496-501G	Leyland Atlantean PDR1/1 NCME H42/31F

1969

| 502-11 | VTG 502-11G | Leyland Atlantean PDR1A/1 NCME H42/31F |

1970

| 322-4 | YTX 322-4H | Leyland Leopard PSU3A/4RT Plaxton C49F |

1971

(Ordered by Rhondda 1970, delivered in Rhondda livery to Western Welsh 1971)

| 325-34 | BTX 325-34J | Leyland Leopard PSU4A/2R Willowbrook B45F |
| 512-20 | BTG 512-20J | Leyland Atlantean PDR1A/1 Alexander H42/31F |